Assault of the Killer B's

Theatrical artwork from 1987's *Slumber Party Massacre II* (courtesy New Concorde)

Assault of the Killer B's

*Interviews with 20
Cult Film Actresses*

JASON PAUL COLLUM

McFarland & Company, Inc., Publishers
Jefferson, North Carolina, and London

LIBRARY OF CONGRESS CATALOGUING-IN-PUBLICATION DATA

Assault of the killer B's : interviews with 20
cult film actresses / Jason Paul Collum.
p.   cm.
Includes index.

ISBN 0-7864-1818-4 (softcover : 50# alkaline paper)

1. Motion picture actors and actresses— United Sates— Interviews.
2. B films— United States.   I. Collum, Jason Paul.
PN1998.2.A83   2004   791.4302'8'092273 — dc22   2003028284

British Library cataloguing data are available

Cover image: J. J. North and Brinke Stevens in *Hybrid* (courtesy Fred Olen Ray)

Manufactured in the United States of America

McFarland & Company, Inc., Publishers
Box 611, Jefferson, North Carolina 28640
www.mcfarlandpub.com

For Mom
(Thanks for treating me like an adult only when absolutely necessary)

Contents

and Tony Pines at New Concorde for their compassion and understanding in my need to make this book as visually attractive as it is.

Michael D. Moore for giving me the opportunity to become a screenwriter and director.

All of the actresses written about in this volume, for allowing me to meet you and intrude on your personal and professional lives.

Finally, to Dennis Smart, without whom I would never have been able to begin my true journey in Los Angeles.

I will forever be indebted. Anyone else I may have forgotten — I'll thank you in the next book.

Acknowledgments

When I got the idea of gathering my previously published articles into a collection, I mistakenly assumed it would be an easy project with little to no effort involved, as they technically were already done. Well, we all know what can happen with assumptions... I realized along the way that without the help of family, friends and colleagues, there was no way I could accomplish this task on my own, nor would I even have this opportunity without the help and love of others along the way. So my "thank yous" must begin.

To Aunt Barb and Uncle Tim Vanderhoef, for their long hours in front of a computer while I was enjoying the Hawaiian sun and my best friend's wedding.

Mom and Dad (Kathy and Larry Campeau, Jr.), for trusting me to go off on my own to the Big City, and giving me the brains to survive it.

Julie King, for being my longest supporter, inspiration, friend, and teacher.

"Jodie" Randall, Carole Vopat and Carol Jagielnik for teaching me how to write, and encouraging me to pursue it as a career.

The Vanderhoefs (all 86-and-growing of you), Campeaus and Collums, who have shown fresh excitement with every new project. Darcey Vanderhoef for being more than a relative, but a best friend as well: I promise to make you famous some day.

Auntie Christine Mapel, who reminded me why I *love* meeting these actresses— I hope you enjoyed meeting Cassandra and Julie as my "thanks."

Bill "Baroo" Krekling, Karen "Big Red" Dilloo, Michele "Meesh" Fredericks-Ludvigsen and Adam Zurawski (and all of their other halves) for being my best of friends in my worst of times, and making me believe I *could* do it.

Brinke Stevens, J.R. Bookwalter and David DeCoteau for helping me get that first foot in the door.

Lisa Coduto, without whose contagious laughter I would have gone insane long ago while in the offices of *Femme Fatales* at three in the morning.

Frederick S. Clarke, Celeste Casey Clarke and Bill George for making my dream a reality and officially making me a journalist.

Tony Timpone and Michael Gingold of *Fangoria* for printing what may seem like long-forgotten little thoughts, but gave me the courage and feeling of being "a writer."

Robert MacDonald C.S.A. and Perry Bullington C.S.A. for helping me locate some of the "missing" actresses— though I'm still on the hunt for Donna Wilkes.

Robert Shaye and Robin Zlatin at New Line Cinema, and Germaine Simmiens

Introduction

Never in a million years, while growing up in the relatively small community of Racine, Wisconsin, did I believe I would one day sit across from the same women I had been watching on television at 11 P.M. on no-budget horror shows like WPN's *Saturday Night Frights*, and *Movie Macabre* and USA's *Up All Night*. I had watched them scream, jump and either die or barely survive. Their clothes were usually torn, their hair and makeup disheveled. Yet I felt an odd sort of bond with them, almost as though I already *knew* them, which is why when I finally became a journalist and discovered there were ways to access these ladies, it became more and more surreal to me.

I discovered something else which would eventually become my niche in the world of entertainment journalism. While some actresses remained active within the business, others had vanished from the silver screens over the years. Though their movies were forever considered cult classics, their audiences weren't growing younger. A new generation was filling theaters and, to my dismay, many of them didn't care about any movie which was older than they were, even to the extreme of refusing to watch anything made more than five years ago. It became my personal duty to remind audiences that these great films, and the women who starred in them, still existed.

I set out in late 1999 to recapture the stories behind one of my all-time favorite B-movies: *The Slumber Party Massacre*. It had been quite popular with kids my age back in the mid–1980s, and though its sequels were somewhat disjointed, they were of the variety you grew to love after repeated viewings. The First Question: "How do I find these actresses and crew members?" The Answer: Call the Screen Actors Guild. The Problem: Most of them were no longer around. They had agents listed and phone numbers for contacts, but the majority of SAG's info was obsolete. In fact, they still had an "active" listing for an actress who had been deceased for four years! Still, I trudged ahead, and after almost a year of research and interviews, submitted my first retrospective to *Femme Fatales* magazine.

Then-editor Bill George (who left in 2001) and publisher Frederick S. Clarke (who passed away around the same time) quickly replied with a "Yes!" My first professionally written piece was going to see publication! As a bonus and an ego boost, it would become the cover story for the August 11, 2000, issue, which became one of the magazine's best sellers. I was on my way.

With the retrospective a success, I decided retros would be my main focus. I would get to meet the actors I adored and talk about the movies I loved, all while reminding viewers old and new of these wonderful horror and camp classics. Over the next two years I would go on to have over 50 retrospectives, interviews and critiques published.

I had already published unpaid articles in the short-lived *Independent Video Magazine*, the industry trade-paper *Video Business Weekly* and *Fangoria* magazine, which has been my bible since age 15, and which also published my earliest letters and critiques in their "Postal Zone." This gave me the confidence to become a journalist in the first place. With many thanks to editor Tony Timpone and managing editor Michael Gingold, I would later find myself *paid* for articles in *Fangoria* as another "unattainable" dream which came true.

I was grateful to the various magazines for printing my work, and remain grateful, but became a bit disturbed when some of the articles were altered upon publication. Though not disgruntled, I was bothered to find the tone of my *Slumber Party Massacre* piece had a negative spin put into it, with comments from critics and other filmmakers whom I had not interviewed suddenly appearing within the body of the text. I understood editing was required for space constraints, grammar correction and deletion of certain topics which didn't fit into the "political agenda" of the magazines (i.e., why would *Femme Fatales'* assumed straight male readership want to read about any actor or director's homosexuality?). However, I was slowly discovering some major overhauls.

Occasionally, my articles were so severely altered from their original versions they had become completely incoherent, often with quotes stopping in mid-sentence, while one paragraph blended not-so-smoothly into another with topics completely unrelated. One article in particular, an interview with my all-time favorite comedian Julie Brown, was so butchered I was actually humiliated and embarrassed to show it to her. I made up my mind I would one day gather all of my work and put it out — topics intact and uncensored — for other film fanatics to read.

I'd originally wanted to title this tome *Jason Paul Collum: Uncut — Discussions with Cult Celebrities*. Alas, my name isn't famous enough. However, the ladies contained within *are*, with extensive résumés as proof.

I can honestly say I *love* these women. They have been my heroes ... my saviors. As my turbulent teens blasted forth and I needed someone with whom I could identify, they stepped in. Whether battling hockey-masked camp stalkers or fending off drill-wielding maniacs, they helped me believe I could win the fight against life's worst situations... I could survive *anything*.

Others would make me laugh when I had only been in the mood to cry. Befriending fuzzy tomatoes, trying to keep their low-budget television crews from vacating the set during PMS rampages, or taking on entire puritanical townships with hysterical consequences, three of these actresses reminded me there was always a brighter side beyond the darkness. To all of them, I will forever be grateful. It is also why I felt it necessary to share their life stories, their often underappreciated or overlooked performances, with the world.

So let me now invite you — the reader, the film fanatic, the 15-year-old trying to find his way in the world, or the 70-year-old remembering the bumps and jumps which kept you up at night as a child — to re-experience, or to meet for the first time, some of the most talented actresses who have put their lungs on the line in as little as one popular horror flick, or over 100 turns as crimson divas, and even a few who helped us laugh at the same horrors we recall, and love, ever so fondly.

Surviving Night of the Living Dead

Judith O'Dea

It's a slightly crisp day in Long Beach, California. In a small cafe known as "The Library," she's easy to pick out of the crowd. Her short hair is laced with silver and blonde, her eyes a splendid blue, her personality welcoming and warm. Almost 35 years after she leapt into cinema history as the pale, waifish Barbara in the original *Night of the Living Dead*, she's even more elegant and demure than ever.

"I started my career in theater in Pittsburgh when I was 15," she begins, her dialect proper and sincere. "Throughout the years from 15 to 23, when I got the role of Barbara, I worked with many of the people who ended up either producing, directing or acting in the film. At the time they were casting [*Night of the Living Dead*], I was in Hollywood … and was called back to Pittsburgh by Karl Hardman ('Harry Cooper'). He wanted me to … audition. I had done a lot of commercial work for Karl and Marilyn Eastman ('Helen Cooper'), so I flew back, auditioned, and got the role."

The majority of the cast and crew had previously worked together, mostly for George Romero, Russ Streiner and John Russo's production company Latent Image, which would later expand to Image 10 for production of *Night of the Living Dead*. The company had focused on commercials and documentaries and were located near Hardman's recording studio. O'Dea had performed a number of voice overs for them.

"My shooting was hard-core for about two weeks in August 1967. Then I came back and did some pick-up shots in the cemetery several months later. I think the rest of the film was shot with the other actors for about a month," she recalls. "Putting the film together took a while. Plus I think shooting the scenes in Washington D.C. took some time…. There was about a year between my pick-up shots and the [release]."

What followed the premiere of *Night of the Living Dead* on October 1, 1968, at eight P.M. in Pittsburgh's Fulton Theater was nothing short of a permanent shift in modern horror cinema. Zombies were no longer dullards wandering through mist and fog. They were flesh eaters, hungry and graphic in their need to feed. They were people you knew, friends and family. They were children … and they had no mercy. While most people would join forces to beat the evil setting in upon them, it was this small group of civilians' *inability* to join together which lead them to the slaughter.

Gone was the horror which was tidy and happy, or at least offering a glimpse of hope by the resolution. Only Hitchcock's *The Birds* (1963) had tried for a somewhat nihilistic conclusion. *Night of the Living Dead* didn't just try … it succeeded. Romero

3

was quoted in *Cinefantastique* magazine, "American International turned the picture down on the basis of its being too unmitigating. They told us that if we would reshoot the end of it, they would distribute it. Have Ben survive and come out somehow."

Romero declined and kept the original ending. The film's power is still felt today.

"I honestly had no idea it would have such a lasting impact on our culture," O'Dea confirms, wide-eyed, almost mystified. "I just loved doing it. I love film and I *love* stage. Doing *Night of the Living Dead* gave me the wonderful opportunity to do something I love. At that age, at that time in my life, was as far as I went with it. I was thrilled it became as successful as it did, but never expected it."

Playing the character who is referred to in one of cinema's most chilling and famous lines ("They're coming to get you, Barbara.") wasn't a negative experience. "I interpreted her on my own," the thespian recalls. "When I was a little kid, I was *terrified* by *House of Wax* [1953]. So it wasn't difficult for me to get scared easily, even though I knew it was just a film. It just sort of came out of wherever I was at that time in my life."

She reports she is still recognized frequently. "It's amazing," she exclaims. "Just about every week of my life! Whether it's on the street or through my own business [teaching oral presentation], somehow somebody always realizes who I am. It's always *so* wonderful!"

She sits back in a sort of euphoria. "It has literally changed my life. It's brought a notoriety to my name. It's amazing to me the power of notoriety. You have the choice to either abuse it or honor it, and be humbled by it. Over the years it has enabled me to go places and do things I possibly would not have been able to do otherwise. People treat you differently. [I'm] ho-hum Judy O'Dea until they realize [I'm] Barbara from *Night of the Living Dead*. All of a sudden [I'm] not so ho-hum anymore! I'm a different person from having made the film. I'm *extremely* grateful."

Among the many people she's grateful to is director George A. Romero. "Oh, he was just great. George is a very 'inside' man. I think there's an awful lot going on inside his head of which I was never aware … yet he's a regular guy … a very wonderful Pittsburgh fellow. Very normal. I admire his creativity. With the small amount of money we had to make *Night of the Living Dead*, he did wonderfully unique things. He was very easy to work with."

When O'Dea is queried about improvisation on set, she laughs, "Oh, all the time! I don't know if there was an actual working script! We would go over what basically had to be done, then just did it the way we each felt it *should* be done. We didn't have a lot of film stock to spare, so we didn't do many retakes. The sequence where Ben [Duane Jones] is breaking up the table to block the entrance and I'm on the couch and start telling him the story of what happened … Johnny (Russ Streiner) with the candy … it's all ad-libbed. This is what we want to get across … tell the story about me and Johnny in the car and me being attacked. That was it … all improv. We filmed it once. There was a concern we didn't get the sound right, but fortunately they were able to use it."

O'Dea reports other unintended elements fell right into place. "I did my own stunts … lots of running," she laughs again. "In fact, there's a scene where I fall down and lose my shoe. [It] was completely by accident. I really did slip and fall. So we built in another shot where I fall and lose my other shoe so I could be running barefoot for the rest of the movie."

She even acknowledges some minor mishaps along the way which didn't make the final cut, like "the scene were I run across the field to the gas pump and stop, see the house and run again. Well, the gas pump was real, but was very old. So when I ran up to the pump, I careened right into it and knocked it over. We didn't realize it was so loose. It nearly fell and crushed George, who was lying on the ground with the camera shooting up!"

There were, however, some decisions which focused on making the film stand out, most blatantly the then-shocking graphic violence perpetuating the zombie rampages. "In today's horror films, most of which I'll admit to not seeing, the focus is on killing. Just killing. In our film, people were *eaten.* "Yes, the truck blew up, but the zombie came by and *ate* the humans. *Donner Pass*

Judith O'Dea being directed by George A. Romero (**center**) in *Night of the Living Dead* (**photograph courtesy John Russo**).

[1978] way before it was made. How many horror films really show people being eaten? I don't think we thought of it that way. All I knew was that we were making something very different from anything which had been done before."

Reflecting momentarily, she continues, "I honestly think everyone hoped to make this little movie with very little money, which would do well and afford them the opportunity to make more expensive and better features. I don't think they expected, or hoped, for anything more."

One has to wonder if in our post-modern world of *Scream* (1996), hip references, CGI and rapidly paced MTV-style editing, does *Night of the Living Dead* have

Ben (Duane Jones) takes on a parental role for the childlike Barbara (Judith O'Dea), who becomes nearly catatonic after her trauma in *Night of the Living Dead* (1968) (photograph courtesy Hollywood Book and Poster).

the same effect on current audiences as it did on those in 1968. "I think our film is very severe," O'Dea surmises. "It's nothing compared to what's out there now. I don't know if young people look at it the same way. In fact, I'd bet many of them laugh at it, because they've already seen so much graphic violence. I don't know if *Night of the Living Dead* would affect them at all. Yet it still creeps many people out. It seems rightfully so, if anything like the events in the film could actually happen, because it almost seems like a documentary. That smacks of 'close to home,' which is why it's so frightening."

Indeed, *Night of the Living Dead* is a paranoia kind of fright. Not of the "Boo" variety, but something which affects the viewer's mind. It terrifies you from the inside out. It makes you feel they really are coming to get *you*. You're all alone. There's no way to escape it. You *will* be conquered.

"This is one of the special things about *Night of the Living Dead*," O'Dea offers. "It really did change the way horror films were made. *The Texas Chainsaw Massacre* [1974] was in that same era where the good people don't survive. Up until that time, the white knight always arrived at the last moment to save the day, but *Night of the Living Dead* didn't let that happen. It mimicked real life. Sometimes the good people don't win the battle. *That* is what is so frightening about *Night of the Living Dead*."

Which is why Barbara's final scene is possibly the most terrifying and psychologically damaging in the film. "That was the most difficult scene to do and was truly terrifying to film," O'Dea confirms, a sudden unease filling her face. "Again, I knew it was only a movie, but when they said, '*Action!*,' I became the character and suddenly it really was very frightening for me. I was being dragged off into this crowd of dead people. [As] an actress, that sometimes happens. The horror on my face is real. I was honestly scared.

"I remember my parents getting telephone calls from irate people asking how they could let me be in 'a film like that,' even though I was 23 years old. 'It was so frightening and affected our children.' It really bothered me for quite a while ... that a film I was in had truly scared not only young children, but older ones as well."

She ponders a moment, then adds, "I think there will always be somebody somewhere who will look at films like that, or *Die Hard* [1988] or any film with violence, and want to run with it. What we see on television today concerns me tremendously. These media are so powerful, there's a great responsibility to not only put the truth out there, but to be aware of how powerful an effect you can have on very malleable minds which can be affected in the wrong way. What we show on screen does have some effect.

"I remember one incident were I was doing a Q&A [at a film convention] and I noticed this little girl in the audience. She had asked me a question, so after I finished I walked over and asked why she liked horror films. She said, 'I like to see how many different ways people can get killed.' It just took my breath away. When I was a little kid, death was terribly frightening to me. I thought about it and worried about it all the time. When we'd go to hotels, I'd figure the safest way out in case there was a fire! To have a kid so taken with that sort of thing amazed me. I'll never forget that."

O'Dea is quick to point out she isn't blasting the genre which made her famous. In fact, she admits to seeing the first official *Night of the Living Dead* sequel, *Dawn of the Dead* (1979) — though she did skip the third film, *Day of the Dead* (1985). "I'm not as familiar with the trilogy as many of the fans are," she confesses. "I'm actually quite embarrassed to admit that. My gut feeling on *Dawn*, though, is that of all the zombie movies made after *Night of the Living Dead*, it came closest to hitting the same mark. It is its own mark.

"I saw the *Night of the Living Dead* remake. I was sort of sad they changed Barbara's character. I could understand being in 1990 it would tend to go that way. It showed the change between the times. I think they both stand on their own and have individual merits. I don't think the original was outdone by the remake's color, fancier makeup FX and bigger budget. They're entirely different entities. In many ways, the original still holds its own. It is definitely the stronger of the two and will probably outlast the remake. Sorry to everyone who made it, but that's how I feel."

Amazingly, O'Dea remained oblivious to much of the immensely huge fan base her debut performance had developed over the years. While many of her co-stars and counterparts took advantage of their cult celebrity through conventions and fan clubs, O'Dea didn't know horror conventions existed "until just a few years ago when [friend and publicist] Marty White got me somewhat involved in it. I've only been to three or four. I was amazed at how much there is out there relating to *Night of the Living Dead*. The posters and comic books, plus all the other things related to horror films, and how many people show up to trade and buy items and meet actors. It's like a life of its own."

Seeing her peers raking in a few bucks and capitalizing on their fame, with many of the femmes turning themselves into "Scream Queens" is something O'Dea has never really desired. "It never appealed to me," she says. "Being in *Night of the Living Dead* was just another wonderful thing to add to my own base of knowledge. In fact, people tell me I should go to all these conventions and have people pay for my autograph, but that would be a very difficult thing for me to do."

What the actress would like to do is again work in front of the cameras. Would she consider returning to the horror genre?

Judith O'Dea today, in a photograph by Ward Boult (photograph courtesy Ward Boult Studios).

"I'd have to read the script," she states. "I did *The Pirates* [1977] for Warner Bros. and still love doing stage work. I certainly would love to see what's out there and consider it, because I would like to get back into the medium. What I really would love to do is get my own screenplay made. I'm in the midst of finishing one called *Play Me Again, Sam.* I love films which truly affect people's lives in a variety of ways. My script will touch people in a way where they'll say, 'Gosh, I can relate to that. I felt that.'"

So why exactly did O'Dea disappear from the film scene? "I have continued to remain active in theater over the years, and worked for some film producers like Mel Frank, but I had two children to raise. My marriage ended in 1975 and I had to support them. They've been with me through a lot of stage work. I couldn't leave. I always had to have my foot in it. There's *nothing* like being on the stage. Now that I'm retiring from Corporate America," she wants all filmmakers to note, "I'm ready to dive right back into it full-time!"

Are there any notes ingenues should take from the thespian? Some very simple words of wisdom: "Persevere. Don't sacrifice your values. Practice your craft. Listen."

Judith O'Dea sips the last of her coffee and smiles. Does she have any difference of opinion regarding *Night of the Living Dead* from her first viewing compared to three and half decades later? "I think it was one of those special efforts which was put together by people who had no idea it was going to become what it did. It still has magically wonderful moments to me today, so I think it's still a viable, special film. Being in it, and then seeing it on screen causes me to have some sort of disassociation with it. You're involved with those people when you're making the film, but you don't really connect to them when you see it on the screen as you did in person."

She hesitates one last time for the right words. She smiles, and, like looking at one of her own children, concludes, "I never dreamed it would ever become what it is."

The Girls of The Slumber Party Massacre

The Slumber Party Massacre: 20th Anniversary

You know the drill: A group of comely coeds gather for a night of pillow fights in their scanties and are "unexpectedly" slaughtered by a maniac with a phallic power tool. Oscar material it's not, but during the 1980s, the *Slumber Party Massacre* franchise successfully duplicated the slasher subgenre and unintentionally inspired T&A sinema in the two decades which followed.

A product of Roger Corman's New World Pictures, 1982's *The Slumber Party Massacre* was feminist in its tone and arguably the *Scream* (1996) of its time. One of the most exploited horror films about exploitation horror films, it remains a wickedly amusing blend of camp, serious slasher and eye-winking to its core audience, forever endearing it to B movie fanatics worldwide. From its degrading sexploitation-driven title (altered from the more respectful script *Don't Open the Door* and shooting title *Sleepless Night*) to its promotion as a movie made entirely by women, *Slumber Party Massacre* is one of two things: a hard-hitting, satirical slap at the females-in-peril films of the early '80s, or a females-in-peril film which, by chance, appeared to be the first idea. Assuming the laughs were as intentional as the scares, consider *Slumber Party Massacre*'s positive points and origins.

Halloween had made a killing at the box office in 1978, officially kicking off the original slasher trend. Though *Twitch of the Death Nerve* (1972), *The Texas Chainsaw Massacre* (1974), *Alice, Sweet Alice* (1977) and more specifically the identical *Black Christmas* (1974) pre-dated the Jamie Lee Curtis classic, *Halloween* defined the stalk 'n slash formula: a group of high school girls, one of them a virgin, spend a holiday evening (or special event) smoking pot, having sex, and drinking, all without parental supervision. As the night progresses, an evil entity stalks the girls and any boyfriends who happen by, kills the sinners and rule breakers, leaving the hapless virgin to discover the bodies. She then has to survive multiple violent attacks for the remaining half hour of the feature.

Though writer-director John Carpenter and his partner Debra Hill never meant for this formula to be taken as a "lesson" for the wayward youth of the 1970s, it was eagerly capitalized upon over the ensuing years. Blood-splattered teens filled the big screens in a gamut of good and bad slashers like *Terror Train* (1979), *He Knows You're Alone* (1980), *Happy Birthday to Me* (1980), *Prom Night* (1980), *Hell Night* (1981),

(**Left to right**) Diane (Gina Mari), Trish (Michele Michaels), Jackie (Andree Honore) and Kim (Debra DeLiso) are ready for a good time at *The Slumber Party Massacre* (copyright 1982, Santa Fe Productions/Concorde).

Graduation Day (1981), *My Bloody Valentine* (1981) and the expected *Halloween II* (1981). The year 1980 offered the largest amount of masked killers with over 20 films seeing theatrical release, but it was that year's surprise box office smash *Friday the 13th* which upped the gore and nudity quotient, thereby rounding out the formula and, essentially, setting it in stone.

After *Airplane!* (1980) carved the spoof as a new comedy subgenre, Paramount attacked the slasher trend with *Student Bodies* (1981), a send-up of everything attributed to the "dead teenager" movies. The same year, Rita Mae Brown, feminist author of *Rubyfruit Jungle* and *Educating Rita*, submitted a screenplay to New World Pictures which delivered the standard formula, yet used a humorous, less-obvious spin on the story.

Keeping events and dialogue with tongue firmly in cheek, Brown made the girls smarter, the boys dumber, the nudity less and the killer nastier, but with a quirky comical bite. New World didn't go for it at first, but when ingenue director Amy Holden-Jones (writer of 1993's *Indecent Proposal*) discovered the script some time later, she gathered a small crew, used short ends (leftover pieces of film), and shot the opening scenes for $1,000 over a weekend. The M.I.T. graduate later showed the product, complete with musical score, to Roger Corman. Pleased, he put up the remainder of the $250,000 budget and sent Jones out to finish her debut movie.

The lead cast was a collection of mostly newcomers. Among them were Michele Michaels (Trish), Robin Rochelle Stille (Valerie), Debra DeLiso (Kim), Gina Mari

(Diane), Brinke Stevens (Linda), Jennifer Meyers (Courtney), Andree Honore (Jackie), Joe Johnson (Neil) and David Milbern (Jeff). Rounding out the adult roles were Michael Villela as the killer Russ Thorn, Ryan Kennedy as the nosy neighbor Mr. Contant and Pamela Roylance as the rather butch Coach Rachel Jana.

Over 100 films later, most of them horror, Brinke Stevens would later be christened a "Scream Queen," DeLiso and Johnson were reunited in *Iced* (1988) and Roylance moved into TV's *Little House: A New Beginning*, only to be *Hexed* in 1993. The remainder of the cast also remained active within the film industry. Mari danced her way through *A Night at the Roxbury* (1998), Michaels dialed *976-Wish* (1997), Villela smelled *Wild Orchid* (1990) and its 1992 sequel, while Milbern dealt with the Academy Award–winning *Gods and Monsters* (1998). Pizza victim Aaron Lipstadt, who also produced *Slumber Party Massacre*, went behind the camera to write, produce and direct nearly 20 movies and television series including *Law & Order* and *Seven Days*. Stille, who dropped her last name and appeared in a few other horror efforts like *Sorority Babes in the Slimeball Bowl-a-Rama* (1987), passed away on February 9, 1996. (See "In Memoriam.")

With Brown's feminist tone mostly intact, the plot is kept simple (escaped mental patient terrorizes a group of basketball playing girls at their high school and a slumber party with his portable, very phallic power drill). Through Jones' use of inspired symbolism, the audience is asked if what they're viewing is entertainment, and if the women are truly being exploited. In one scene, as Diane is about to be slaughtered, the camera watches her cowering between the maniac's spread legs … his long, spinning drill bit dangling from his crotch waiting to "screw her."

The scene clearly points out the male antagonist and his fascination with both empowerment and manhood … a common theme of the essential slasher film (Jason Voorhees and his machete, Leatherface's even more enormous chainsaw, etc.). To similar effect during the climax, Thorn holds his drill to Trish's waist, insisting "You know you want it … you'll love it…." Moments later, his weapon is erect towards Valerie, at which point she chops his drill bit in half with her machete, thereby "castrating" him. He looks at the small remnant of his "tool," dismayed and at first humbled, then furious.

Brown filled her script with mechanically inclined women (such as carpenters and telephone repair workers) and heroines who don't run … they brandish their own tools of destruction. Strong female characters abound in roles commonly given to male stereotype. Rachel Jana is both the basketball coach and is also set up to be the protagonist-savior. After beating the killer down, however, she is caught off guard. As she falls victim, the remaining heroines take charge.

Valerie brandishes both a buzzsaw and a machete; Trish implements the biggest kitchen knife (used effectively in a great slow-motion attack of her own); and junior high age Courtney (who admittedly looks a lot older than her supposed 12 years) uses her own body twice to trip and tackle Thorn.

To further heighten the feminism angle, the male leads are demoted to the "bimbo" roles. They are wimpy, dense and more feminine than the girls. Sample this dialogue between them on the way to crashing the slumber party:

JEFF: "Let's scare the girls."
NEIL: "They'd beat the shit out of us…."

JEFF: "Well, we did fail gym."
NEIL: "Yeah … twice!"

They are excessively ineffective in not only trying to save the girls, but quickly and too-easily become victims themselves.

While obvious in its commentary, *The Slumber Party Massacre* does not take itself too seriously. Walls in the gymnasium feature posters which read "Emergency *Drill* Instructions" and "Join the *Drill* Team." Boob jokes abound, as in the shower room sequence when a nude Linda enters and a girl says, "Hey, I think your tits are getting bigger," to which the entire room chimes, "Mine?!" (Stevens reports that during the shooting of the scene, "several of the girls refused to appear naked, so they put tape over their breasts so the director couldn't use shots of them.") Other moments have a morbidly dark sense of humor.

When Trish and Jeff, money in hand, think the pizza delivery boy is at the door, they query, "What's the damage?" The voice on the other side responds, "Six … so far." Upon opening the door, the boy's eye-less body falls into the house. Later, as the girls await rescue, Jackie becomes hungry. In the most enjoyably repulsive scene, she pulls the pizza from the dead boy's hands. As she places it on his back and starts to eat, the other girls gasp in disgust, but Jackie replies, "I feel better when I eat…" She takes a second bite and says, with a full mouth, "See, I feel better already."

Though the dark humor swiftly attacks viewers, Holden-Jones (who also went on to write, produce or direct 1983's *Love Letters*, 1987's *Maid to Order*, 1989's *Mystic Pizza* and 1997's *The Relic*) never lets her audience forget they're watching a horror movie. In

The Driller Killer, Russ Thorn (Michael Villela), closes in on Linda (Brinke Stevens) at school in *The Slumber Party Massacre*.

doing so, *The Slumber Party Massacre* accomplishes what most satirical scare films do not — riding the fine line between horror and comedy. While the chuckles are deliciously corrupt, the darker, meaner side lurks throughout and strikes when least expected.

Early on, solid suspense is delivered when Linda, in the throes of an assault, hides beneath a counter in the shower room, her arm profusely bleeding from a gash. As the psycho stands on the other side of the counter, she reaches up and grabs a towel to stop the bleeding. The tension of whether or not the killer will see her hand is certain to keep even the most hardened viewer's breath still.

Stevens (1984's *Body Double*) remembers this scenes as "very difficult. There were about five of us crammed into this tiny area to get the shot. It was literally a closet, but Amy pulled it off and the scene worked really well." In fact, Stevens has only fond memories of the shoot and her director. "Amy was so great. She really knew what she wanted and how to get it. She's one of the hardest working directors I've met. She cared about her crew. My role was initially bigger. I was supposed to attend the slumber party, but I got another acting job, so Amy reworked the scenes so I could do both."

Stevens' role was small, but out of her 100-plus films she remains most recognized from her debut. "I'm still getting fan mail about it. A few years ago I even got a bath towel from a fan in honor of my shower scene. It's so amazing my role and the film have stuck with people this long. People are still renting it on a regular basis!"

One the many factors keeping *Slumber Party Massacre* a mainstay on renter's lists is Ralph Jones' electronic organ music. Often accentuating the horror, his music builds the suspense and scare sequences to tense climaxes. Though occasionally overbearing at times, the overall sound reminds one of the haunting sounds of silent classics like *The Phantom of the Opera* (1925), adding to the dark, foreboding mood.

The Slumber Party Massacre accomplishes more than its title or unfair T&A reputation would lead one to believe. Is it a witty satire with commentary on its exploitation roots, or a movie so predictable in the clichés of its subgenre it simply appears to be humorous?

It does promote women and simultaneously pokes fun at their exploitation in other features. At the same time, though, it exploits its own actresses, perhaps for "the cause." Maybe this is its intent. It's possible someone never even thought about it, and therefore it contradicts itself. Regardless, it remains a fun, scary and, yes, suspenseful film which utilizes dark corners to its best imitation of *Halloween*, keeps the murders gory and the action quickly paced. Combined with Brown's intriguing feminist slant and decent acting from its green cast, it is easy to comprehend its ongoing cult status, and why it spawned a trilogy and a parade of imitators.

Though not a massive success during its 1982 theatrical run, *The Slumber Party Massacre* was released on video in 1985, and became one of the biggest successes of the year. (It mustered additional profits when it was re-released theatrically in France during the summer of 1999 on new 35mm prints.) Corman's newly founded Concorde Pictures immediately set out to duplicate the profits with *Sorority House Massacre* (1986). Though the theme and title of the shocker was similar, it was artistically directed by Carol Frank, who had been Holden-Jones' personal assistant on *Slumber Party Massacre*. Frank's film featured inspired visuals and drew more of its mood from the sorority house-themed *Black Christmas* and the newly popular *A Nightmare on Elm Street* (1984).

Although Frank's direction had made the worn material seem fresh, the slasher trend was already near death by the time of its release. So when Concorde sought to reap more profits from its sleepover success, but fearing a slasher backlash, they decided to adapt the unique elements of *Sorority House Massacre* with the name value of their previous hit and devise not only a truly bizarre concoction, but another huge success to boot.

One of the few horror sequels of the 1980s to continue the storyline set by its previous installment (witness the *Howling* series to understand what the average franchise was destroying), *Slumber Party Massacre II* (1987) picks up five years later. Young Courtney Bates (now played by *Wings* star Crystal Bernard in her film debut) is now a high school senior living with her mother (Jennifer Rhodes of 1989's *Heathers*). Older sister Valerie (here portrayed in quick flashes by Cynthia Eilbacher of 1985's *Thunder Alley*) remains locked away in the loony bin while Courtney has started having issues of her own.

During recurring nightmares, Courtney dreams "The Driller Killer" has been reincarnated as an evil rocker (Atanis Ilitch of 1992's *A Private Matter*) using a wickedly humorous electric guitar with an excessively more phallic drill protruding from its neck. In an attempt to relax and escape the sexually tinged nightmares, Courtney and her friends Sheila (Juliette Cummins), Sally (Heidi Kozak) and Amy (*Playboy* Playmate Kimberly McArthur) head to Desert Springs, an empty development

Sally's (Heidi Kozak) "actual" death is far less graphic than her imagined one, but still disturbing in *Slumber Party Massacre II* (copyright 1987, New Concorde).

community where Sheila's father has just purchased a new condo. Hoping to become a rock band, the girls' plan is to practice for an upcoming dance and celebrate Courtney's seventeenth birthday. When her nightmares begin to meld with her "real" world, however, their weekend slumber party turns into a case of severe insomnia.

Slumber Party Massacre II is definitely one of the few sequels which attempts to expand upon the original premise. While going to great lengths to prove it can stand on its own, it simultaneously buys into the same trend most of the other late 1980s horror films attempted to capitalize from: copy Wes Craven's icon Freddy Krueger. A two-year span saw *Dreamaniac, Paperhouse, Slaughterhouse Rock, Bad Dreams, Deadly Dreams, Dream Demon* and scores of other dream stalkers assault audiences … and *Slumber Party Massacre II* was no exception.

Lensed as *Don't Let Go*, the movie put its heroine into the same delusional state as Heather Langenkamp's Nancy Thompson, but blatantly borrowed the more commercial green and red lighting set up during scary sequences from *A Nightmare on Elm Street 3: Dream Warriors* (1987). The Driller Killer also went from a psychopathic creep to a wisecracking musician. Kozak (TV's *Dr. Quinn, Medicine Woman*) remembers, "It wasn't what I'd thought it was originally going to be, because it wasn't *Slumber Party Massacre II* when we started filming. [Scenes] changed throughout the shoot once it became a sequel, but I think they may have known all along they were making another *Slumber Party Massacre* movie."

Some sources claim Bernard, then known for her role on TV's *It's a Living*, was less than happy when she learned of the title change, yet remained professional

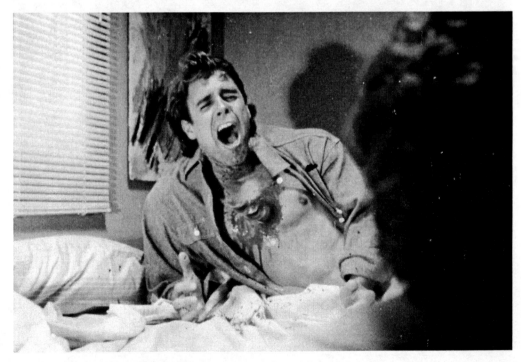

Matt (Patrick Lowe) experiences the best FX death sequence of the franchise in **Slumber Party Massacre II** (photograph courtesy New Concorde).

throughout the shoot. Kozak simply remembers Bernard as "a blast to hang out with. She was always spirited and fun."

Kozak had no complaints upon seeing the final product at its theatrical premiere, recalling, "The cast and crew all sat together and had a lot of fun. We were a really close group. Everyone was around the same age and just connected. I thought the movie was pretty silly, but also fun. It's total camp ... it was supposed to make you laugh, and it did."

Slumber Party Massacre II continued the humor of the first installment, though it was played more on the lighter side and offered less of a feminist influence. (Concorde again heavily promoted the "written, produced and directed by women" angle.) It also picked up on the influence of rock band soundtracks, having its female leads warble soft rock love ballads like "If Only" and "Why" by Wednesday Week and "Tokyo Convertible" by Man Alive.

The follow-up did have its share of darkness, mostly during the massacre sequences. Victims had the guitar from Hell dragged across their faces, backs, stomachs and legs before they were eventually disemboweled. In one of the most shocking — and effectively gruesome — scenes, the giant drill bit bursts from the bare chest of Courtney's boyfriend Matt (Patrick Lowe). Writer-director Deborah Brock (1989's *Rock 'n Roll High School Forever*) proves she can kill with the same wicked sense of humor as her male counterparts.

In one of the series most memorable murders, Sheila, already sporting a dripping gash in her arm, is chased through the house by the maniac as he drinks champagne, dances and sings the song "Let's Buzz." Upon cornering her in a hallway, he thrusts his drill into her stomach, sending humongous chunks of meat spinning out of her. In a particularly cruel touch, Courtney and Amy are on the opposite side of the door hearing the attack, but refuse to help her or let her in for fear of placing themselves in danger (a scene similar to the original film when Trish refuses to let Jeff come through the back door).

Kozak participated in perhaps the most infamous death scene in horror history. During one of Courtney's many hallucinations, she "sees" Sally's face grow into a giant pimple which explodes yellow puss directly into Courtney's screaming mouth. Kozak gleefully laughs, "When I got the part, Deborah asked if I was claustrophobic. I said no because I wanted the job, but I actually had no idea. Then I found out I would have to wear this latex on my face. The process took a lot longer than they'd originally anticipated, with the zit forming [in various stages]. I [was in the makeup] for over 12 hours, but it turned out great. It didn't leave any bad effects on my skin ... I'd gladly do it again!"

The actress, who drowned at the hands of Jason Voorhees in *Friday the 13th, Part VII: The New Blood* (1988) and dealt with the monsters of *Society* (1989), admits dying on screen is one of her favorite things to do. She giddily confesses, "Oh, I love doing death scenes! I think they're really fun. I love to scream..." She also offers an amusing side note. "After we wrapped, someone told me Concorde shot *The Nest* [1987] using the same building. They used real cockroaches and after the shoot was done they couldn't get rid of them, so the building had to be destroyed because it was so infested."

Kozak, who won a Best Actress award from the Hollywood Actors Theater for her stage role as an abused teenager in *Whores*, has only positive words concerning her director. "Deborah was so nice ... and great to me. I didn't want to do nudity and almost turned down the part. Deborah came to my apartment to talk about it. She asked what she could do, what could be compromised. I said, 'Put me in lingerie. I will wear any sexy bra you want,' and she said, 'Okay.' I know [the producers] were mad at her, but she stuck up for me," Kozak smiles. "They tried to pressure me later, but she [again] told them no. She went to battle for me on several occasions, [which] I've always truly appreciated."

Cummins, who also appeared in *Friday the 13th, Part V: A New Beginning* (1985) and *Psycho III* (1986), agrees that Brock's influence on set made filming relaxed. "*Slumber Party Massacre II* was fun because the director let me do what I wanted with the character," she says. "It was great to make [the character] Sheila who I thought she should be, not somebody else's impression. Deborah essentially just said, 'Go ahead.'"

This sense of ease is apparent in the actors' performances, as they truly seem like a group of friends. It also gives the film the feel of live-action animé mixed with a teen bubblegum movie on acid. Director of photography Thomas Callaway gives the films a soft, gentle look, aided by pastel set designs and costumes. Yet the violence which erupts and the manner in which it is portrayed seems, at times, entirely implausible in human realms. In addition to the giant zit, characters are attacked by headless chickens, eat severed hands and dodge the drill burrowing through floors and walls.

Throughout the film, only Courtney hears and sees the killer. Even as he laughs aloud preparing to impale Matt, Courtney sees him and gets out of the way, but Matt has no clue he's about to die. Elsewhere, the killer stands behind the bushes where the kids are eating, but Courtney is the only one who sees and hears him cackling at them. This is supposed to make the characters wonder as well if their friend is losing her mind like her sister. After Matt's mutilation, however, Courtney, doused in blood, runs to her friends, who now realize her "nightmares" are real, and now they too can inexplicably see the villain.

As each of the teens meet their grisly fate, Courtney tries to explain where he came from and how, but is never truly able to give an answer. At the conclusion, the camera pulls back to show Courtney lying on a urine-soaked cot in a mental hospital, screaming and insane. This leaves the viewer with three assumptions: One. Courtney did see the killer in her dreams and he was able to punch into our reality as flesh and bone, *ala A Nightmare on Elm Street 2: Freddy's Revenge* (1985). However, his charred remains are never found after the fiery climax. Two: Courtney only imagined the killer, while *she* was actually killing her friends during emotional distress. The best answer might be Three: The events of the previous 90 minutes never actually happened. Courtney has been in the institution the entire time. Her friends and the new massacre are merely creations of her warped mind.

If the final example was the intent, then the proceedings take on a certain level of unexpected sophistication. If not, then *Slumber Party Massacre II* is simply fluffy, enjoyable kitsch with a couple of scares and ultra-gooey gore.

Like its predecessor, *Slumber Party Massacre II* had little box office clout, but hit record numbers when released to video, becoming Concorde's biggest VHS hit of the 1980s. With many copies still in circulation over 15 years later, Cummins recalls, "I believe it went platinum in video sales … just phenomenal numbers. It was also a huge hit in Japan and Europe." As expected, at least one more chapter was in order.

By the time *Slumber Party Massacre III* hit theaters in the fall of 1990, slasher cinema was, no pun intended, dead. Silver screens had been taken over by latex monstrosities like *Tales from the Darkside: The Movie* and *Nightbreed*. The few slashers left, like *Friday the 13th, Part VIII: Jason Takes Manhattan* (1989), *Maniac Cop 2* (1990) and *Leatherface: The Texas Chainsaw Massacre III* (1990) sank fast at the box office. Their ilk was retreating to the same arena where most horror films found their profit salvation.

Slumber Party Massacre III (filmed as *Nite Lite* and temporarily titled *Stab*) was slated for video release in April 1991, but Concorde, among others, found dealings with distributor MGM to be less than satisfactory and withdrew their product from the Lion's lineup. By the time *Slumber Party Massacre III* was finally released to video in 1992, Concorde had developed it own video distribution arm, Concorde–New Horizons (now simply known as New Concorde), which became one of the few supporters of low-budget horror and science fiction-fantasy during the genre's lowest period in history. Likewise, it followed the growing trend of releasing alternate versions of movies, offering the last chapter of its trilogy in both "R" and "Unrated" formats.

Instead of continuing the storyline, writer-producer Catherine Cyran (1993's *White Wolves: A Cry in the Wild II*) and director Sally Mattison (1991's *Eye of the Eagle 3*) essentially retold the original movie, even recycling the character names. A group of girls celebrate one of their last summer evenings before their friend Jackie (Keely Christian) moves away.

Among the girlfriends are Diane (Brandi Burkett), Maria (Maria Ford), Janine (Hope Marie Carlton), Juliette (Lulu Wilson) and Susie (Maria Claire). Perverted neighbor Morgan (M.K. Harris) leers at the girls through his telescope. Unwanted troglodyte Duncan (David Greenlee) worms his way into the party posing as a pizza boy, unaware the real pizza girl (Marta Kober) has just been disemboweled behind him.

Eventually three mischievous boys, Michael (Garon Grigsby), Tom (David Kriegel) and Frank (David Lawrence), show up and scare the girls. They're allowed to stay once Jackie and Diane discover (in an effectively scary *and* funny moment) a creepy prowler (Yan Birch) outside the back door. Soon after, Ken (Brittain Frye), the final guest, arrives. Minutes later, Juliette is found stuffed inside a coat bag in the closet (a variation on a scene involving Trish in *Slumber Party Massacre*) and panic ensues. This is where *Slumber Party Massacre III* surprisingly picks up inspiration.

Instead of bumping off characters one at a time until only the final girl discovers the bodies and runs around screaming for the last 20 minutes, the initial murders and discoveries occur during the second act. More shocking, the teens actually decide to stick together (a unique concept indeed), though the killer, large portable drill in hand, manages to assault them anyway with a few clever moves.

Typically just wounding them at first so as to get a better stab at them later with less resistance, *Slumber Party Massacre III*'s Driller Killer has a more established psychotic personality … and it's ugly. The murderous appetite stems from horror's favorite motive: sexual abuse as a child. The difference in this circumstance is the molestation occurred from his favorite uncle. (Russ Thorn's motives were never established.) So here is a maniac who, when triggered by advances from one of the girls, has somewhat of a "reason" for his rampage. Unfortunately, this anger is aimed at the females when, in retrospect, it should be directed towards other males.

In the most shocking and unnerving scene, Maria is repeatedly sliced, punched and raped before finally being drilled to death, all while three of her friends watch, too terrified to help her. The sheer brutality and realism of the depiction is a credit to Ford's (1989's *Stripped to Kill II*) intense acting, but is also the point at which the movie is no longer camp or fun. It has truly become a horror film.

Burkett (1997's *Liar, Liar*) recalls, "I was on set thinking, 'How is [Maria Ford] doing that?' [The actor] was extremely intense and extremely there in the scene. It was disturbing, and I remember thinking, 'Gosh, I'm glad that's not me,' in more than one way. [The actor] being as powerful as he was, and the vulnerability Maria must have felt."

Burkett closes her eyes a moment and takes a deep breath, then adds, "Regardless of whether you're playing a character or not, you're still affected. [Somehow] Maria made it through, and I thought she did a great job." The subject of rape and abuse plays heavily into the remainder of the film.

Susie pays homage to Jamie Lee Curtis by hiding out in a closet. Once he locates her, the killer breaks in and savagely beats her unconscious. This unexpected mean-spirited tone is what gives this film its own identity. Where *Slumber Party Massacre* was a dark-humored, feminist commentary on slasher films and *Slumber Party Massacre II* tried to be more commercial and light-hearted, tapping into the trends of its immediate time, *Slumber Party Massacre III* derives more of its inspiration from Wes Craven's gritty and horrific *The Last House on the Left* (1972). Though *Slumber Party Massacre III* never equals the intensity or controversy of that revenge classic, it does create a sense of undefeatable doom. You dread what each character will have to endure before the end credits role. This can be viewed as either an accomplishment … or a sadomasochistic fantasy.

With brutality focused on the women (the men's deaths are typically quick, whereas the women's are more drawn-out), it seems the feminism attributed to the original film has been completely forgotten. Burkett's opinion differs. "I never though of it as feminist when we were shooting," Burkett relates, "but now when I see the film I think [the characters] were all strong individual females and it showed in their camaraderie and intelligence in taking care of the business at hand. I don't know if it goes as far as the first film, but I definitely see the whole message as feminist, portraying women who are strong-willed and independent."

Kober (1981's *Friday the 13th, Part 2*) has a drastically different view, cracking, "It was the basic plot with the set formula: You can't smoke pot, screw or take your top off. If you do, you die." She rolls her eyes and adds, "Then you've got the little blonde girl who doesn't do any of those things, runs around [screaming] and lives. It's just your average horror slasher."

The film, which was the first speaking role for Burkett (then 17), did surprise her on many levels. She smiles, "I was shocked at how the gore looked, because when you're shooting, the blood is just this sticky stuff which gets on everything and you're thinking, 'Oh, whatever.' Then when you see it on film, it looks real ... and I liked it. I liked it a lot!"

She was equally impressed with the action sequences, recalling, "Hope Marie Carlton [1988's *A Nightmare on Elm Street 4: The Dream Master*] said, 'Oh, I looked so stupid,' after she jumped through the glass door. Seeing it completed, I thought, 'Wow! She had no reason to feel bad. It looked awesome!'"

During the five-week shoot, Burkett insists, "The cast and crew were like family. We were almost always together." She also found Mattison's direction to be a wonderful learning experience. "Sally was great. I think I'd met her before briefly when she was a casting director. *Slumber Party Massacre III* was her first foray into directing. She was very patient with us and understood the need for rehearsals. She knew what she wanted and handled a cast of ten people, and was appreciative as well."

Burkett insists Mattison's attitude helped keep the set professional but relaxed. "She'd show her joy and communicate with us. Some directors just want to get the shot and move on, but Sally always said, 'Good job, guys,' or 'I'm not sure I liked it. Let's try again.' She was very honest and sincere."

Whether or not Mattison and Cyran were making a social commentary (as is hinted at in the 1998 documentary *Some Nudity Required*, in which Cyran implies they wanted to put the violence against women in men's faces in a sort of "You want it? Here it is" way), *Slumber Party Massacre III* stands apart from its subgenre and emulates it simultaneously. Like its predecessors, it is equally sparing in its use of expected nudity, has likable, humorous characters, and occasionally scenes of true horror. For Burkett and some of her co-stars, it furthered blossoming careers.

"*Slumber Party Massacre III* definitely helped me in the industry," says Burkett. "Concorde is known for breaking in new talent, and it certainly helped me get [auditions]. I was on a role pretty much afterwards. Everything about the movie was very positive and did a lot for me as a person and an actress. It took me to a whole new confidence level, and everyone in the industry was saying, 'Wow! She worked for Roger Corman's company. This is good. She has some real experience.'"

Most of the final chapter's cast continued to find work in film and television. Christian walked down *Hollywood Boulevard II* (1989) and met her *Earth Angel* (1991). Kriegel tried to stay *Alive* (1993), then found himself at high *Speed* (1994). After creepy Birch led *The People Under the Stairs* (1991), he helped *Bless the Child* (2000), while Harris said *I Love You, Don't Touch Me* (1998) and boarded *Babylon 5: A Call To Arms* (1999).

The impact of *The Slumber Party Massacre* and its sequels continues to be felt 20 years after it slashed across film screens. Further knock-offs had the titles *The Last Slumber Party* (1987), *The Stay Awake* (1987), *Sorority House Vampires* (1998) and the two-for-one deal *Sorority House Slumber Party Massacre* (1997). In fall 1998, Concorde announced its own spoof on the slasher resurgence, *I'll Scream If You Know What I Did Last Halloween at the Slumber Party Massacre*. When a number of similarly titled spoofs (which were later retitled and released as the box office smash *Scary Movie* and the less-successful *Shriek If You Know What I Did Last Friday the 13th*) were announced, Concorde put their project out of commission.

The success of the *Slumber Party Massacre* trilogy even inspired *Sorority House*

Massacre II (1992) which, directed by Jim Wynorski and filmed as *Nighty Nightmare*, utilized the left-over set from *Slumber Party Massacre III* and incorporated footage from *Slumber Party Massacre* as flashback sequences, using an altered storyline and voiceovers. Wynorksi also used this footage in future flicks like his similar *Hard to Die* (a.k.a. *Tower of Terror*, 1991).

Though there are currently dozens of Internet fan sites, a successful DVD re-release of the trilogy in 2000 and a profitable theatrical run of the original film in France, plus mention of the series in magazines and even on sitcoms like TV's *Will and Grace*, there are no current plans to revive the franchise. In 1994, 1998 and again in 2000, following the original publication of this article, spec scripts for *Slumber Party Massacre IV* were submitted to Concorde, but refused by Corman. The year 2003 will see the release of Concorde's *Cheerleader Massacre*, produced by Roger Corman, Jr., and lensed by Jim Wynorski. Filmed as *Slumber Party Massacre IV*, and featuring Brinke Stevens as "Linda" who survived (based on an idea lifted from the earlier submissions). The title was changed by the elder Corman, who has reportedly long deplored the series for its depiction of violence against women. Oddly, *Sorority House Massacre III* has recently wrapped production.

No one ever said *The Slumber Party Massacre* was a threat to the legacies of classics like *Psycho* (1960), *The Texas Chainsaw Massacre*, *Halloween* et al. It is, however, a scary, suspenseful movie which utilizes its dark mood, enjoyable characters and clear narrative … traits generally lacking in most slasher fare, spoof, satire or straight. Wynorski summarizes, "*Slumber Party Massacre* was very well done for the budget and tight scheduling. It was the launching pad for turning Brinke Stevens into a horror film legend, it was a starting point for Amy's career and, bottom line, its enduring legacy is that it was a fun film of the 1980s."

Brinke Stevens: 20 Years Later

Being Brinke Stevens has never been an easy job. Sure, there are the conventions, the film shoots, the glamourous makeup, the fan club, the tours and promotions, the photo shoots… Then, there's the conventions, the film shoots, the glamourous makeup, the fan club, the tours and promotions, the photo shoots….

The actress, who first arrived in the City of Angels in 1980 and shortly thereafter made a permanent mark on the horror psyche of two generations of fans, still loves what she does, even though she admits to some off days. On the twentieth anniversary of her first speaking role (and probably her best-known) in 1982's *The Slumber Party Massacre*, Stevens confirms she's ready to make some drastic changes. We'll get to that a little later; first a bit of back history….

Stevens hasn't always been an actress, model, writer and producer. In fact, she hasn't always been Brinke Stevens. Born Charlene Elizabeth Brinkman to her Army father Charles Brinkman II and mother Lorraine, who riveted bolts on WWII aircraft, the tyke was named after Charlemagne," a Roman Emperor around A.D. 800. The name meant "courage," and little Charlene has produced her fair share of it.

With a heritage of three-quarters German and one-quarter Mongolian, she, and younger brother Kerry often confused others concerning their nationalities. Her above-average intelligence coupled with an innate obsession with science fiction and

Star Trek, made the little girl a prime target for ridicule amongst classmates and neighbors in their 400 population township of Crest, California (20 miles outside San Diego). Of course, while her peers were skipping rope and making out in the back seats of cars, she had convinced her parents to buy her a microscope and dissecting kit, and spent her afternoons scraping road kill off back roads for inspection.

As she grew into her teens (and cut her hair and eyebrows to look like Spock), sea creatures began to grab her attention more than splattered possums. She recalls originally wanting to become a xenobiologist (an astronaut who studies alien life forms), but when she realized her ambitions were decades ahead of science, she opted to pursue oceanography instead. Meanwhile, she had embraced her "uniqueness" amongst classmates, but as she was developing into the face and body which would eventually land her in front of cameras, boys in school began to take notice. During her high school senior year, she was voted Senior Christmas Princess. A star was born ... only she hadn't realized it yet.

Double-majoring in biology and psychology at San Diego State University might seem a daunting task, but the shy girl on campus had maintained a 4.0 GPA (even while learning seven foreign languages) and scored exceptionally high on her SATs. She was accepted into Scripps Institute of Oceanography to obtain her Masters degree, which she received by studying the vision of seals. She was also a standout at the campus, not necessarily for her beauty, but because she was female ... the sole lass in the entire program. It seems her much publicized problems began there.

While the administration clearly told her she was to study only seals and sea lions, her heart led her to secretly research dolphins at Sea World. When the Institute found out, she was promptly expelled from the program and barred from receiving her desired Ph.D. (Over a decade later, possibly with fame on her side, she was awarded an honorary diploma.) During the next several years she worked a variety of ecological jobs, but was never truly satisfied. After the loss of her last science job due to budget cuts, the now twenty-something lady was ready to enter the second phase of her life.

In 1980, Charlene Brinkman married college sweetheart and *The Rocketeer* artist and creator Dave Stevens, but her their union was short-lived. She had sold everything she owned and moved to Los Angeles, where he was working as a storyboard artist for Steven Spielberg's *Raiders of the Lost Ark*. In their spare time, he had his wife pose as Betty Page, the popular 1950s pin-up girl. Interestingly, the drawings and storylines for *The Rocketeer* were echoing relationship troubles between them.

In *Cinefantastique* 22:1, the former Mrs. Stevens said, "One of the most popular images of Betty Page is the T-shirt artwork where she's bound, gagged, slung over the Rocketeer's shoulder, and wearing little more than an angry expression. I posed for that sketch, bound, gagged, leaning over the edge of a sofa, trying to communicate with Dave with this 'Will you hurry up and take this picture!' type of glare." Much of the comics dialogue, she says, was verbatim transcripts of their real-life conversations.

As her husband's work began to receive notice, her own modeling career unintentionally flourished as well ... a development which made Mr. Stevens uncomfortable. Furthermore, she had made it clear she still wanted to pursue a science job in L.A., not remain a stay-at-home wife. Jealousies soon put a strain on the relationship,

and within six months the
marriage had dissolved. This
is where her Hollywood career
truly kicks into high gear.

Desperate for income,
Stevens searched for, and
landed, modeling jobs. She
started with simple print
work, then eventually worked
her way up to posing for men's
magazines like *Playboy*, *Penthouse* and *Oui*. Meanwhile,
Famous Monsters magazine
creator Forrest J Ackerman,
whom she had met as a teenager at a convention in 1973,
was about to introduce Stevens to her first film experience.

"I realized recently that
if I'd never met Forrest J Ackerman, my whole reality
might be different," she smiles
affectionately. "When I was a
teenager, I attended a Comic
Con masquerade as Vam-
pirella, my favorite comic
book heroine at the time.
Forry was a guest of honor,
and after I won first prize we
posed together for publicity

Stevens maintained a steady income in her early career
by modeling (photograph courtesy Brinke Stevens).

photos. It was the most amazing night of my life, to hear the cheering of an admiring crowd, plus the chance to meet someone I totally revered. I credit that one experience for dispelling my painful shyness and giving me a huge boost of self-confidence,
which served me well for my acting career.

"Forry and his wife, Wendayne, soon became like my godparents, often inviting me to their L.A. home and showing me around the town. Soon after I'd moved
to L.A. myself, photographer Dan Golden saw my Vampi photo on Forry's wall and
hired me for my first [University of Southern California] student film."

Golden, who photographed Stevens for the premiere cover of *Femme Fatales* in
1992, sought out the model to make her true screen debut, sans dialogue, in *Zyzak
Is King* (1980). Stevens, who had changed her first name to Brinke (a favorite nick-
name) and retained her married name, portrayed a witch named Sara. Though the
student film saw little release, it set off a spark in her.

"If not for Forry, I might still be in San Diego working as a scientist," she chuckles. "The other person I must credit for my acting career is my ex-husband. If [Dave

and I] hadn't gotten married, even though our union was short-lived, I would never have moved to Hollywood in the first place. He got me here and gave me a great last name, for which I will always be thankful."

Modeling jobs continued to roll in. One day, after leaving a modeling agency which had closed early, Stevens passed an open office door. Stopping a moment to peek in at the movie posters covering the walls, she heard a gruff voiced demand that she enter. The man, Jacob Bressler, asked to see her modeling portfolio, then immediately cast her as an extra in the comedy *All the Marbles* (1981). The rest is history.

Bressler continued hiring Stevens for work as an extra in what she reports to be "nearly 100 films." She soon discovered that shedding her clothes on camera, still sans dialogue, would earn her larger paychecks. Being completely comfortable with her body, Stevens was often cast alongside Michelle Bauer and Linnea Quigley, each performing similar duties. Then came the day she won her first speaking role as Linda in *The Slumber Party Massacre*. The tongue-in-cheek slasher film, written by Rita Mae Brown (1983's *Educating Rita*) and directed by Amy Jones (1987's *Maid to Order*), went on to become a cult favorite, and suddenly Brinke Stevens was no longer just a model or an extra ... she was an actress.

Though she's quick to admit her roles were far from meaty, and she was still required to shed her clothes for most of them, it remains a fact some of her early films had some decent names, and box office. Among her list of once-popular and occasionally still enduring early work: *The Seduction, Terminal Velocity* (1982), *Star 80, The Man Who Wasn't There, Private School* (1983), *This Is Spinal Tap, Body Double* (1984), *Savage Streets,* TV's *Days of Our Lives* (1985), *Three Amigos* and *Psycho III* (1986).

Around the release of *The Slumber Party Massacre* and her appearances in several volumes of *Playboy Video Magazine*, a surprised Stevens began receiving a hefty number of fan letters. She was advised to begin attending conventions. Unlike the few other actresses who appeared, Stevens gave out her photos and signatures to fans for free. As her popularity and fan base grew, she began making conventions a regular part of her routine, and formed an official fan club selling materials from her growing list of features, modeling photos and original material. She frequently dealt with her fan club members, at its peak numbering well over 15,000, on a one-to-one level, spending most of her free time hand-writing personal responses to each letter she received.

"Ten years ago, it was at least an eight hours a day job for both me and a personal assistant: processing 50 to 100 letters a day, filling fan club orders, returning calls, booking travel and appearances, packing or unpacking, restocking products, to name but a few typical requirements," she reports. "Thankfully, it's quieted down a bit. I now spend my mornings at home doing fan club tasks, putting in four hours 'til noon. Then I devote another couple hours to running fan club–related errands, like going to my mailbox, the post office, bank, office supply, etc. Late afternoon 'til bedtime, I work at my desk doing e-mail, magazine articles, interviews and such. Pretty predictable and not too exciting. Once in a while I splurge and rent some horror DVDs and make a big bowl of popcorn. It helps me to feel like I have a life..."

While she maintained a steady rise in both film-television work and fan base, she soared to the level of big-time horror star in 1987. It was the dawn of the video

Brinke Stevens "ran, screamed and died horribly" for the first time with her first speaking role in 1982's *The Slumber Party Massacre* (photograph courtesy Brinke Stevens).

age, and video stores were popping up at every other corner across America. With no franchise competition, most of them were "mom and pop" owned. There was one dilemma: Most of their shelf space was empty. Drive-ins were vastly disappearing, so B-filmmakers needed a new way to get their product seen. Wisely, they found their niche in the direct-to-video market. Stevens, along with Linnea Quigley and Michelle Bauer, plus a few other ladies, became the nubile, and frequently naked, stars for this market.

Hired most often by Fred Olen Ray, Jim Wynorski and David DeCoteau, Stevens, Quigley and Bauer appeared in a glut of kitschy, campy and typically fun horror fodder. *Sorority Babes in the Slimeball Bowl-a-Rama*, *Slavegirls from Beyond Infinity* and *Nightmare Sisters* were among the first of the terrifying trio's efforts to attract public attention, and the "Scream Queen" era was born.

Quigley (1985's *The Return of the Living Dead*) was often called as the leader of the three. Her little blonde cheerleader with punk undercurrents, produced with a giggly persona, worked wonderfully opposite Stevens' intelligent, sultry attitude and Bauer's (1987's *Hollywood Chainsaw Hookers*) outgoing, funny presence and perfect body.

"As an actor, I'd supported myself just fine since 1980," says Stevens. "Then, around 1987, the whole Scream Queen phenomenon took off. Suddenly I was riding

(*Left to right*) Linnea Quigley, Michelle Bauer and Brinke Stevens starred in the 1987 cult favorite *Nightmare Sisters.*

in limos, flying to foreign countries for film festivals, appearing on dozens of popular talk and entertainment TV shows, and truly feeling like a glamourous movie star. It was the most wonderful time of my whole life. The only thing which might ever top it would be my future success as best-selling author or artist."

Stevens readily admits that much of her fame and frequent work were based on her willingness to strip in front of the camera. "In the early 1980s, so few actresses would do nude scenes. I was among a small group who were willing to be body doubles and do shower–hot tub scenes, so we got a lot of work and were able to support ourselves at the start of our careers. When video hit the scene in the mid–'80s, B-movies filled a new niche by offering near-naked babes, and it was obligatory for us to do at least one topless scene in any film. If I had refused, I could not even remotely have supported myself, nor would I have garnered such a tremendous fan following from those sexy B-films." She insists it's a task she's never regretted.

"Quite the opposite," she confirms. "I've always felt comfortable being naked, from my early days in San Diego when I went with friends to a nude beach. I like my own body, and I was just a natural at posing for the camera. I'm also proud so many others have enjoyed looking at me, especially since I'm a small-breasted woman in an age of impossibly large, siliconed bosoms." The actress, who refuses to even get her ears pierced, maintains she will never get implants.

She adds, surprisingly, she has never felt any uncomfortable pressure to film a nude scene "except when it's part of a love scene. I've never enjoyed having to simulate sex or an orgasm for an audience. It's just plain embarrassing. Fortunately, I haven't had to do much of that at all."

As the video-boom began to die out in the early 1990s, and many of the true Scream Queens began vanishing from the market, Stevens managed to remain on top, and busy. Her fan club continued to expand, and her mini-empire began to include the series of comic books *Brinke of Eternity* and *Brinke of Destruction*. Trading cards, personal effects (such as wardrobe from her films) and her personalized *Private Collection* entries sold big numbers. She was dating active members within the industry like Fred Olen Ray, writing her own screenplays (like 1991's *Teenage Exorcist*) and magazine articles, voicing her own 1-900 horror hotline (an award winner as the best 900 number in the country), was animated for cartoons like *Garfield and Friends*, and mascoting as "Evila" for *Famous Monsters* magazine. In 1994 she was deemed the reigning Scream Queen by *Entertainment Weekly*. Then the market crashed.

By 1995, video shelves were overstocked, independent video stores had been devoured by politicized franchises and "used" bins at Blockbuster were filled with the movies which had made Stevens and her co-horts famous. The horror market itself was considered officially dead. Quigley had stepped down from her throne, Bauer retired ... several times ... and the directors who had cemented their own legends as horror auteurs could typically only find work with Band's Full Moon Pictures and Corman's Concorde–New Horizons. *Basic Instinct* (1992) had made erotic thrillers the over-whelming trend of the mid-'90s, which is where the few remaining B-thespians could find jobs. Stevens was among them.

Though work was slow to nil for most actors and actresses, Stevens persisted, and prevailed. She managed to appear in 14 new movies and documentaries and continued to thrive on the convention circuit. With the notice in *Entertainment Weekly* came legitimacy as an actress. Her required nude scenes were becoming fewer, her dramatic roles increasing. Her appearance as straight-laced and dependable Aunt Beth in 1995's *Mommy*, written and directed by author Max Allan Collins, garnered her critical raves. Her performance in the 1997 sequel, *Mommy 2: Mommy's Day*, brought even more interest and positive reviews.

Her transition from nubile coed to respectable actor can be viewed from two angles. Stevens had entered the acting and modeling game late. She was already 26 when she portrayed 17-year-old "Linda" in *The Slumber Party Massacre*. Thanks in most part to her prolonged youthful appearance, she continued playing high school and college girls well into her late thirties. Even as she progressed into slightly older characters, typically in their late twenties, like 1996's overlooked *Hybrid*, she was still being considered a sexual object. However, in entering her mid-forties, she could no longer pull off the teenager (though at age 42 she still portrayed an 18-year-old in 1998's *Victoria's Shadow*). In fact, she'd already been aged, in what is possibly her most terrifyingly effective role, to a crazed mother in *Grandma's House* (1989). With most female characters within the horror/sci-fi/erotic thriller genres typically aged around 19, Stevens was being boosted into the roles of "the aunt" and, by the early 2000s, "the mother."

The other angle is that Stevens was becoming more aware of her craft. She was paying attention to characterization, motifs, background. She had honed her craft for so many years (without ever taking a single acting class), her talents and on-set experience had finally caught up with her. She, however, is the first to admit that having a career based on her appearance rather than performance can result in some harsh realities about ageism.

"Our culture is so horribly youth-oriented, making it seem like a crime to grow old," she seethes with disappointment and a tinge of disgust. "I look at it logically ... it's inevitable. No one likes it, but that's the way it is. Given that age span from college babes to moms, I actually think the older roles are so much more interesting. Those moms and aunts I've played recently were all very developed, complex, fully realized characters. Can you say that about a teenage cheerleader?"

The late '90s were an incredibly slow period for both Stevens and all B-film actors. By 1999, she was burned out from the frustrations of Hollywood. Her *Buried Nightmares* script, which had been bought and put into pre-production on a number of occasions, was repeatedly delayed, and she was ready to give it all up.

Stevens poses in the early 1990s for photographer Dan Golden (photograph courtesy Dan Golden).

"Although I've suffered a few serious injuries and creative tensions on set before, it's never been enough to make me think of leaving the business. However, there was one year, 1999, when I was so utterly burned out I wondered if I could continue as an actor," she reveals. "I took that year off and only did one day of filming, instead of my usual half-dozen movie projects. I planted a garden, learned gourmet cooking, pursued my hobbies like stained glass, mosaic tile and oil painting. I also wrote three screenplays with one of my favorite collaborators, Ted Newsom [1985's *Attack of the B-Movie Monster*]. It completely revitalized me, and by the next year I'd shot 11 movies, which is the most ever in a single year."

Indeed, Stevens again pulled a swift one-two. Typically, when an actress grows older and takes time away from the business, it spells the end to her career. (Hollywood's sexist mentality tends to allow male actors less trouble evolving into older roles.) With the success of *The Craft* and *Scream* in 1996 and, more importantly, 1999's shot-on-video cultural phenomenon *The Blair Witch Project*, B-movies, shot on both film and video, were once again in hot demand ... as was Stevens.

Movie offers literally poured in at such a rapid pace it left the actress's head reeling. Her film roles have numbered nearly 35 in just the past three years, with another four set to go into production by summer 2003. With most of her counterparts from her '80s heyday long gone, and the likes of Debbie Rochon, Tanya Dempsey, Debra Mayer and Holly Sampson rapidly rising up the B-movie ranks to claim the throne, it seems odd that Stevens would have regained popularity at such a speedy clip. She theorizes, "In my early years, I built up a good reputation with both fans and filmmakers. As such, my name has remained in demand for over two decades. Also, many of my 13-year-old fans have since grown up to become writers and directors themselves [sample *Witchouse 3*'s J.R. Bookwalter, *Hell Asylum*'s Danny Draven, even yours truly]. They now all want to hire and work with me. It's a fun twist of fate where everybody wins!"

She's even returned to working with one of the men who made her famous. In August 2001, Stevens rejoined reining B-Movie director David DeCoteau on the set of *The Frightening*. "David was as relaxed and easy going as he's always been ... and he's still only willing to give you one take," she laughs. "Unless you have a heart attack on the set, you'll only get one shot at any scene. Fortunately, I knew my lines and hit all the marks, so it went down quickly and smoothly ... just the way we like it."

The supernatural horror flick, about a teenager (Matt Twining) who realizes his school has some dark, ghastly secrets in its basement, finds Stevens as the tormented kid's mother. In a true rarity for the actress, she portrayed a character who doesn't scream, get naked or turn into a monster. She's just normal ... well, relatively anyway.

"Well, obviously, what you're describing is lots more fun," she giggles, "but having just finished *Witchouse 3*, where I spent two hours getting into horror makeup every day, it was a relief to look fairly normal and plain. I was ready for something simple and easy like *The Frightening*, where I even got to play one scene in my bathrobe and slippers!"

She reveals playing good vs. evil characters—caked in demonic makeup—are still among her favorite roles. "One can't exist without the other, and I enjoy them equally," she smiles. "My favorite role is both good and evil, where I start out normal and end up either insane, demon-possessed, or a vampire. Some of Fred Olen Ray's earlier movies allowed me to play that range, like *Haunting Fear, Spirits, Bad Girls from Mars, Warlords* and so on.

"I've always enjoyed Fred Olen Ray's films. He's challenged me as an actor and given me some memorable roles in almost a dozen movies. "His style is relaxed, yet efficient, and I've learned so much about directing from him as well."

Her thoughts turn to another co-worker. "I have to praise Debbie Rochon, with whom I've shared [five] projects: *American Nightmare, Bleed, Witchouse 3, We're Coming to Help* and *Dr. Horror's Erotic House of Idiots*. She's an incredibly hard worker, not afraid to tackle the wildest roles or delve into the darkest emotions. Despite her fierce intensity, she's a very light, spiritual, generous and knowledgeable person who's fun to spend time with off-camera, too. If anyone deserves to be crowned the 'New Queen,' she does," Stevens insists.

The fact that Stevens has outlasted most of her female peers remains an intriguing topic. After all, being labeled a Scream Queen was only cool from 1987 to approximately 1992. The title carried a stigma with it, attached to direct-to-video schlock in most cases, and throughout the 1990s Stevens found herself surrounded by other so-called Queens at conventions. A horde of busty young babes had invaded the circuit, and Stevens soon learned any girl who had the money to rent a table could, and was, slapping down snapshots on the polycloth coverings, charging $5 and up for an autograph, typically wearing only what was required by law under their vampire capes, and introducing themselves as "Scream Queens." Making matters worse, not only didn't these "ladies" have a single film credit to their names, but it was rumored that any male fan could pay for five minutes of some "special attention" in a bathroom stall or a none-too-heavily guarded stairwell. Both the dignity and credibility of the conventions, and the girls who appeared at them, became tarnished.

The result was lower attendance, fewer dollars earned at tables and a negative backlash against the horror moniker. Stevens attempted to ditch the title for a period, but realized her image had been etched in horror history stone. Rather than run from it, she forged ahead. "The sheer joy of doing it has kept me going," she says. "Eventually, I think it became old hat and tedious for the others, and they simply didn't get what they wanted from it. I've never lost interest in making movies and seeing all my fans at the shows."

She notes that the industry itself has changed quite a bit since her early days. "I can only speak for myself, by noting many young filmmakers have had far less experience than me. So they tend to allow and welcome my input on set, which leads to a very cooperative, creative atmosphere for everyone. It's such a reward to be respected for my wisdom now, rather than merely being told to 'Stand over there and say your lines,'" she chuckles.

For all the zany, twisted and amusing characters the actress has portrayed on screen, she admits there are a few roles she's long desired to portray. At her peak, Stevens was awarded the chance to audition for Francis Ford Coppola's *Dracula* (1992) as one of the three vampire brides. After numerous call backs, she "made it to the final cut of seven girls out of 500, but didn't get in the last round. In retrospect, I'm glad I didn't have to have snakes crawling through my hair…" Another regret is not accepting a larger role in *The Slumber Party Massacre*. As it stands, Linda meets her maker within the first 20 minutes of the flick. Originally, however, Stevens was supposed to make it well into slumbering before she bit the phallic drill bit. A prior modeling commitment kiboshed the opportunity, but director Jones liked the actress so much the script was rearranged to fit her in.

Other roles she's longed to play haven't been lost to other actresses, but by languishing in pre-production hell. She insists on looking at the positive side, which is the remaining possibility she still has a chance to get these characters on screen. "For my own project, *Buried Nightmares*, I will soon have a chance to play twins with two very different personalities," she says of the script, which she first sold nearly five years ago. "It's further complicated when Twin A murders Twin B and assumes her identity. It's an actor's dream, if you can just keep it all sorted out in your head!"

Her excitement grows as she continues, "Another fun new challenge will arise for *Sim Siren: Chloe*, where I will voice and model for the titular blonde animé character, set in a cybertech future. I contributed to writing that script, and will also be a co-producer."

Of the projects, *Buried Nightmares* is the one she has longed to film the most.

"[It] was my fourth script sold, and the first time I insisted on being a co-producer [as well as an actor]," she says. "My partner and director, Gene Vine, was a big shot at Paramount Studios who's now retired from the grind, but is still eager to dabble in the film business. His lawyer, who was in charge of our growing investment money, did a horrible thing last year — he skipped town with nearly a million dollars, some of it our movie budget. The lawyer is in jail now, but he refuses to reveal where he hid the money. So now we're starting from scratch to raise the funds."

She pauses, then adds, "It was extremely disheartening, because we've worked so hard for a couple of years to make this movie a reality. On the positive side, I have learned so much about producing from Mr. Vine, a real hands-on education you can't get in film school."

With all of the challenges the actress has faced over the last two decades, it's a bit strange she's never tackled the stage … and doesn't really plan to. "I prefer movies, because you generally shoot one take and then it's over," she says. "A stage play requires weeks, or even months, of group rehearsals, and then you have to perform it over and over for several more weeks or months. I really lack the patience for that sort of thing. Some people say they perform better in front of a live audience, but I don't need that adrenaline rush to pull out my best performance."

She considers the topic a second more and adds, "The closest thing I did to a stage play was Joe Casey's *We're Coming to Help*, an ensemble piece with seven actors [including Rochon]. We were required to memorize an entire script and shoot it all in one take, over and over again. It was a real challenge, not only in terms of memorization, but also of patience. It was, however, an interesting experiment and will prove to be something very different from the usual low-budget science fiction film."

In the 2001 action-drama *Real Time: Siege at Lucas Street Market*, Stevens led a cast during a hostage situation seen through the eyes of the store's security cameras. Not only did the entire cast have to run upwards of 20 minute blocks of dialogue, hitting all their marks along the way, but Stevens got to play possibly the first female hero who was seven months pregnant!

Stevens seems to be relishing new opportunities and leaving her sexpot image behind. One look at her forever expanding résumé justifies her position as one of the top B-film actresses in history, yet even with thousands of adoring fans, she found the people she wanted to impress the most weren't viewing her career choice the same way.

"At first, it was very difficult for my parents to accept and understand my new acting career," she divulges. "My father had hoped I would become a medical doctor and discover a cure for cancer. It wasn't until *Mob Boss* [1990] played on prime-time, network television that they felt a swell of pride for my chosen path as an actor. The following day, we all went out to a restaurant, and my dad glowingly told the waitress, 'You may have seen my daughter on TV last night … she's an actress!' It was a real breakthrough moment, when I first felt their approval and support."

With her career back in full swing in the new millennium, Brinke Stevens finally seemed to be back on top. Then, in October 2001 came a blow so close and personal, it changed her entire outlook on life, love, and career. Brinke lost her mother. On the day of a photoshoot for the tenth anniversary cover of *Femme Fatales* at Ward Boult's L.A. studio, Brinke joined Julie Strain and Lisa Wilcox in a cloud of orange and yellow smoke. It was a hot day, and everyone noticed Brinke wasn't as lively and boisterous as usual. She looked exhausted and defeated. Her mother had been severely ill for several weeks, and the actress was trying to maintain her career and care for both her parents simultaneously. She had only an hour to shoot, as she needed to rush back to San Diego to be with them. Hours later, Brinke's mother passed away in her arms.

"My mother was also my best friend. When she died, I felt like my heart had been ripped out. Part of me just wanted to give up, to become apathetic and withdrawn. On the other hand, the concept of 'mortality' really hit home ... to only have a limited time to accomplish your dreams. If anything, it accelerated my efforts to achieve my as-yet unfulfilled goals, such as writing children's books and novels, or having a gallery showing of my paintings. Now, moreso than ever, I'm really clear and focused about what I truly want in my future ... and I'm much more determined to make it a reality."

She's humbled a moment. Yet her energy is forthright and determination solid. "My mother's death clarified a lot of things in my head, like where I've been so far, and where I want to go in my life," she says. "If the first act of my life's story was me as a scientist, and the second act has been me as an actress, then I want the third act to be my fulfillment as a writer.

"Although I've sold four screenplays and penned scores of non-fiction articles, I still don't feel completely fulfilled at that career. I've started, and have yet to finish, countless children's books, juvenile fiction and a sci-fi novel. I'll need to create the proper time and space to finish those projects. It could mean a major shift in my life, like isolating myself in a mountain cabin for two years—[and] I might just do it!"

Among her immediate plans are to revamp and essentially eliminate certain factors of her fan club, scale back on the number of films she does each year and even move away from the heart of the entertainment world. "Soon, I plan to phase out my hard-copy annual Newsletter, which gets mailed to about 15,000 fans. By now, most people have access to the Internet, and it just makes sense to save all that paper and expense [like printing and mailing]. Regularly, I do updates on my official website www.brinke.com, like sharing my latest movie news, convention appearances, new products and so on. It's surely a better way for my fans and I to stay in touch, so let's do it that way and save a few trees," she smiles.

The move from Los Angeles is based both on her prior convictions and the unfortunate economy. "In L.A., housing prices have skyrocketed to an impossible level. A simple 'two bedroom-one bath' 1950's tract-house now costs half a million dollars," she exclaims. "For practical reasons, I first started to look at more affordable homes up to 90 minutes outside the city. Meantime, I suddenly realized that I've grown to hate L.A., and I just don't want to be here any more. The stress factor is enormous; it's like living in a giant pressure cooker. I used to think I needed to be in a big city for the wealth of culture and entertainment. Lately, I'm drawn to a more peaceful, quiet, rural setting."

Do these changes in any way imply Stevens is looking to eventually retire from the film business itself? "For as long as they'll want to hire me, I'll work as an actress," she confirms, surely prompting a sigh a relief from film fans across the world. "It's just too much fun to ever give it up entirely. I'm also eager to continue my work behind the scenes as a writer, director and producer. Nonetheless, I've decided to devote a larger portion of my time to writing, including journalism articles, short stories and novels. Undoubtedly, something else will have to be sacrificed to free up that valuable time. This year, I'll drastically cut back on conventions, since less travel means a lot more hours at my computer desk."

Does she really have designs on competing with the boys club and scooting herself into the director's chair? "Working on over 100 films, I've been keenly observant and have absorbed a lot of filmmaking technique. I once was an assistant director on a Utah project called *First Loves,* which was a very delightful and educational experience. I think I'll be pretty good at it, especially in dealing with the actors and encouraging their best performances. I've learned both what to do—and what *not* to do—from all my previous directors."

Looking back at the last 20 years, Stevens admits to a desire to change very little about her career and life path. There is, however, one nagging detail she occasionally dwells on. "I'm genuinely surprised I never made it as an A-movie star," she reveals. "I think I did the right things: hustled for auditions, had good agents and presumably possessed the looks and talent. It just never happened. I believe in fate and destiny, so I have to think it's all been perfect just as it is now."

With the unexpected career path life has thrown her, it makes one curious as to whether or not Stevens regrets not going further with her science career. "I was so certain I'd be a marine biologist for the rest of my life. But my path took a sharp turn in 1979, when I was literally kicked out of school for some unauthorized experiments—and I accidentally became an actress the following year. For a decade, I felt such shame about my aborted science career, until I went back for a ten year reunion and discovered how much my former colleagues admire and support my new path. They made me feel I was the lucky one for getting out when I did!"

Still, there must be some desire to return to her childhood instincts. "I've toyed with the idea of going back into dolphin research," she ponders, "but technology and equipment have changed so much in the last 20 years. I would have to go back to graduate school to get re-educated, and I just couldn't face any more schooling at this point in my life."

Her honesty is appreciated, her life enviable. These traits, combined with an appreciation for knowing fans on personal levels, and a gratitude for those who helped her to succeed, have given Brinke Stevens a sort of plausible accessibility. To many, she isn't a character on the screen. She's a real person ... a friend. Who is the real Brinke? Most probably envision her in a dark castle atop a gloomy mountain surrounded by stone gargoyles. She is seen as a diva and vamp, even during her slumbering hours. The truth is, however, movie star Brinke is a completely separate entity from the homebody Charlene Elizabeth, a name only used by her immediate family and Forrest Ackerman.

Stevens' quaint home hides in the jungle-like culture of the Valley. It is littered with crystals, candles and antiques. She is a very spiritual person, her door always open to friends ... pot roasts and fresh vegetables from her garden cooking in the kitchen. She is a caregiver to those who know her best. She wants others to succeed, and tries to send them down the correct paths by offering guidance, support and even an introduction or two. When all is said and done, she is simply a human being.

"When I'm not appearing on-camera or at an event, I stay home wearing no makeup, hair in a bun, casual sweatpants and slippers," she confesses. "I prefer flannel pajamas to sexy lingerie. I don't go to many Hollywood parties. Instead, I'm a homebody who likes to read, watch videos, tend my garden, cook meals for my friends, feed the ducks at a nearby lake and work on my hobbies. I cherish the moments when I *do* become a glamourous vamp ... but it really isn't my natural state."

Stevens has clearly earned her place in cinematic history. Whether chasing teenagers with chainsaws, battling inner demons or making men across America yearn for a gentle kiss, she's proven herself a lasting commodity to her co-workers, fans and friends. Surely, she plans to one day write an autobiography encompassing her career and unique life ... right? "I've been shot by some of the greatest glamour photographers, like Ken Marcus, Jeff Dunas, Peter B. Kaplan and so forth, and also drawn by some of the most remarkable artists like Julie Bell, Boris Vallejo, Clyde Caldwell, Dorian Cleavenger, etc. It would be lovely to collect it all in one hefty volume," she decides.

The title of this lavish coffee table book? *Brinke: A Body of Work.*

Brinke Stevens Filmography*

Acting on Impulse (1993) a.k.a. *Eyes of a Stranger; Roses are Dead; Secret Lives* ... Waitress

All the Marbles (1981) ... Extra

American Nightmare (2002) ... Lisa

Apocalypse (2003) ... Sister Anna Maria

Attack of the B-Movie Monster (1985) (new footage 2002) ... Dr. Nikki Carlton

The Bad Father (2002) ... Shady

Bad Girls from Mars (1991) ... Myra

The Bad Movie Police (vignettes) (2005) ... Mayor

Birth Rite (2003) ... Mona Proctor

Bleed (2003) ... Phyllis Patterson

Blood on the Backlot (2001) ... Sabrina Morgan

Blood Reaper (2002) ... Sosha

Body Double (1984) ... Holly Does Hollywood

Carmilla (2003) ... Juliet

Cheerleader Massacre (2003) a.k.a. *Slumber Party Massacre IV* ... Linda

Chinatown Connection (1990) ... Missy

Corpses Are Forever (2003) ... Dr. Thesiger

Cyberzone (1995) a.k.a. *Droid Gunner; Phoenix 2* ... Kitten

Dark Romances (1989) ... Dianna

Dark Romances 2 (1990) ... Dianna

Days of Our Lives (TV) (1985) ... Dance Troupe Leader

Deadly Stingers (2003) ... Harry's Wife

Delta Delta Die! (2003) ... Rhonda Cooper

Demon Treasure (2003) ... Archaeologist

Demon Lust (1997) a.k.a. *Eyes Are Upon You* ... Amanda

Demon Skull (2003) ... The Dark Lady

Dr. Horror's Erotic House of Idiots (2002) ... Herself

Emmanuelle 4 (1984) ... Dream Girl

Fatal Games (1984) a.k.a. *Killing Touch; Olympic Nightmare* ... Shower Girl

5 Dark Souls, Part III: Retribution (2003) ... Sandra

The Forgotten Ones (1984) ... Gangster's Girlfriend

The Frightening (2002) ... Mrs. Peterson

Garfield and Friends (1996) (animated) ... Brinke, the Horror Hostess

Girls of Penthouse (1984) ... Ghost-Town Woman

Grandma's House (1989) a.k.a. *Grandmother's House* ... Mystery Woman

*Stevens has appeared in bit parts in so many features on which she did not receive credit, *she* doesn't even remember all of them. Therefore, it would be incorrect to call this list complete. However, it is as thoroughly researched as I could accomplish. Dates are intended to reflect the year of release, not of the filming.

Haunting Fear (1990) ... Victoria
Heads Are Gonna Roll (2003) ... Bartender
Hell Asylum (2002) ... Leader of the Dead
Brides
A Hell of a Night (2002) ... Dr. Gates
Hollywood Scream Queen Hottub Party
(1991) ... Herself
Horrorvision (2000) ... Toni
Hybrid (1996) ... Dr. Leslie Morgan
Illicit Dreams 2 (1996) a.k.a. *Death &*
Desire ... Dianne
Invasion of the Scream Queens (1992) ...
Herself
Invisible Mom (1995) ... Dr. Price
Jack-O (1995) ... Witch
Jigsaw Murders (1988) ... Stripper #1
Julia Wept (2000) ... Kathryn
The Kid with the X-Ray Eyes (1999) ...
Agent X11's Sexy Girl
L.A. Street Fighter (1985) a.k.a. *Ninja Turf;*
Chinatown ... Boss's Girl
Let's Do It!(1982) ... Jogger
The Man Who Wasn't There (1983) ...
Nymphette
Mark of the Astro-Zombies (2002) (billed as
"Victoria Munro") ... Cindy Natale
Masseuse (1996) a.k.a. *American Masseuse*
... Hotel Manager
Mob Boss (1990) ... Sara
Mom, Can I Keep Her? (1998) ... Jennifer
Mommy (1995) ... Aunt Beth
Mommy 2: Mommy's Day (1997) ... Aunt
Beth
Monsters and Maniacs (1988) (documen-
tary) ... Hostess
More Candid Candid Camera (1983) ...
Horse Rider
Munchie (1992) ... The Band
Murder Weapon (1990) ... Girl in Shower
Naked Gun (1988) ... Running Girl in
Shower
Nightmare Sisters (1987) a.k.a. *Sorority Suc-*
cubus Sisters ... Marci
100 Years of Horror (1996) (documentary)
... Herself
100 Years of Horror: Scream Queens (1996)
(documentary) ... Herself
100 Years of Horror: The Count & Company
(1996) (documentary) ... Herself
Over the Wire (1995) ... Jenny
Phantom of the Mall: Eric's Revenge (1989)
... Girl in Dressing Room

Playboy Video Magazine, Volume 1 (1982)
... Marie in "Ribald Classic"
Playboy Video Magazine, Volume 4 (1983)
... Flashdancer in "Dream Lover"
Playboy Video Magazine, Volume 5 (1983)
... Horse Riding Student
Private Collection (1992) ... Hostess
Private Collection II (1994) ... Hostess
Private Collection III (1996) ... Hostess
Private Collection IV (2000) ... Hostess
Private School (1983) ... School Girl
Psycho III (1986) ... Body Double for Diana
Scarwid
Quicksand! (1999) ... Diana
Quicksand! 3: Tierra Del Diablo (2001) ...
Lead Investigative Reporter
Real Time: Siege at Lucas Street Market
(2001) ... Janet
Repligator (1996) ... Dr. Goodbody
Roots of Evil (1991) a.k.a. *Naked Force* ...
Candy
Savage Streets (1984) ... School Girl in
Locker Room Fight
The Sensual Spirit (2003) (co-wrote screen-
play with Ted Newsom)
Sexy Shorts (1984) a.k.a. *Red Hot Rock* ...
Miss Utah
Shadows in the City (1991) ... Fortune
Teller
Shock Cinema, Volumes 1-4 (1991) (docu-
mentaries) ... Hostess
Sideshow (2000) ... Madame Volosca
Slavegirls from Beyond Infinity (1987) ...
Sheila
Slice 'N Dice (2003) ... Reporter
The Slumber Party Massacre (1982) ...
Linda
Sole Survivor (1982) ... Jennifer
Some Nudity Required (1998) (documen-
tary) ... Herself
Something to Scream About (2003) (docu-
mentary) ... Hostess
Sorority Babes in the Slimeball Bowl-a-
Rama (1987) a.k.a. *The Imp* ... Taffy
Spirits (1990) ... Amy Goldwyn
Square Pegs (TV) (1984) ... Student
Submerged (2000) ... Bartender
Surf II: The End of the Trilogy (1984) ...
Student
Tales from the Darkside (TV) (1988)
"Basher Malone" ... Wrestling Match
Groupie

Teenage Exorcist (1991) … Diane (also wrote screenplay)
Terror Toons 2 (2003) … Wicked Witch
Theater Dark Video Magazine (1996) (documentary) … Herself
This Is Spinal Tap (1984) … Derek Small's Girlfriend
Three Amigos! (1986) … Actress in Silent Movie
To Dance with Death (2000) … Angel of Death
Transylvannia Twist (1990) … Betty Lou
24 Hours to Midnight (1985) … Devon Grady
The Vampire Hunters Club (2001) … Brinke
Vicious (2002) … Hiker

Victoria's Shadow (1998) … Victoria
Warlords (1988) … Dow's Wife
We're Coming to Help (2002) … Rachel Alcina
Web of Darkness (2001) … Intensity
The Witching (1972) (new footage 1983) a.k.a. *Necromancy* ; *Rosemary's Disciples*; *A Life for a Life*; *The Toy Factory* … Black Sabbath Member
Witchouse 3: Demon Fire (2001) … Lilith LaVey
Zombiegeddon (2002) … Laura Reynolds
Zyzak is King (1980) (student film) … Sara, The Cave Witch

Debra DeLiso

I've always been a huge fan of the *Slumber Party Massacre* series. Why? It comes down to is this: One man's crap is another man's gold. I thoroughly enjoy this type of film … the B movie. I also *love, adore* and *appreciate* the actresses who appear in them. Hence, my 16-months-in-the-making retrospective of the *Slumber Party Massacre* franchise which appeared as the cover story in *Femme Fatales* 9:3.

During my hunt for the actresses, I had to accept the sad fact that, in the 20 years since the series began, most of them had faded into oblivion. Some retired, some simply gave up on the business and others, sad to say, had passed away. After months of research, I decided that anyone I hadn't tracked down was unreachable. Happily, about a month after the issue hit stands, one of the "unfound" actresses saw the issue and found me. And, although she was only one of the original sleepover victims, I must say, I was beyond delighted to have a chance to meet her … and discover she has flourished as both an artist and a human being.

Debra DeLiso began her career in Hollywood as many other ingenues: Small, non-speaking roles in a variety of features, plus work on stage which lead to bigger roles. She considers her first "official" role to be a dancer in the 1977 Gene Wilder comedy *The World's Greatest Lover*. It was 1982's *The Slumber Party Massacre* , however, which garnered her the most recognition, and her first speaking role on film as spunky tomboy Kim.

"She was such a fun character," DeLiso begins as she makes herself comfortable in a chair at Hoy's Wok in Hollywood. "She brought the 'mowie-wowie' to the party. She had a real personality. She was the jokester."

The still-vibrant actress settles back and giggles, "It'll be interesting when my daughter sees the film and I sit with her as Mom and tell her not to do everything I'm shown doing. It'll be a while, yet. She'll have to wait until she's much older."

Not necessarily as old as many of the students she now teaches at the prestigious Academy of Dramatic Arts, or the high school students to whom she taught dance for several years. "I still get recognized from the film, mostly by the students," she chuckles. "It never fails. About halfway through every semester, a group of them walk in smiling and say, 'Ms. DeLiso, we saw a movie you did….'"

DeLiso shakes her head, "It never fails. The guys look at me, then look directly at my chest and all I think is, 'Oh, god … Is this ever going to die?' I can only laugh now and fondly enjoy it." She adds the connection to her past doesn't end there.

"I actually got a phone call a few years ago and the voice on the phone asked, 'Is this Debra DeLiso?" she reminisces with wide eyes. "I said 'Yes,' and he said, 'This is Russ Thorn….'" Though understandably unnerved at first, the actress later discovered it was a friend of someone with whom she was doing a play, someone who had recognized her name in the theater program and decided to pull a prank. "It's just amazing to me how many people have seen this movie," she says, clearly astounded.

"There are a lot of fond memories surrounding the shoot," she insists. "I *loved* showing up for work every morning. We drove out to this house in LaVista, California, and there was always a lot

Debra DeLiso today. She was among the first women to begin drama programs for women in prison (photograph courtesy Debra DeLiso).

of excitement. It was a bunch of young actors [Gina Mari, David Millbern and Brinke Stevens, to name a few] who were thrilled to be making this movie."

Unfortunately, DeLiso's favorite shot never made it to the final cut. "There was a ouija board scene in one of the bedrooms," she informs. "There was a strong connection between the actors and I think everyone felt really confident with their work that particular day. I think it got cut because it didn't forward the plot in any way." Others who knew of the scene said it lent a supernatural twist to the story which, in turn, seemed out of step with the rest of the slasher picture.

DeLiso found the cast delightful. "Meeting and working with Joe Johnson [Neil] was so wonderful and fun," she beams. "I was very close to Robin Stille [Valerie], Michele Michaels [Trish] and Andre Honore [Jackie]. I also liked working with Brinke Stevens [Linda]. About a year after the movie came out, the Academy of Science Fiction, Horror and Fantasy had a special showing of *The Slumber Party Massacre* and invited me, Joe and Brinke to have a discussion period. We did a lot of schmoozing and had fun with it. Brinke went on to become this huge success as a Scream Queen and is such a great person. I really like her."

Method acting among some of the other cast members kept DeLiso and some of her co-stars more distant. "I didn't get very close with Gina Mari [Diane]," she admits, "but I think it was because of our characters. It was really interesting to work with Michael Villela [drilling maniac Russ Thorn]. He was a Method actor who literally would not have conversations with any of us during the shoot. He would stand off and just stare at you. It was genuinely creepy and definitely served its purpose."

Villela's eerily silent manner finally changed, to some degree. "When we had the wrap party, he came up to me and said, 'I just want to apologize. I kind of feel like this person who has this huge amount of guilt … this movie took a much larger toll on me than I thought it would.'"

While much of the time on set was almost ethereal, there were some dark periods to endure. Among her least favorite memories, "filming the shower scene," she says, shaking her head. "It was shot very mechanically. There was nothing organic about it. It was very 'rush rush rush' and none of us really knew how much the camera was getting of our bodies."

There was a bit of brightness for the then nerve-wracked teenager. "The one good thing about that day," DeLiso smiles, "was my friend Leslie. She knew I was having so much mental angst and she knew we were having extras that day, so she asked if I wanted her to be an extra for the day and shoot the scene with me. I figured it would make me more comfortable, so she actually did it! She's in the shower scene! So I got through the hardest scene to shoot because a friend came in to support me."

With a sigh of relief, DeLiso continues, "What you see of me is actually less than what they filmed. I thought that was wonderful of [director] Amy Jones [1987's *Maid to Order*] because she knew what a problem I had with it, especially since I had to do a second scene where I change my top at the party."

Brief on-screen nudity became a big off-screen deal amongst many of the actors. Brinke Stevens reported in *Femme Fatales* 9:3 that the shower sequence found many of the ladies covering their nipples with tape so shots of them could not be used. DeLiso notes, "Gina Mari refused to do any nudity. So, for the scene where she's in the car making out with her boyfriend and he starts fondling her breast, they actually had to use Michele Michael's breast for the closeup!"

According to DeLiso, Michaels was far more accommodating to the 1980s horror standard of T&A. "Michele seemed to be more comfortable with the nudity than the rest of us," she says. "Amy was getting stressed out because she had an actress who wouldn't do the required nudity and finally said, 'I'll pay extra money to whichever one of you would be willing to do [the close up] in this scene.' So Michele said, 'Okay….'"

Although she found her director intelligent and respectful, DeLiso states, "She was very hard to work with. She was put into a very difficult position. In order to get the job, she had made a seven-minute short version of the film. (The much talked-about, never-seen footage is something DeLiso knows existed but says, to her knowledge, was the beginning pages of the original script. Neither were used in the final feature.)

"The script was originally titled *Sleepless Night* and was written by Rita Mae Brown [an author best known for her novel *Rubyfruit Jungle*], which thrilled me because I was a huge fan of her work," DeLiso continues. "I remember getting the

Trish (Michele Michaels) and Kim (Debra DeLiso) scream as their attacker approaches in 1982's *The Slumber Party Massacre* (copyright 1982, Santa Fe Productions/New Concorde).

script and being in awe of doing something which had been written by her.* Aaron Lipstadt [the eyeless pizza boy], who was also the Line Producer, told me about the audition.

"I was very excited to be in this film," she adds. "When I first read the script, I took it to be a full-on satire of low-budget horror films. I believe that's how Rita Mae Brown intended it. Either Amy didn't have the power or the ability to control what was written and what she wanted to do from being transformed into a lot of T&A. I think Amy was pressured into making it more of a true slasher film."

DeLiso sits back and shakes her head. "We kept finding out every day something new had been added involving shower scenes and changing our clothes ... again. So I sort of have bittersweet feelings about the whole experience. It definitely affected all of us, because it kind of felt like we didn't matter. I mean, at that point I had a Bachelor's Degree in theater. I would ask questions about my character and her motives and Amy seemed to be more interested in just getting the shots done. I think she was also stressed with some of the actresses who weren't experienced and had to be guided through a lot of the making of the movie. So, little by little, I think her stress and the tensions whittled down the camaraderie on set."

The actress is quick to add it wasn't necessarily a case of the corrupt director vs. the young, naïve and nubile cast. "Amy did protect me when it came to the nudity,"

*It's said that once Brown submitted this original work, she was never involved in rewrites.

DeLiso smiles. "I started asking how much they were going to show and became very concerned. All the shots of my body basically got cut out, so I'm very grateful."

Risqué scenes aside, DeLiso was in for another shock after completion of the feature. Keeping in mind the film was lensed as *Sleepless Night*, DeLiso first learned of the new moniker "after the fact. They called [Andree Honore] to do the poster, [and no one else]. [Unknown models were used instead.] I found out they only wanted large breasted girls for the artwork, which I didn't think was very nice. One of the girls who did do it told me about the title change and I was like, 'Oh ... my ... god ... I'm in a movie called *The Slumber Party Massacre*.'" DeLiso demonstrates how far her jaw dropped, then laughs, "I was shocked, but what's your alternative? To be upset, or take it and make it a part of your life?"

DeLiso sums up with, "I don't think the movie turned out to be the comedy it was intended as. A lot of people would disagree with me, though. I know many people who think it's an absolutely frightening movie which serves its purpose and has a lot of appeal. I mean, it's over 20 years later and I'm still here talking about it. It's enduring."

The actress wishes she had remained in touch with her castmates whom, for the most part, have gone on to different lives (although she still counts Joe Johnson among her best friends). "I would love to see all of those women again! I think we should have a little *Slumber Party Massacre* reunion. It would be so fun!"

When queried on their whereabouts, DeLiso reports, "I used to see Michele Michaels for a while," she says. "I was in a play with a friend of hers, so I'd see her frequently. Andree Honore and I keep in touch occasionally. She married a Denver Bronco and started a family. I get Christmas cards and pictures every year. I also saw David Millbern in *Gods and Monsters*, which starred Ian McKellen, whom I had the pleasure to study with in London in the early 1990s. It's like a big circle."

She suddenly becomes somber and says, "You know, I didn't know Robin Stille had died until I read the article in [*Femme Fatales* 9:3]. It was so sad. I had no idea she was depressed or disturbed. After we filmed *Slumber Party Massacre*, she moved to Florida and called me from there. I know she dated Wayne Newton for a while, and I saw her in *People* magazine dating Sylvester Stallone. She was hanging around with big celebrities and hoped it was going to help her get big roles, because she was a very good actress and was such a beautiful woman. She was very centered and direct and nice, which is why it came as such a shock."

She lightens the mood by reflecting on a friendship which not only blossomed after the completion of *The Slumber Party Massacre*, but led to her next film role. "I *am* very close to [co-star] Joe Johnson," she chirps. "He wrote the [lead] part of Trina for me in *Iced* [1988]. I'm just so proud of him for having written something which got produced because it's such a difficult thing to accomplish. We had a great time doing it."

The icy slasher saga (a.k.a. *Blizzard of Blood*) was filmed in Snowbird, Utah, and starred DeLiso as the object of a scorned man's obsession. Many years after she chooses one man over another, she retreats to a mountain resort with her new husband and friends (including Lisa Loring of television's *The Addams Family*). As expected in any 1980s slasher flick, the desolate surroundings become a bloody playground when the maniac decides to enact revenge on said retreaters (including Loring in a literal "hot" tub).

"I had an interesting relationship with Lisa," DeLiso recalls. "She was such a trip. Her life was pretty rocky at that point. She and Doug Stevenson, who played my husband in the film, were married in real life and were in the process of breaking up. She went on to have a relationship with [adult film star] Jerry Butler [1982's *Taboo III: The Final Chapter*]. I hope she's doing well now."

She found the cast and crew to be equally wacky and close knit—including her husband, Dan Smith. "It was such a blast to film. The [location] was gorgeous. [Director] Jeff Kwitney was very nurturing with us."

The actress was also fond of her character, whose personality and self-image changes throughout the course of the film. "[Trina] is such a good girl," she smiles. "She wants to have the perfect image and life. Then she winds

In the 1980s Debra DeLiso continued her career as a professional dancer (photograph courtesy Debra DeLiso).

up becoming the victim, but also becomes strong and learns to fight for herself. I really appreciate that Joe wrote the part for me."

Her views of the finished project seem somewhat mixed. "Ultimately," she begins, "I think it's very campy. I don't think it's what Joe envisioned when he wrote it. The script had a lot more suspense and humor, which didn't come through. It has some scenes which are funny, but I think the difference between *Iced* and *The Slumber Party Massacre* is that *Slumber Party Massacre* intentionally had a lot of laughs."

Of course, the years in between her first and second lead roles were not uninteresting. "[After *Slumber Party Massacre*], I did what every actor in Hollywood does," she informs. "I waited tables for about two years. Got really sick of that, so I started to teach high school. I kept doing that five hours a day for eight years which was great, because I could still go out on auditions.

"I also received my Masters in theater during that time and went on to study at the Royal National Theater in London. Then I went to the Edgar Festival in Scotland and played Agnes in *Agnes of God* and Joanne in *Come Back to the Five and Dime Jimmy Dean, Jimmy Dean*."

Reviews of her performances were golden. One wrote of her *Agnes* performance. "Both [other actresses] are put in the shade by Debra DeLiso, a revelation as the neurotic, tormented yet endearing Agnes." Another said of *Jimmy Dean*, "The show might be worth a visit just to see Debra A. DeLiso as the sex-changed store cleaner returning to set the record straight."

Appearances in other plays continued to garner glowing remarks. A critic for *The Scotsman* paper wrote of her play *Isle of Dogs*, "in Debra DeLiso, beautiful, quicksilver, lightning-timed, they have a star for Julius Caesar to single out. The Dubin Street Baptist Church should be magnified a hundred fold to win her the audience she deserves."

A turn on stage as Blanche in *A Streetcar Named Desire* earned the well-respected thespian some of her greatest reviews. *The Pasadena Weekly* wrote, "Debra DeLiso's portrayal of Blanche carries the play from beginning to end with great delicacy and care. She seemed to float effortlessly across the stage from one place to another…"

Added Ron Secor, a *Tribune* Theater critic, "Debra DeLiso plays Blanche Dubois with such total commitment and such wounded, painful sensitivity that it is hard to imagine her in any other part."

The critics' darling also filled her time with appearances on television shows like the action comedy *Sledge Hammer*. "I had such a great time," she grins enthusiastically. "I played a punker named Angel who wore this crazy outfit … probably the craziest I've ever worn. Lots of leather and chains. My character's boyfriend is put in jail so he makes his one phone call to me and I gather all the gang members and go down to the police station and raid it." She found the series stars, David Rasche of 1995's *Out There* and Eddie Benton (a.k.a. Anne Marie Martin) of the hit 1980 slasher flick *Prom Night*, "so wonderful to work with. David was so funny! Eddie [as Rasche's sidekick] was also really great. She saw me in my punk outfit and said, 'Oh, I have one of those at home.'"

DeLiso also got work in the 1987 Shelley Long-Bette Midler comedy *Outrageous Fortune*, but never appeared in the film, despite credit in the closing crawl. "Oh, that's a sad story," she frowns. "Arthur Hiller had a casting session where all these girls had to line up and out jetté each other. They drew lines you had to jump to and from so they could find who could jump the furthest [as a double for Long's cliff-jumping sequence plus an earlier classroom scene]. I'm an athlete and was a competitive gymnast for eight years and out-leapt the other girls. So I got the part."

She smiles for a brief moment, then disappointment fills her expression. "When the day came to film the scene in the dance class I showed up, but they were behind schedule and never got around to shooting it that day. Then they never called me back and gave it to another girl. Then they called me to shoot the cliff-jumping sequence, but I had another commitment and couldn't do it. So they used the choreographer instead. I still got paid and received credit in the movie anyway."

The actress continued to perform in theater, teach and further her own education through and beyond production of the 1989 oddity *Dr. Caligari*. A sequel to the 1919 silent classic *The Cabinet of Dr. Caligari*, the story follows the grandchild of the infamous insane asylum doc continuing the family business by running an asylum in which the patients are used as guinea pigs for hormone experimentation. Directed by Stephen Sayadian of the infamous sex classic *Cafe Flesh* (1982), *Dr. Caligari* received mixed reviews, but almost always was given kudos for its stylish look and approach to the bizarre themes. "I played Grace Butter," DeLiso smiles. "I had been Caligari's grade school teacher. I'm made into a stew and get eaten."

She laughs a moment, looking back to the production which also involved *Permanent Midnight*'s Jerry Stahl. "It wasn't a gross scene. It was actually extremely stylized. The scene everyone remembers most is this huge tongue which would bathe everyone in saliva…" The actress pauses, then adds, "It was very stunning … visually…"

Licked by giant tongues, chased by drill-wielding maniacs and threatened with blood-soaked icicles would seem to be highlights of anyone's career. DeLiso, however, proved her merit and continued to expand her talents, as well as emotionally reaching out to those less fortunate throughout the last decade.

"I wrote a one-person show while I was at UCLA," she begins, "which is a wonderful thing to do as an actor becomes an artist — to see from the creative point of view of the writer. Now I teach Developing the One-Person Show at the American Academy of Dramatic Arts, among other classes."

The actress also took her knowledge into the humanities field, initiating one of the nation's first-ever programs for prison inmates. DeLiso says, "I had a grant from the California Arts Council to be an artist-in-residence at a women's prison. That has been some of the most rewarding work I have ever done. I feel like I'm actually changing people's lives."

Through the program, DeLiso works with the inmates directly, using their personal situations to bring out the women's unseen talents. She has them dance, write monologues and plays and perform on stage. In an interview with *The Press-Enterprise*, DeLiso said, "They are in prison for various crimes, but there is a common bond in their stories—family cycles of addiction, abuse and inherited belief systems…" She added in another issue, "You try to enrich their lives in ways that can create some kind of drive within them… Being able to express themselves in a non-threatening environment is emotionally beneficial, physically beneficial and ultimately, spiritually beneficial. The dances are so personal. They bring you themselves. They're putting their hearts and souls into it, and you're moved by what they do because it's so honest."

DeLiso does admit in the article to being intimidated at the beginning of the initial class, but knew she couldn't show the women those fears or she would have no control. "I realized these women are just like me, who made a bad decision along the way and they're here. They're individuals now. They're not 'women in prison.'"

DeLiso admits the project was not easy, but was none the less rewarding. After the initial meeting of her first class in 1997, emotional walls began to crumble amongst the women. In the March 18, 1999, *Press-Enterprise*, the actress-educator-therapist said that over ten inmates dropped out because "they couldn't handle the heavy emotions that arose once they began delving into their past to write the assignments. Those who remained said they fought their fears.

"This is the other side of making low-budget horror films," says DeLiso with admiration for her students. "I'm actually dealing with some women who are in prison for trying to save themselves from violent situations and relationships. I've gone from portraying women who experience violence to helping real women who experienced it [first hand]. "It's also helped me to learn a lot about human behavior and about our belief systems, cycles of abuse and the human psyche. Most of the women have written some extraordinary things through the program."

One has to wonder how the actress views the entertainment industry's emphasis on brutality and its impact on society. "The hardest part about having been in these movies is my very strong feeling about women [subjected to] violence," she says. "When I did *The Slumber Party Massacre*, I felt good about doing it because I truly felt it was a parody of slasher films. Women ultimately prevailed and were the strong ones. [But] I wondered what it said about me as a person doing that sort of film. I've always been a very strong woman. People I know have thought I was very courageous for making the film, going to that dark place. Others were like, 'How could you make that movie?' It all makes me feel as though I was very brave for being able to 'go there.'"

DeLiso also believes there are better ways to get to those dark corners of cinema. "I really do enjoy suspense and I can enjoy horror, but I like the psychological thrills better than the juxtaposition of 'Ooh, that was scary... What a turn on...,'" she says. "There's a part of me which believes in freedom of speech. A part which believes in the artistic creativity which we should all be able to express. I do have strong issues about what should be shown on television which any child could come across."

Making her issues and experiences a part of her performance is the ideal way DeLiso deals with the subject and uses them to her advantage. "In my theater programs, I now create stories which address these theories in healthier ways," she informs. "I'm writing a one-woman show based on my own life in which I am a strong, independent woman who has to confront her own past of having been in these films."

She snickers a moment and alludes to her most famous role winding up on stage. *Slumber Party Massacre: The Musical*?! Not exactly...

"I've written a play called *Slaughterhouse Sleepover: The Musical*," she smiles, a twinkle in her eye. "It's a dark comedy about the making of *The Slumber Party Massacre*, or a film of its nature. The experiences of an actress appearing in her first horror film."

While she makes light of her foray into the world of underdressed damsels in distress, one wonders whether she regrets making the picture 20 years ago. If she was then who she is now, would Debra DeLiso make *The Slumber Party Massacre* all over again?

"I would do a version of it," she contemplates. "The way I thought it should have been done from the beginning. I would take the genre it represents and milk it for all its worth in a more humorous way, and take a look at why we're so fascinated with it. I wouldn't make the exact same movie. It would have to be made with people who all understood which direction the movie was going."

Still, she's delighted that the film, which she last saw about five years ago, continues to thrill audiences and maintain a strong cult following. She laughs, "I last watched it with a group of acting buddies and the funny thing is they loved it, but it scared them! It's still a pretty tight little film."

So would the actress, who continues to teach writing workshops and has just premiered her self-written show *Cock Tales* (a bend on *The Vagina Monologues*), advise her own daughter to follow in her footsteps? Debra DeLiso sits back and mulls it over.

"I would just tell her to get some excellent training first," she decides. "I would suggest she spend more time concentrating on the process and not the result. I think once you understand what you're doing and you feel like you have a skill, you're not going to just jump at any job. I have no regrets about what I've done in my career, because it has brought me to where I am today."

In Memoriam: Robin Rochelle Stille, 1961–1996

Through months of research and attempts to locate actors from the *Slumber Party Massacre* franchise, one actress' whereabouts became an obsession. Several key players had simply retired from the business, but locating Robin Stille, who portrayed heroine Valerie Bates in the 1982 original, always seemed "this close."

The Screen Actors Guild still lists her as an active member. In retrieving her agent's phone number, I figured I could contact her with relative ease. Unfortunately, the agent had not been in contact with her for some time, and did not know her current residence. Several of her former castmates and directors reported seeing her occasionally "a year or two ago," yet none knew exactly where she was living other than in Los Angeles. Then one shared a rumor: She had passed away.

No one could confirm her death or even offer details. I checked newspapers, the Internet, the film companies which had produced her features ... all turned up zilch. I even had my Internet whiz cousin, William Vanderhoef, Jr., do intense digging. He came up with a few leads and phone numbers, but of all the calls I made, not one person responded. I had given up hope and wasn't sure if the rumor should even be mentioned in the retrospective. The day before I printed the final draft, there was an unexpected stroke of fate.

Brinke Stevens, who co-starred with Stille in *The Slumber Party Massacre* and *Sorority Babes in the Slimeball Bowl-a-Rama* (1987), was attending a horror film convention in Chicago. Rhonda Baughman, a longtime fan and poet, approached Stevens and in passing conversation confirmed Stille's death. Baughman informed Stevens of minor details and where to pursue more information (www.imdb.com).

Robin Rochelle Stille was born in Philadelphia, Pennsylvania on November 24, 1961, to Jere Stille and Sarah Bridge. She grew up with sisters, Dawn and Melanie, and brother Jere, Jr. After moving to Los Angeles, the raven-haired beauty immediately landed numerous modeling gigs and shortly after won the lead role in *The Slumber Party Massacre*. Her co-stars remember her as "fun" and "a delight to work with," but also recall how she longed for stardom.

Her next credited role was 1986's *Winner Takes All*. Soon after, she seemed to temporarily take hold of the burgeoning "Scream Queen" trend. She dropped her last name, dyed her feathered locks blonde and, billed as "Robin Rochelle," regained lead screen time with Brinke Stevens, Linnea Quigley and Michelle Bauer in director David DeCoteau's *Sorority Babes in the Slimeball Bowl-a-Rama*. As Babs, she's the evil sorority sister who delights in tormenting the initiates, even before she is possessed and transformed into a leather-clad dominatrix complete with punked-out hair.

Stille, center right, laughs with her director David DeCoteau and co-stars on the set of *Sorority Babes in the Slimeball Bowl-a-Rama.*

She next battled the *Vampire Knights,* and was seen dating high-profile celebrities like Sylvester Stallone and Wayne Newton, then disappeared from screens again until a 1990 episode ("God Bless the Child") of TV's *Jake and the Fatman.* With her last name changed back to Stille, her next and final known credit was as Sarah, the lead heroine in 1991's kung fu saga *American Ninja 4: The Annihilation.* Some time thereafter, she gave birth to twin boys, Justin and Joshua. The ensuing years remain somewhat of a mystery.

Robin Rochelle Stille took her life on February 9, 1996, in Burbank, California, a tragic loss not only for the family she left behind, but because the industry in which she strived so hard to succeed in never knew she was gone.

Although Stille may not have considered herself a star, her many fans did, and will forever. Rhonda Baughman certainly thought so. The opening of *Carnal Capers, Book 2: Logorrhea,* her book of poetry, reads "In Memory of Robin Stille."

Heidi Kozak

Perky, award-winning actress Heidi Kozak has been a staple of family television throughout the past two decades. If you've seen any horror films bordering on extremely bizarre, chances are you've seen her bright persona followed by her blood-curdling screams. Occasionally brunette, usually blonde, the University of Southern California graduate has traveled through almost every genre of television and film.

As she enters a Brentwood, California, Starbucks for a cup of hot chocolate, Kozak looks as though she could still pass as one of the exuberant high schoolers she frequently portrayed in the 1980s. When asked about her career, her thoughts immediately turn to her favorite character: bubbly, Oxy 10–obsessed songwriter Sally Burns from *Slumber Party Massacre II* (1987).

"I *was* Sally! I got the audition the same week I graduated from college. At that point, the movie was called *Don't Let Go*. They brought me back, like, a million times to read again, then finally it was between me and one other girl. I went in to do the scene where I'm telling someone a story and I start laughing. All of a sudden I fell off my chair! It was a weird-shaped chair and I just slipped right off! So I just went with it … started cracking up all over the floor, and I think that's what got me the job. It was one of those fluke things … even the director [Deborah Brock] was [laughing]!"

Though *Slumber Party Massacre II* was her film debut, the Denmark, Copenhagen–born actress had been a frequent guest star on TV sitcoms and dramas during her college years. "I was in the Repertory Theater Company at USC on a full scholarship," she informs. "I was doing about four plays a year — Shakespeare, Chekhov, everything. My education, room and board were paid for, and I had an agreement with the university that I could work professionally and get out of class if I needed to."

While many a college student would be seething at her circumstances, Kozak utilized her benefits. "I started doing TV shows like *The New Twilight Zone*, *Silver Spoons*, *Growing Pains*, *Mama's Family*— a lot of sitcoms all through college."

In her *Twilight Zone* episode, she and a group of friends (including *L.A. Law*'s resident transvestite Rob Nepar) get into a car which transports them back to the 1950s. "It was a weird episode, but really neat. While we were traveling back in time we'd see all these freaky things and have to figure out how to get back." She found herself back in the present on *Silver Spoons* with future *N.Y.P.D. Blue* heartthrob Rick Schroder. "He is the nicest actor to work with. On my first day he and Alfonso Ribeiro [TV's *The Fresh Prince of Bel-Air*] took me and my friend and co-star Helen Udy [who later starred with Kozak on *Dr. Quinn*] out to lunch to make us feel welcome."

Sitcoms were not her only source of income, and on a special two-hour episode of *Jake and the Fatman*, the actress took her first step towards the darker side of entertainment. "I played a teen hooker who gets murdered. It was a really moving episode. I still get a lot of mail from fans about that episode," she smiles. She continued her dark descent into an episode of *Matlock* in which she played a shy girl who must testify against a criminal. "That was a really emotional episode too."

As job offers increased, Kozak's college days were winding down and she found herself unsure of her talents and future. She recalls, "The week I was graduating I suddenly thought, 'Oh, God, now I have to fend for myself. What am I going to do? Can I really make a living as an actress?'" Those fears lifted the same week when she was invited to a certain slumber party.

Since the slasher trend parodied in the original *Slumber Party Massacre* (1982) was mostly D.O.A. by 1987, the sequel took a bizarre direction. Playing as part slasher, part *A Nightmare on Elm Street* rip off and part animé-style gore, *Slumber Party Massacre II* remains one of the '80s most indefinable shockers. As surfer babe Sally, Kozak found herself having the time of her life — and quickly became the victim of one of horror's most infamous death scenes...

During her audition, Kozak was asked by director Deborah Brock (1989's *Rock 'n Roll High School Forever*) if she was claustrophobic. She laughs as she remembers, "I had to do a full face mask and I'd have to be under the [plaster] for quite a while. I told

Heidi Kozak endured over 12 hours in FX makeup for the exploding zit scene in *Slumber Party Massacre II* (1987) (photograph courtesy New Concorde).

her 'No, not at all,' but I really had no idea if I was or not. I just wanted the job." She later found out the appliance she'd be molded for was a gigantic pimple which, at its most extreme, explodes yellow puss all over co-star Crystal Bernard (Courtney).

Though Bernard's character may not have appreciated the soupy surprise in her face, Kozak revels at the infamy. It wasn't always a blast, as she recalls, "The zit make up took a lot longer than was originally anticipated. I had to go through all the progression of the zit forming, and when I had the final makeup on I couldn't eat, drink or move my face, so I had to sip liquids through a straw. I pride myself on being very professional, and I never complained once about it. I [was in the makeup] for over 12 hours, but it turned out great."

While a number of actors who have done time under latex often claim they'd think twice before repeating the torture, Kozak would endure it again. "Oh, yeah! There weren't any bad effects on my skin and I had a great time. The one bad part was smelling dinner, but not being able to eat it. Plus, [food] combined with the smell of the latex wasn't that great, so I escaped to my trailer. [Unfortunately], there's a [SAG] rule that you have to be served dinner or they have to pay you extra. So they brought the food to my trailer!" After arguing with the crew, the human zit finally won, sending the food away. She went home with an empty stomach, but got a nice bonus in return. Still, revenge awaited her.

Kozak also recalls arguing over her attire with the wardrobe department, saying, "The wardrobe lady wanted to dress me like Annie Hall! I told her Sally was a surfer girl with tank tops and jean shorts and drumsticks in her back pocket. She kept saying, 'No, no, no— this is how you're going to dress...' I was like, 'Hey! This is my character and this is how she acts and should dress. [It was] why I got the part in the first place, and that's what they're expecting me to do.' So I stood my ground."

She got her way, with the support of Brock, and remembers suddenly seeing cast mate Kimberly McArthur (Amy) in the Diane Keaton outfit. She laughs at her come-uppance. "My jean shorts suddenly started getting shorter every day. Somebody was cutting the fringe a little more each morning until they were so short I eventually had to get a new pair."

Remaining good-humored about the shortcomings, Kozak only recalls the entire shoot as, "great! Everyone got along really well and had a lot of fun. We worked really long hours, but we laughed all the time."

When *Slumber Party Massacre II* premiered in theaters, Kozak and company continued their camaraderie. "The first time I saw it was at a screening with the cast and crew. We all sat together and had a lot of fun," she laughs. "We were a really close group, all around the same age and just really connected."

She thought the final outcome of the movie was "pretty silly," but still enjoys the picture and the fan mail it brings her. In fact, of every project she's done, she insists her favorite scene is the pillow fight sequence between her, Bernard, McArthur and Juliette Cummins (Sheila). "The feathers flying everywhere ... that's definitely my favorite scene of everything I've done — though I really love the scene where I walk into the house after everyone thinks I've been killed. That was pretty [amusing], too."

Heidi Kozak reprised her Sally character in 2000 for a photo shoot to coincide with the magazine publication of a *Slumber Party Massacre* retrospective (photograph courtesy Jan Deen).

After the experience ended, most of her co-stars went on to further horror projects. Cummins wound up having *Deadly Dreams* (1988), Joel Hoffman (T.J.) paid for his sins in *Pumpkinhead* (1988) and Jennifer Rhodes (Mrs. Bates) battled the *Heathers* (1989) and *Night of the Demons 2* (1994). Kozak was no exception, and on Friday, May 13, 1988, she took a fatal dip in Crystal Lake.

As Sandra in *Friday the 13th, Part VII: The New Blood*, Kozak was more of a set piece for the battleground between the ever-rotting Jason

Voorhees (Kane Hodder) and his telekinetically charged foe Tina Shepard (Lar Park-Lincoln). She recalls with disappointment, "[Sandra] was a completely different character from the original script. She was a swimmer and had a lot more [depth], but by the time we got the shooting script there was nothing left to her."

Still, she insists her time on set was pure, bloody bliss. "*Friday the 13th, Part VII* was such a fun shoot. We were all in Mobile, Alabama, and had the best time. We'd go bowling and hang out. I remember it rained for an entire week when we were supposed to be doing outdoor shots, so we eventually started getting crazy and wild and made it the best time. Lar [1987's *House II: The Second Story*] was so nice and Kevin Blair [1983's *The Hills Have Eyes, Part 2*] was so sweet. [Then there's] Kane Hodder … the nicest monster I've ever met," she chuckles.

Blair, who is now credited as Kevin Spirtas on *Days of Our Lives*, reciprocated the fondness. He remembers, "Heidi was great. She was a lot of fun to work with. I remember we were both heavily into the horror movie thing at the time, but we've both gone beyond it. I haven't seen her for years, but I liked her a lot and remember what a great time we had doing *Friday VII*."

Kozak also speaks of her admiration for the film's director. "John Carl Buechler [1990's *Ghoulies III*] was so caring. A really, really great guy. You could tell he cared a lot about his actors. He was so sweet to all of us. He, and the entire production, treated us wonderfully," she smiles.

While she claims she would never do another *Friday the 13th* movie, she maintains it's only because of her cardboard character and her dissatisfaction with her body double. "I didn't see the movie until there was this big screening in Hollywood. When I saw the girl who was supposed to be me, my mouth dropped. Anybody who knows me could tell immediately that wasn't my body. I wasn't even on the set that day. They literally just got some girl from the town to do it, and she looked like she always hung out at the Dairy Queen!"

Kozak confirms, "I've never done nudity. I had the body double in *Friday VII*, and in *Slumber Party Massacre II* I didn't want to do it, so I almost turned the role down. So Deborah Brock came to my apartment and talked to me. She asked what we could compromise to keep me in the film. I said, 'Put me in lingerie. I will wear any sexy bra you want.' She said, 'Okay.' I know the producers were mad at her, but she stuck up for me."

Nudity became an issue again in her next genre feature, Brian Yuzna's ultra-warped *Society* (1989). The controversial film, which was finally released theatrically in 1992, concerned a young man (Billy Warlock) who discovers his adoptive family and their Beverly Hills associates are actually flesh-eating monsters who sacrifice humans in blood-drenched orgies. Kozak, who played Warlock's bitchy girlfriend Shawna, steered clear from the kinky carnage.

"I was up for all the female leads, but the nudity came into play again, plus I just decided I wanted to play Shawna," she says. "I was originally supposed to play Billy's sister, but the role wasn't as fun." Kozak reveals she was also slated to play the films black widow, a role which first went to 1984's *Friday the 13th, Part IV: The Final Chapter* veteran Judie Aronson. After conflicts, however, the role was finally awarded to Devin DeVasquez. Kozak maintains her own decision was right on. "At my final audition, I told the producers I would give them a great Shawna.

"I really do love [my character] Sally. She was my favorite character to play, but I loved Shawna, too. I can easily play both. Some people can only do the 'good girl' or the 'bad girl.' I just loved being a stuck-up, snotty bitch in *Society*."

It's easy to assume the actress truly enjoyed her participation amongst Screaming Mad George's sexual monstrosities, not to mention a 400+ group of rowdy teenagers. Her eyes brighten as she pulls out her photo album to show pictures of the shoot. "I loved it! Absolutely loved it! There was one day in particular when we were shooting at Taft High School for the pep assembly scene. Real students had been brought in and they were totally out of control..."

Kozak shows a photo of herself on an auditorium stage in a blue and yellow outfit, perfecting the stereotypical cheerleader you either loved or loathed in high school. "The kids were really loud and the director was going crazy, so I decided, 'I can take care of this.' I got up on stage and led a Q&A time with the students. I just took control of the auditorium. I felt really useful and think that, in a way, I helped direct that scene."

She smiles proudly and offers up a glistening reference for her boss, who went on to produce and direct a number of the horror genres biggest cult classics, including *Bride of Re-Animator* (1989), *Silent Night, Deadly Night 4: Initiation* (1990) and *Return of the Living Dead 3* (1993). "Brian Yuzna is such a great director. Fun and smart and talented — totally great. I would definitely work with him again in a minute."

Society marked Kozak's final turn in horror, but with three cult hits back to back, one has to wonder why her bountiful screams never labeled her. "The Scream Queen thing just never happened. I think it was because I kept doing so many other [projects] like TV," she theorizes. "Maybe it was because I only did three horror films. It never really mattered. I try not to label myself as anything. I'm just an actress."

After horror film boot camp, many '80s screamers had two choices: Continue the cycle into the dwindling rental market and make a career out of erotic thrillers, or venture full-speed ahead into the television and bit parts in smaller movies. Considering Kozak's TV success, her choice was an easy one. She also returned to the stage in the early 1990s, accumulating rave reviews and even a Hollywood Actors Theater award for Best Actress in the play *Whores*. In the lead role, Kozak gripped audience emotions as an alcoholic teenager raped and impregnated by her father, whom she later tries to kill. "It was a very serious play," she recalls. "It was this wonderful story dealing with a lot of women's issues. I got a lot of recognition from it."

After a few years on stage, she found herself back in front of the camera as Emily in the CBS favorite *Dr. Quinn, Medicine Woman*. In the pilot episode, Dr. Quinn (Jane Seymour) and her friend (Diane Ladd) save a dying Emily as she attempts to give birth. Having to resort to a Cesarean section which, for television standards, was quite graphic, Dr. Quinn manages to save mother and child. It turns out viewers weren't the only people reacting with tears. "It was very intense and emotional," she reminisces. "When it was over, everyone on the set was crying and recalling the birthing stories of their own children. It was such a wonderful experience, just incredible."

Slated to appear only in the pilot, Kozak was delighted when producer Beth Sullivan asked her to consider being a series regular. The day the show was picked up by CBS, Kozak learned she'd be spending a lot of hot days in the Old West. Kozak giddily remembers, "One night my phone rang and this voice on the other end said, 'You're on it, baby!'"

For the next two seasons, Emily became Dr. Quinn's best friend in hilariously tackling the sexism and methods of the period. During this time Kozak became close to the crew and even got her mother, choreographer Madeline Taylor, a job on the show developing dance sequences.

Towards the close of the second season and with the show's popularity increasing, Emily was suddenly hiding behind large objects and wearing loose fitting outfits. Since her character remained unwed throughout those years, Kozak's real-life pregnancy had to be hidden. "I was pregnant and wanted to take maternity leave. So I worked up through my eighth month and they just kept hiding me behind props. On my final episode, Emily got married and was moving to another town. So they had me in this huge wedding dress with this big bouquet of flowers over my stomach the whole time."

When the next season began production, Emily was scheduled to return, saying her husband was abusive, but the joy of motherhood prompted Kozak to continue her leave indefinitely. She remained close with Seymour and the crew, whose persistence to get her to return continued into the reunion production of 1999's *Dr. Quinn: The Movie*. She politely turned it down.

Asked whether she would ever return to splatter cinema, Kozak laughs and shakes her head. "I don't know. It would depend on the part. I wouldn't do a slasher movie unless it was something like *Scream* (1996). I'm at the point where I don't need to work, so I only take roles which look fun to me, or whom I would be working with."

Kozak isn't attacking the genre. In fact, she thinks today's growing rate of teen violence can be attributed to internal factors. "I think the problems come into play when you've got teenagers who are already screwed up. Our society is screwed up because of poor parenting. When you put the combination of a child who has not been nurtured, loved or parented properly, who then already had mental problems, movies can be a problem. For a 'normal' person, however, these movies are just fun and scary and can be put into proper perspective."

These days, the actress

Actress Heidi Kozak

prefers to concentrate on her children and produce projects which they, and other children, can enjoy. Currently on her agenda is an already-in-the-works CD of music for young children. Kozak has written and sings many of the songs herself.

No longer nervous about the future of her career, Heidi Kozak holds her head high as she offers up advice to any of the ingénues seeking the same dream she has accomplished. "If there is anything else you want to do with your life, do it," she exclaims. "You have to really, *really* want to be an actress with all of your heart and be willing to work really hard at it. It's a business. It's not the kind of thing you can just tiptoe in and out of — you've got to take your work seriously." With awards, television favorites and cult classics filling her résumé, it's obviously good advice.

Juliette Cummins

At a glance you recognize her: saucy eyes, porcelain skin, quirky smile — and of course the flaming red hair. Maybe you've seen her as a mother zooming at light speed to prepare Mission Tortillas. Or as the reprimanding wife who keeps her husband on a leash as he chases the "new" Plymouth Prowler. You may even remember her Pepsi commercial homage to *Field of Dreams* during a recent Superbowl. To fans of horror, though, the former pre-med student was a genre staple of 1980's B favorites including *Psycho III*, *Friday the 13th , Part V: A New Beginning* and *Slumber Party Massacre II*.

Whether victim or victimizer, this sexy vixen has lent her talents to numerous television dramas and big-screen screamers, working alongside some of Hollywood's most eclectic actors, including Anthony Perkins, Crystal Bernard, Eric Stoltz, Xander Berkley, Jeff Fahey and Angela Lansbury.

When agent Nora Sanders spotted a 15-year-old Cummins at a restaurant, her career was launched. Sitting back in her chair at Santa Monica's Coffee Bean & Tea Leaf, Cummins marvels at the luck which dropped at her feet that day. "I never wanted to be an actor," she reveals. "I was in a restaurant when Nora saw me and asked if I wanted to do film. She called me the next day and sent me out for an interview and I immediately got the part in *Running Hot* [1983] with Eric Stoltz. My character is being raped by her father and Eric comes in and shoots him. That's how I got into the business. It was pure luck."

Maybe. Or perhaps it was her natural talent, which prompted casting agents and directors to admire her. Carolyne Barry called her "an original who could break your heart or make you laugh out loud." CSA casting director Jackie Burch refers to the actress as "a cross between a genius and [someone] totally insane."

Luck or not, Cummins' performance quickly had her on casting director's lists and she was soon a fixture in television guest spots. Among her credits are *Whiz Kids*, *New Love American Style* and *Black Widow*. On TV's *Simon & Simon* she was Sophie, a high school terror who dressed like Cyndi Lauper and acted like a gang girl. Just before her *Simon & Simon* gig, she was cast as a teen prostitute on *Murder, She Wrote*. "I got both jobs the same week, so I was supposed to shoot *Murder*, then run over to *Simon* the next day. Unfortunately, the *Murder* shoot ran over. So I looked at both roles and had to decide which one I wanted to play — the punk or the hooker. I chose the better guest-starring role. Then they had no time to recast on *Murder*, so instead they gave my part to some girl who was an extra on the set."

She shakes her head and pets her dog, Romeo, who has been observing passersby. "Isn't that amazing? It happens all the time. This whole business is based on luck ... and talent and perseverance. It's about who you know and what they know about you."

Cummins found herself as yet another misguided youth, taking on one of the 1980's biggest pop icons. "Oh, *Max Headroom* was fun! I played a British punk rocker who didn't know what books were. I would sell books because they were a big commodity. They were like money." The icon's show faded quickly thereafter, but Cummins' career took a sharp turn into the woods, heading her into the genre for which fans love her most.

In late 1984, Cummins was cast as disturbed Robin, one of the many troubled teens at a half-way house in — where else — Crystal Lake. Unfortunately for her character, she came face to machete with a certain hockey-masked marauder.

"*Friday the 13th, Part V: A New Beginning* [1985] is the best shoot I've ever had. I love that movie the most of everything that I've done. Some of the scenes were really well directed and the actors were great to work with. And the blood...!"

Yes, like any nubile *Friday* femme, poor Robin had her heart literally torn by Mr. Voorhees. Her portrayer, however, happily looks back at her gory demise, saying, "The same type of death scene had been done [to Kevin Bacon] in the original and again [to Los Angeles newscaster Tracie Savage] in *Part 3*, where you actually see the spear come up through the person's chest. That's how it was done with me, but for some reason the body mold didn't turn out right.

"The crew had cut a hole in the bunk bed, so just my head stuck through. I sat in a chair underneath and they slid the fake body up to my neck. As soon as the machete comes up through me, I look at it and scream. I guess the chest just didn't look real enough. They did two body molds, but neither worked. So they wound up doing a cut away."

The average person might get queasy at the sight of non-stop gore and grue for weeks, but Cummins gleefully reminisces, "It was cool to see how the chubby guy, Joey [Dominick Brascia], got his arm chopped off with the ax!"

Director Danny Steinman's sequel, in which Tommy Jarvis (Corey Feldman/John Shepard) and his peers are stalked by Jason imitator Roy (Dick Wieand) as revenge for his son Joey's murder, was critically blasted (as is any *Friday* film). However, its 1985 box office and subsequent video success warranted another sequel. It also put a new edge on Cummins career: horror star.

Through various scenes of slashing and mutilation in the films which followed, Cummins became accustomed to shrieking and hiding in dark, foreboding places. Her 1986 visit to Hitchcock's old Bates Motel in *Psycho III* furthered it.

During her stay in Room 12 as Red, Cummins got to roll around in bed with Jeff Fahey (1992's *The Lawnmower Man*), share an underwater grave with director-to-be Katt Shea (1999's *The Rage: Carrie 2*), meet Norman (Anthony Perkins) and his Prozak-deprived mother. "Oh, my God," she exclaims, throwing her arms up in the air. "My interview for *Psycho III* was with Tony Perkins. I walked into his office wearing these tight jeans and I didn't know he was going to be there with the producers. All I remember is ad-libbing my lines and at the end I said, 'Oh, yeah,' and I got right up to him, put my middle finger in his face and said 'Fuck you' and walked out the door. I guess he looked at the casting director and she looked at him [speechless] and he said, 'That's my Red!' That's why I always take a chance. That's when I get the roles."

Her boisterous audition not only got her the part, but a lot of physical activity as well. In addition to a sleazy striptease and getting violently thrown off a porch into a parking lot (a stunt she devised and performed herself), the actress also had to wrestle with Mrs. Bates and a bloody butcher knife in a shattered phone booth, and later endured hours of underwater torture.

Attempting to escape from a watery grave, Norman pulls back some garbage and seaweed, suddenly exposing Red's white, bloated face and wide open eyes, giving audiences one of the sequel's best scares. Cummins describes, "We were in this big tank and I had a fake bloated face on. The tank was so murky we had to keep shooting it over and over again, [because] you couldn't see me. Then you couldn't see my eyes, so [makeup FX artist Michael Westmore] had to put in

Juliette Cummins as Red in *Psycho III* (photograph copyright 1986 Universal).

contact lenses and I couldn't see at all. I had to be steered around the set. You wouldn't believe how many electric cords there are on a movie set! My face was completely covered in [swollen face] makeup, which took three hours to apply."

Perkins apologized to her one of the last times they spoke for what he believed was a poorly made film, yet Cummins is proud of the movie. "Tony said, 'I'm so sorry, Julie. The movie should have been so much better.'" She contends, however, that working with Perkins was a joy.

Actress Brinke Stevens, who stood-in for leading lady Diana Scarwid (Maureen) during pick up shots, concurs, "It was so amusing to watch him yell 'Action!,' jump in front of the camera, later shout 'Cut,' and then race off asking all of us 'How did I do?'"

Stevens and Cummins also shared similar territory, each falling victim to the driller killer of the *Slumber Party Massacre* series. By the time her role as nympho

Sheila came about in 1987's *Slumber Party Massacre II*, Cummins was getting used to laborious hours in bloody latex and being chased by maniacs with steel appliances. With dripping wounds and runny mascara, her disembowelment by electric rock guitar drill remains one of the series' campiest phallic highlights. Not only does the rockabilly maniac (Atanas Ilitch) send chunks of her innards flying throughout the house, he sings the John Juke Logan song "Let's Buzz" during the mayhem.

Cummins expressed utter joy of her nights with the guitar from hell and its Freddy-esque owner, recalling, "Atanas was great. So much fun! Crystal Bernard [Courtney] and Heidi Kozak [Sally] became great friends. We were always having a blast. *Slumber Party Massacre II* was [really interesting]. I believe it went platinum in video sales … just phenomenally huge numbers."

The actress next popped up in 1988's *Deadly Dreams*, the Kristine Peterson–directed sleeper about a college student (Mitchell Anderson) who has visions of the wolf-masked man who slaughtered his family on Christmas Eve years earlier. It received favorable reviews and had an interesting ensemble cast. Cummins played Anderson's back-stabbing girlfriend Maggie who, alongside Xander Berkeley (1992's *Candyman*) as his brother, might be responsible for the night scares.

Mention of her final horror feature, 1992's *Click: The Calendar Girl Killer*, brings a confused look to Cummins face. Why? It is a movie she never knew she made!

Lensed by and starring B-movie regulars Ross Hagen (*The Phantom Empire*) and Troy Donahue (*Tin Men*), *Click* tells the story of a fashion shoot plagued by a maniac who takes out his childhood aggressions on a number of hapless models. Barely on camera for more than ten minutes, Cummins shows up to take a literal blood bath in a hot tub. "I have absolutely no idea what you're talking about," she says with total seriousness.

After much deliberation, she comes to the conclusion her death scene is something she shot in the mid–1980s as part of a clip show for the promotional reel of a "never developed" feature. Apparently, Hagen and Donahue purchased these clips and spliced them into their feature, which would explain the film's uneven appearance. "Amazing," she laughs, shaking her head. "You can shoot something and never know what it's going to be used for."

She continued to make appearances on weekly television, but in the early 1990s Cummins' career took a distinct turn onto a path she still follows. "Throughout the '90s I've mostly done commercials. My friends call me the 'Commercial Queen' because I'm always doing one. I [recently had] about nine running on the air [at once]: Mission Tortillas, Pepsi, Mobil Oil, Burger King, Crest, Eggos and Aamco," she says, then mentions additional commercials on radio.

Cummins laughs and continues, "I also did an HMO for breast cancer which is great, because women don't realize they can get breast cancer at this young of an age. It lets [them] know it doesn't have to be genetic. They can still get it and need to get checked. I'm really proud of that commercial."

Averaging six to eight commercials per year over the past decade has kept her busy, and her label has even lent her notoriety among casting directors. This past spring an advertisement appeared in a trade paper requesting "an actress along the lines of Juliette Cummins for commercial work." She was ecstatic when her agent called her with the news.

With the label of reigning commercial queen, it's bizarre that Cummins was never labeled a Scream Queen during the time when any actress who appeared in more than two horror films was either clinging to or running from the moniker. She insists it wasn't her doing.

The conversation is abruptly cut off as, nearby, a small child makes a sudden dash for the busy street and his mother screeches for him to halt. Once the child has been recaptured and scolded, Cummins observes the situation, impressed, and states, "There's something to be said about not letting children take control. It's great to see [a parent] taking control of their child, not letting them just run out into the street [metaphorically speaking]."

As she continues to watch the parent and child, the issue of her horror career and its effect on children comes into the discussion. "I don't know if I would allow children to watch horror movies," she contemplates. "There are so many

Juliette Cummins circa 2000 (photograph courtesy Juliette Cummins)

other beautiful and engaging, wonderful movies for a child to watch. It's like, why bring a loaded gun into the house? I'm afraid it might be used accidentally.

"I don't think small children should see horror movies. I saw *Jaws* [1975] when I was little and it devastated me. I remember walking back to the parking lot afterwards and not even talking to my mom. I didn't talk for days. I was so scared I wouldn't even take a shower. I think it's a great film, but not for a child."

Cummins regains her spirited composure, recalling the number of fans her scare fare has brought her. "I've never had any problems with fans," she smiles. "They've all been wonderful. [One] actually flew in from Tennessee to meet me. We met at Universal Studios and it was so funny. We were chosen to be Klingons on *Star Trek* together! We were in the audience and out of 250 people we were both picked to be on stage at opposite ends of the fleet. They did the facial makeup and everything. He said it was a dream come true."

She hopes her continued luck will soon carry her back to the sound stage and movie theaters, deciding, "It's time to do more feature films. I've done a lot of commercials and made great connections. Commercials are fun and so easy to do—two or three days of work each, but it's time for me to do more film work. The great thing about the movie industry is that it's like shooting craps. There's times when you win big, but there's also times when you lose. It's 100 percent craps."

Brandi Burkett

It's a sweltering day outside Canters restaurant in West Hollywood, California. Inside, however, a pixie-like twenty-something coolly skims the deli. She resembles Sharon Stone, but actress Brandi Burkett has carved an impressive career of her own in the industry. In fact, it's still difficult to believe she hasn't just graduated high school.

"I was only 17 when I did *Slumber Party Massacre III* [1990]," she begins. "It was really bizarre. I went in for the audition, which itself was really strange, because they were ready to start shooting the following week. [Director] Sally Mattison was also casting and it was a one-shot deal. Normally you do the audition, then meet the producers and have screen tests—usually about five or six interviews. I went in, not expecting very much, and read for [the character] Diane. Then Sally was called in; I read again and went home. That afternoon they called and said I was booked! I was blown away..." Soon after, the teenager had her first real taste of Hollywood.

Born and raised in Conyers, Georgia—which also bred Academy Award winner Holly Hunter—Burkett began her career in musical theater at age nine, eventually growing into performances in *Chicago* and *Pippin*. During her teen years, Burkett was preened for Broadway, but the night an agent saw one of her performances her goals were altered.

Burkett reminisces, "I was originally going to New York to do Broadway after I graduated high school." The talent agent in the audience that fateful evening changed Burkett's intention and set her up with a management company. "The opportunities in [Los Angeles] came up and I figured I couldn't say no, but I am still singing," she smiles.

The then 16-year-old obtained her G.E.D. and was legally emancipated so she could work without the child labor law. She moved out and headed for the land of dreams—and occasional nightmares.

Upon arriving in L.A., Burkett landed some bit parts in movies like the Ned Beatty vehicle *Time Trackers* (1989) ("I was an English lady with a chastity belt"), then won her first real acting gig on an episode of *Who's the Boss*. She fondly recalls the cast as "a great group of people. They had done the show for so long they'd created their own family and were really comfortable with each other. Tony Danza sent me flowers on taping day and Alyssa Milano invited me out for sushi..." Confidence boosted by her initial experience, she continued onward to her only horror movie—and a date with a driller killer.

Burkett now thinks "someone at Concorde saw me in *Time Trackers* and that's how I got *Slumber Party Massacre III* so quickly." The former ingenue ventured into her first prominent film role with enthusiasm and pride. I was ecstatic when I got the job. I was playing a character I was really comfortable with: the cool best friend. It wasn't a big stretch for me, which was good because it was my first film. I wanted to get used to the cameras and how the whole process worked. We shot one of the last scenes of the movie first and, being the naïve girl I was, I thought films were shot in sequence. So I had this huge bloody gash in my side and was like, 'Where did this come from?'"

Burkett recalls the grisly prosthetic as "sticky, and it itched so bad! I just wanted to scratch it off! I would reach around to scratch it and it would feel like a real wound!" Surprisingly, she preserves the latex nightmare in a baggy in her keepsake trunk as a souvenir of her battle with Brittain Frye, the final "driller killer."

"Brittain [1987's *Hide and Go Shriek*] is extremely intense. I don't want to call him a Method actor, but he's extremely focused and concentrated. He's a perfectionist with his work, which is great," she says fondly of her co-star, whom she knew previously from acting classes.

"I ran into him after one of our sessions and said, 'I just got a movie!' He said, 'So did I' and told me it was *Slumber Party Massacre III*. I'm like, 'No you did not! I just got *Slumber Party Massacre III*. We'll be working together for five weeks.' So we were buds from the start." This companionship proved in her favor during the violent climax.

Masking her embarrassment, or perhaps a smirk, Burkett covers her mouth and confesses, "We were shooting the scene where I bonk him on the head with a polo mallet and I accidentally hit him for real. I'd never done a staged [fight] sequence before and I just whacked him! It was good we'd already been friends for almost two years, because he probably would've been a lot madder at me.

"I absolutely adored everyone. Hope Marie Carlton [Janine] and I had the best time. She was one of my favorite people to work with. She was just a 'good time girl' who had this perfect body and was carefree. I wish I knew where she was."

Burkett knows little about the current status of her co-stars, but has seen some of their work during the intervening years. "Devon Jenkins [Sarah] was the lead in Tom Petty's 'Freefalling' video. I also saw David Kriegel [Tom] in *Leaving Las Vegas* [1996] and another commercial within the past year — I thing promoting boom boxes."

The whereabouts of her other castmates remains a mystery. She recalls meeting up with lead actress Keely Christian (Jackie) a few years ago, but their reunion was brief. "We talked for quite a while, but I never saw her again. I'd love to see Keely again, too. She was so great!"

Her one fellow slumber victim who remains a frequent Hollywood player is the delectable Maria Ford (Maria). Burkett chimes up, "Oh, Maria was wonderful. Very sweet and beautiful. She was like an intangible French model."

Excitement fills Burkett's face as memories long forgotten begin to resurface. "[The shoot] was professional but very relaxed and low-key. We had to share dressing rooms which brought us a lot closer. We were all supporting one another."

One of her most vivid recollections was the opening beach shoot which, "took place in January. We were lying on the sand in our bikinis, freezing, and had to keep waiting for the sun to come out. We were wrapped in blankets between takes and at the last second someone would yell '*Speed!*' We'd throw off our blankets, run to our spots and begin acting and smiling like we were basking in the sun."

After thawing out one evening, the cast thought their day had ended and dressed as they prepared to go out for food and drinks. This, however, was not to be. Burkett groans, "We found out we still had to shoot more scenes and had to change back into our costumes, redo our makeup and start shooting all over again."

This type of stress was not prevalent on the set and was often overshadowed by some mishaps and hot situations. Burkett giggles, "We shot the scene where coals spill onto the deck. Keely Christian kept stomping on them instead of kicking them away and a brief fire broke out!"

Despite cold days, hot nights and occasional bludgeoning, Burkett insists the movie essentially went off wonderfully. When she finally saw herself on the big screen, she was delighted with the outcome. The actress describes the Fall 1990 premiere as leaving her "blown away. I wasn't used to seeing myself on

Brandi Burkett was just as surprised as the audience when her character, Diane, died in *Slumber Party Massacre III* (photograph copyright 1990 New Concorde).

screen for more than a few seconds. Of course I picked myself apart and complained about my hair, etc., but overall the film came out great." Her family's reaction, however, was a bit divided.

"My mom was thrilled to death," she laughs. Changing to an adorable Southern dialect, Burkett restates her parents' thoughts. "[My mom] kept saying, 'Oh, Brandi, you look so cute and so pretty!' My dad was a little disturbed, though. I said, 'Well, dad, what did you think?,' and he said, 'Well … you died, didn't you, Brandi?' … but they were both still excited that I had done my first feature."

Her death scene was actually just as much of a shock to her as it was her parents. Burkett titters, "They had shot an ending where I *didn't* die. When I first saw the screening, I was like, 'Oh my gosh … I died!' I think they used it for the impact."

Circumstances aside, she insists she'd jump at an opportunity to slumber again.

"Oh, definitely," she nods. "I would have to enjoy the script and see who I'd be working with, but I'd gladly do another sequel."

Following *Slumber Party Massacre III*, Burkett began frequenting television sitcoms and dramas. Among her list of guest appearances: *Unsolved Mysteries*, *My Two Dads*, *The Hogans*, *Meego* and others. She was also featured in *Spooners* and landed a recurring role on the ABC hospital drama *Vital Signs* with the late Robert Urich. Playing a character with meningitis, the actress found the role tricky to play because she would have to simulate seizures and other effects for the disease. She contends, "I was happy because I got to look like crap. I had to look sick and never wore makeup. I just walked around in my hospital gown, not worrying about lipstick touch-ups, etc. I was really proud of my performance. It was a good experience for me."

After a year in the industry, the actress suddenly took a leave of absence "for personal reasons" and returned home to Conyers. She remained in Georgia for over a year, but when the time was right, she returned to Los Angeles and her career picked up as though she had never left.

In 1993 she found herself back in teen roles in the comedy *My Boyfriend's Back* and the drama *There Goes My Baby*. More television work followed with roles on *Guys Like Us*, *House Rules*, *Diagnosis Murder*, *Fanelli Boys* and *Step By Step*. She even returned to her musical roots, singing in the TV movie *The Heidi Chronicles*. She considers her appearance on an episode of *Frasier* "a highlight, because I'd always loved the show. Kelsey would run around singing all the time. It was a very professionally run show. Probably the most professional I've ever worked on."

Her expanding résumé also includes the Jim Carrey hit *Liar Liar* (1997), her first big-budget feature, where she appeared as a distraught airplane stewardess. "I was amazed. There were grips that would set up for other grips who set up for the master grips. Plus, I was on the Universal lot, which I remembered being on as a kid and thinking, 'Gosh, I wish I could work here...' Jim Carrey was very energetic [and] nice with the people, and boy, does he know how to improvise."

Since the majority of her work after *Slumber Party Massacre III* has been PG-13 fare, Burkett found nudity was not an issue on set. However, she does admit to her opinions about exposing herself on screen, and that her views today are quite different from those when she first started acting. She speaks seriously, "As an actress, I was very anti-nudity when I started in the business. I didn't understand when your character is in a certain situation, sometimes it is necessary. When I did *Slumber Party Massacre III* I was 'No, no, no. Absolutely no nudity.' Now, I know there are times when it is necessary.

"I will not do nudity unless it's an integral part of the character or scene. I almost think it's more appealing if there is no nudity, but if it's important to the story line, then I'm all for it." She smiles candidly, then mentions a few roles she's turned down because of excessive flesh requirements, including an installment of the *Red Shoe Diaries* series.

Interestingly, while she will agree to do most things on film as long as they pertain to the plot, she puts her foot down "if there's a line which uses the Lord's name in vain. I will try my best to change it, to see if there's something else I can say, because it sets a bad example. I don't think it's necessary. There definitely are other things which can be said." The discussion then turns from religious beliefs to the topic of on-screen violence.

As the list of high school shoot-outs and suburban violence increases, Burkett defends action and horror chaos. She points to parents who aren't overly responsible when allowing their children to view television, play video games, and so on. "At such a young age, children don't have the intelligence to differentiate between what is real and what is a movie. Each child is different. [Some] don't have the knowledge to think, 'Oh, this is a movie.' It's exciting to them and they don't realize it's fiction."

Burkett asserts she has no regrets about her horror credit, insisting she'd love to do more horror. Ecstatic about where her career has brought her, she advises other ingenues to, "...believe in yourself, no matter what anyone says. You are never what people say you are when they say negative things. Remember this is a business. It's not fun and games. Bottom line, you

Brandi Burkett in 2003 (courtesy Brandi Burkett).

have to believe in yourself and your abilities. Stay in acting class. It's not about getting an agent and waiting for calls. Get an agent and work together as a team. Do some theater. Send out flyers, and get into a good acting class so when you start submitting to agencies they'll recognize someone's name and think, 'Oh, maybe she's worth taking a look at.'" The actress smiles and leans back in her seat.

As she meditates on her career, there's a realization everything seems to circle back to her first movie role. She shares, "I got a fan letter after [my appearance] on *Frasier* which read, 'I've been following your career since *Slumber Party Massacre III*,' and I thought that was so cool."

Brandi Burkett takes a final sip of her tea and sums up, "I pat myself on the back because it's not easy, especially when you start young and have to make the transition from being a teenager into [an adult]. I'm still here and there's nothing else I'd rather be doing."

Marta Kober

Screaming and dying at the hands of a maniacal killer in *Slumber Party Massacre III* was nothing new to actress Marta Kober. She'd already been spiked to her boyfriend in *Friday the 13th, Part 2*, was ravaged by the *Neon Maniacs* and fought to survive a life behind bars in *Vendetta*. So dealing with the driller killer—who was less than satisfied with her pizza delivery skills—was mere child's play.

Throughout the 1980s, Kober was one of Hollywood's busiest ingénues. Still a teenager when she debuted in the 1981 follow-up to the previous summer's biggest hit, the young star unexpectedly found herself climbing the ladder. Oddly, it wasn't what she desired.

Presently tackling a *huge* pastrami sandwich, the graduate of New York's famous Performing Arts High School recalls, "I was a kid when I did *Friday the 13th, Part 2*. I'd just graduated and didn't really know what I was getting into. They shot in Connecticut for about nine weeks. It was almost all night shoots and was really cold. It took a lot of work to get through."

One of the more torturous scenes was the forementioned impalement, one of many controversial MPAA cuts and long accused of ripping off a similar scene from *Twitch of the Death Nerve* (1972). As thrill-seeking Sandra Dier, Kober is in bed with on-screen boyfriend Jeff (Bill Randolf) when the couple is rudely interrupted by a pre–hockey mask Jason. With a quick thrust of his handy spear, the lovers get closer than they ever thought possible.

Kober claims, "[The MPAA] cut out a lot of that scene, but it was mostly sex! They did leave most of the gore intact, except when we shot it you actually saw the spear go into my boyfriend's back." She adds it was one of the more uncomfortable scenes to shoot. "They had cut a hole in the bed for me and Bill [*Dressed to Kill*] to slip through and used body molds for the impaling. It took weeks for the entire process to be finished…"

After two months of roaming through freezing woods and lying in pools of sticky fake blood, Kober

Marta Kober and Bill Randolf in *Friday the 13th, Part 2* (copyright 1981, Paramount/Georgetown Pictures).

fled to Europe to rethink her career choice. The actress recounts, "I was so displeased with the experience, I went away for about a year and swore I'd never act again. I think I reacted that way because I was so young and it wasn't as glamourous as I'd expected it to be."

Any *Friday the 13th* actor could tell you the shoots have never been known as glamourous (what with rolling around in rain, mud and dead teenagers), but after a year of rest, Kober returned to the states for the film's premiere. "When I came back, I went to Los Angeles, which gave me the glamour I'd expected," she laughs.

Kober found herself delighted with the final version of the first in a long line of sequels. Even today, its popularity keeps her in fans' eyes. She shares, "I think everybody in the world has seen *Friday the 13th, Part 2*. I still get letters from fans and people get really excited when they recognize me. It's always on television. I mean, it's been [over 20 years] and I'm still getting residual checks! It's probably never going to die..."

Though perpetuating the trend of slander by critics, the film's release did anything but kill Kober's career. Immediately after it opened, the box-office success helped the actress make a career decision. She remembers, "*Friday 2* opened so many doors for me. I did a play in New York for a year with Brent Spiner [*Star Trek: The Next Generation*] and David Marshall Graham [*The Rock*]." Upon completing the play, the still teenaged Kober accepted another offer and found herself nominated for one of the industry's most prominent awards.

Rodeo Red and the Runaway was Kober's follow-up project which garnered her critical raves and an Emmy nomination. "I was still really young. It was one of the very first ABC *After School Specials*. It was so great just to be recognized like that," she smiles. Having added yet more credibility to her name, television and film work flowed in, making Kober one of Hollywood's busiest actresses.

In 1982, Kober found herself in a supporting role as Debra, one of Rosanna Arquette's best friends in the love story *Baby, It's You*. Co-stars included Vincent Spano (*Alive*), Liane Curtis (*Sixteen Candles*), Tracy Pollan (*A Stranger Among Us*) and Matthew Modine (*And the Band Played On*). She was suddenly being typecast as the "teenage best friend," which didn't bother her, because over the next five years her plate was continuously full. "I worked all the time in the 1980s. I was always doing a movie or a sitcom. I got a stint on *Happy Days* when I was 20. It was my first TV show."

Kober's résumé is an encyclopedia of '80s TV favorites: *Cheers*, *Better Days* (on which she was a regular), *Magnum P.I.*, *Matlock*, *Full House* and *The Facts of Life*, plus TV movies like *Children of the Night* with Kathleen Quinlan, *Intimate Encounters* with Donna Mills, *Touch of Scandal* with Angie Dickinson, *Shattered Vows* with Valerie Bertinelli and *Second Sight* with Elizabeth Montgomery. She remembers *Children of the Night*, in which she plays a teen runaway-prostitute, as one of her best roles. It earned her further critical applause, but her appearance on *Facts of Life* almost got the actress her own sitcom. "I think it was called *The Funny Boys*. I turned it down, but I think they shot the pilot and it never got picked up, at least as far as I know." She also turned down a lead role on the NBC sitcom *Nurses* because, "I didn't think it would ever even air." She instead continued her focus on guest spots and movie roles.

During the middle of the "Me" decade, Kober segued back into the genre which launched her. Finding a niche at Roger Corman's Concorde Pictures, the actress appeared in a slew of low-budget cult favorites. First up was *Neon Maniacs* (1985), a scary, ambitious teen flick about demons terrorizing New York, which received positive reviews for its special FX and creepy monsters. Next came the comedy *School Spirit* (1985), about a teenager who dies and returns as a sex-starved ghost. Though the critics were less favorable, Kober asserts, "A lot of my movies are really bad and trashy — just awful. [Yet] people really like them. They've got these great groups of fans, so I guess you could say they've become cult classics."

Another of these so called "trashy" movies has the approval of her most honored fan. Kober laughs and shakes her head, "My mother loves *Vendetta* [1985]. She calls me every time it's on television. It's her favorite of every movie I've made." The women in prison flick was also blasted by reviewers, but its cult status makes up for any embarrassment its lead might feel. "Oh, so many people have seen that one and just love it. It made me a lot of money too! Fox used to show it, like, once a week," she exaggerates. "It was showing on TV all the time a few years ago. It's the same as *Friday 2*. It's never going to disappear."

Following *Vendetta*, the sitcom princess and supporting player briefly abdicated her R-rated movie fare for the family oriented *RAD* (1986). As tomboy Becky, one of a group of teens who perform impressive stunts on their dirt bikes, she and her best buddy Cru (Bill Alley) must stop an "evil" business man (Jack Weston) from rigging a race in which they are competing. Of co-starring with Talia Shire (*Rocky*), Lori Loughlin (*Amityville 3-D*) and Ray Walston (*The Stand*), Kober smiles, "*RAD* was a lot of fun to do. Little boys seem to like that one the best of all my movies. I played one of the BMX bike riders. We shot it in Canada for about six or seven weeks and had a great time. Lori was really sweet ... probably one of the sweetest girls I've ever met."

Kober reunited with Loughlin a few years later on an episode of *Full House* and insists, "She was the same. Really pretty and nice to everyone." It was around this time a friend offered her a cameo in one of her last horror films. As usual, there was a deadly appliance involved.

"[High school friend] Josh Melville was working at Concorde on a slasher movie. He said they needed someone to do a couple nights work as a pizza girl. It paid some decent money, so I agreed." The role turned out to be the doomed pizza delivery girl who gets disemboweled in the middle of the street in *Slumber Party Massacre III*. It's clear why the 5'3" brunette has no mention of the feature on her résumé: "I thought it was terrible!"

The mood lightens as she states, "It was the basic plot with the set formula: You can't smoke pot, you can't screw, you can't take your top off, and if you do any of these things, you die. Then you've got the little blonde girl who doesn't do any of those things, finds her dead friends, runs around for two hours and lives." The driller killer's victim laughs and rolls her eyes.

With her taste of the film industry souring in the 1990s, Kober decided it was time to try something new. She had desired a career in rap music, so with assistance from Melville and another high school friend, the former teen actress kissed L.A. goodbye and returned to New York.

Throughout the majority of the 1990s, Kober (who points out she has no relation to *China Beach*'s Jeff Kober — a question she's frequently asked) continued to pursue her rap ambitions, but took acting jobs "whenever the money was good. I've done a bunch of independent movies like *Washington Square* and *Suburban*. Nothing really major." She cringes at her role in the *Playboy* hit *Inside Out* (1992), then changes the subject, naming other previously unmentioned projects, such as stints on *Law & Order*, *Getting Along*, *The Patty Hearst Story*, *Beth Paley Stories* and *A Very Delicate Matter*.

Mention of 2002's *Jason X* (a.k.a. *Friday the 13th, Part X*) has Kober giggling again, but it's not at the masked maniac's return. Instead, she tells of an amusing situation she found herself in which almost landed her in Mr. Voorhees path again. "My agent sent me to read for a horror movie and I got the role. Afterwards, I found out it was *Friday the 13th, Part VII*! The filmmakers had no clue I'd already been in *Part 2*!" Her original idea was to keep mum, but she eventually gave in and told the casting directors the truth. "I thought it would've been pretty funny, but I don't think they would have been as [amused]."

Marta Kober today (courtesy Marta Kober).

Kober returned to L.A. in the late '90s, but insists her heart remains with the music. "I'm honestly intending to go back to New York again very soon. The people I was working with there have plans to produce a couple tracks, so hopefully that will pan out and I can get a CD released. I've done what I wanted as far as acting is concerned. Now I have something else to say, something I want to do more. That's what's important to me and that's [the dream] I'm going to follow."

Camping Out on Friday the 13th

Lar Park-Lincoln

If the 1980s taught American teenagers anything, it was not to go into the woods alone, not to have sex anywhere near the woods, not to skinny dip in a lake on the shore of the woods, and definitely not to consume any form of alcohol or drugs ... in the woods, or anywhere else for that matter ... especially on any kind of holiday. Basically, don't be a teenager. If you did any of those things, the results were guaranteed: You'd die. Heaven forbid if you were of any ethnicity besides Caucasian. You'd be lucky to make it to the third act.

Of course, metaphorically, the message referred to drinking and driving, overdosing on drugs, and possibly getting a sexual disease with varying results of severity — all things which would destroy your life, and possibly others. In the horror films of the era, however, doing those things really just meant a guy in a hockey mask was going to show up and give you a lick of his machete.

There were, of course, a few ways to survive. Don't perform any of the above mentioned "bad things." Be of the "pretty blonde cheerleader" variety, and have a likable personality. Oh ... and be a virgin. Otherwise you could hold within your psyche hidden telekinetic powers and unleash them at just the right times. Luckily for Lar Park-Lincoln, a former model, her character was all of the above.

The *Friday the 13th* franchise was one of the big three genre staples of the decade. Freddy was the most commercial, and Michael was the most time-honored and respected, while the ugly eldest brother, Leatherface, only popped in from time to time just to remind everyone he was still important. The most put-upon by the general public was Jason Voorhees— the lad who drowned as a boy in Crystal Lake, yet mysteriously kept coming back again ... and again ... and again.

As much as everyone seemed to groan when a TV commercial for each new sequel ran in America, the box office always seemed to say "Keep 'em coming." By the time *Friday the 13th, Part VII: The New Blood* came around in 1988, however, Paramount execs realized it was time to start breathing some new life into the routine. What better way to go than full-on supernatural, and "borrow" an idea from a horror classic?

"Tina was a completely different character," Park-Lincoln says of the character who "cried constantly" and which made her face a well-known commodity among horror enthusiasts. "She was psychic and telekinetic. They were trying to move the series into an area with multiple storylines. Tina was vulnerable but intelligent. Her mental state was being compounded by the lies of the doctor sent to help her. The storyline added a new dimension to the previous shows, and I hope the fans enjoyed it."

She smiles, "I had fun with the film. I felt the storyline was complete and told well-enough that it could stand on its own as a separate movie. I believe that was the intention."

Park-Lincoln began her career playing a true-life teen prostitute in the TV movie *Children of the Night* (1985), followed by 1987's *The Princess Academy*, which the actress "hated shooting. We were in Yugoslavia. I loved the director, Bruce Block, and my character, Cindy Cathcart, but I hated the cold and the storyline was all over the place. However, it's become a cult favorite and is a very early version of *The Princess Diaries* (2001)."

There were also TV guest appearances on *Hunter, Outlaws* and *Highway to Heaven*. Then, in 1987, Park-Lincoln won the role of Tina Shepard through "a casting session with Anthony Bareno. I was brought in very late into the casting process and met with the director [John Carl Buechler]. They were looking for someone who could be tough but show intense emotion and who, of course, had the ability to cry on cue! I went through a lot of contact lenses and learned that crying gives you a real headache!"

Amusingly, she didn't even know for certain she was auditioning for a *Friday* film. "When I read for the [movie], it was titled under another name [*Birthday Bash*].

Lar Park-Lincoln (right) on the set of *Friday the 13th, Part VII: The New Blood* with co-star Susan Blu and director John Carl Buechler.

I suspected from the script it was a *Friday the 13th* movie, but wasn't sure. The audition script was vague and partial. I gathered they wanted to keep the casting as quiet as possible to keep fans under control at the sessions," she winks.

Though a fan of horror films, the actress admits she had only seen two of the previous *Friday the 13th* films at the time of her casting, but "my husband, now deceased, was a huge fan. It was a fun show to do to give him for his library of horror films." She later viewed the other chapters, but has not seen *Parts VIII: Jason Takes Manhattan* (1989), *IX: Jason Goes to Hell* (1993) or *Jason X* (2002).

Taking the role seriously was important to the thespian who, in *Fangoria #84*, revealed, "I took it upon myself to work with real psychics and learn what it would be like to experience a vision, and what a person would go through trying to communicate the experience to other people. I was really serious about trying to do this movie right."

She says the shoot as a whole was "a lot of fun. However, at seven A.M., it is hard to have a TV set flying over your head! Of course now my friends and family tease me about moving furniture around. A lot of the effects were done with magnets and wires and prop men off-stage and below me. I had a great time! We did some reshoots in the forest at a later time ... and it was a different forest than where we did the rest of the film. They needed more 'screaming' shots, which was interesting because there were no bodies to see or scream at — but, hey, that's what actors do."

Jason Voorhees of the *Friday the 13th* films.

Park-Lincoln recalls an ailment encountered by most actresses who do time in Crystal Lake: bruises and battering from performing their own stunts. "I did the stunt falling from the staircase into the basement. [I was] well-padded, but it was still a creepy feeling. Remember, I had to repeat it several times. I also did the stunt at the end of the film on the pier, taking a running, full-frontal dive onto the wood. Now that hurt! Girls, do not try that at home," she laughs. "They gave me an honorary stunt woman T-shirt! I think I proved my boobs were real — no fake boobs could have withstood that stunt!"

Nudity was never an issue for Park-Lincoln in *Friday VII* ... after all, she was the heroine. "Tina didn't have any nudity in question. I have had roles which required a brief passing of nudity, and of course on *Knots Landing* I was in bed *all* the time! Nudity in films doesn't bother me. The scenes I have done were modest, usually just teasing that the nudity was there, which really is more fun anyway … don't you think?"

One of the few things which did bother her were regular sightings of disembodied carnage on her co-stars and other gruesome props (many of which never made it to theaters after the MPAA swung their magic ax). "I did not like a [chopped-off] head bobbing at me at seven in the morning," she trembles. "And of course the crew carrying around body parts … well, it was odd. Having lunch one day with an actress with an ax in her head was really good for dieting!"

Park-Lincoln's sense of humor is clearly strong, as was her trust in her on-screen tormentor during some "hot" situations. "Kane Hodder [Jason Voorhees] was a sweetheart," she says. "I trusted him with the stunts, such as the fire scenes. He would have to pull me away at the right time and put the stunt actress in."

Working with John Carl Buechler [*Ghoulies III*] is also a fond memory for the actress. "He was a good director for *me*. He worked with me most on creating Tina's reactions to the special effects I could not see, as they were added in later. He spoke softly with me, never embarrassed me [in front of] the cast. He didn't need to hear himself talk," she smiles softly.

The first time Lar Park-Lincoln saw *Friday the 13th, Part VII: The New Blood* (which opened Friday, May 13, 1988) was "at a public screening in Brentwood, California. I wore a stupid disguise and was chased out of the theater! It scared me! I had never [experienced] something like that before. I was so foolish to think nobody would know it was me."

Sadly, there were more negative experiences following the film's release. "I've had some problems with fans," she solemnly divulges. "I had a stalker, was attacked by two separate fans, and a bomb threat was made to my home. Most of the fans are just great, but you know the world is full of people who just can't separate reality from fantasy. Those types of instances have also occurred following some of my other shows as well."

Does this lead her to agree with protests against violent films in recent times? Has her opinion changed since she made *Friday VII*, especially now with children a part of her life? "When the films started they were just fun, scary movies. Compared to violent video games, the issues at schools today, etc.… It's different now. I believe each parent must monitor what their child is shown. Yes, that requires *a lot* of supervision. I actually *see* every film before my children are allowed to [view it]. They have to call home from a friend's house before watching a video. We also walk out of films with bad language and storylines which are not appropriate for their ages. I am constantly surprised how many parents, for their own selfish reasons, stay in a theater with children when the film is objectionable. My children have not seen *Friday the 13th, Part VII*. They thought the poster was too scary, so I had to put it away. Many of their friends *have* seen [it], which disturbs me because of their ages."

This is not to say she now disavows the film. In fact, she freely admits to being tempted to some day return to Crystal Lake. "I was asked to do *Friday the 13th, Part VIII: Jason Takes Manhattan*, but at the time my agents and I were concerned about typecasting. *Friday VII* was huge. It made $19 million. At one point I did write a script for *Friday VIII*, but Paramount decided not to use it. I think if we could have been assured a good script with a strong storyline we may have taken it, but I passed on the one they did," she says.

"I love scary movies," she continues. "Not the gory ones, though. I enjoy reading the scripts [people have sent], so never say 'never.' I loved the new direction *Friday VII* brought to the series, and wish they would have stuck with it. Maybe matured Tina and made another film. She could come back now with children who are also psychic ... or she could be a doctor who works with emotionally disturbed young adults. There I go again with my writing..."

Other horror offers did come her way following the success of *Friday VII*, many of which Park-Lincoln turned down ... with one exception. "I did *House II: The Second Story*, but it was a comedy poorly marketed as a scary film. *House II* [which beat *Friday VII* to theaters] is the film I consider my first move towards being a *femme fatale*, which are the roles I seemed to always play from that point on."

Though *House II* was panned by critics and audiences, the actress' memories are fond. (Many of her scenes were either rearranged or cut entirely.) "What a cast," she

Kate (Lar Park-Lincoln) watches husband Jesse (Arye Gross) make out with his ex-girlfriend Lana (Amy Yasbeck) in *House II: The Second Story* (1987).

exclaims. "Bill Maher, Arye Gross ... a lot of them went on to become quite successful. I went in to audition with Arye and we had great chemistry."

Next, in a bit of blasphemy, Park-Lincoln did the unthinkable ... she crossed over to the other side ... of *Elm Street*. Playing Karen in the "It's a Miserable Life" episode of the television spin-off *Freddy's Nightmares*, she got to be another terrorized teen who gets her mouth sewn shut prior to an operation. In *Fangoria* #84, the actress reported, "The makeup people glued my mouth shut with spirit gum.... I had to breathe through my nose for an awful long time. The mouth sewn shut was a major problem; not being able to open your mouth is an actor's nightmare."

With the then-negative Scream Queen label looming over her head, Park-Lincoln skipped into

Lar Park-Lincoln today (photograph courtesy Cody Harris Photography).

dramatic territory with an episode of *Tour of Duty*, followed by a two-year run on the nighttime soap *Knots Landing*. Though still frequently recognized from *Friday VII* , she claims more people associate her with her troublesome *Knots* character Linda Fairgate, who eventually wound up the victim of one of the show's many murder mysteries.

After her stint on the series wrapped, she moved onto an episode of *Murder, She Wrote* and the cable thriller *Fatal Charm* (1992), in which a jailhouse psycho (Christopher Atkins, 1980's *The Blue Lagoon*) is freed and stalks his pretty female penpal (Amanda Peterson, 1987's *Can't Buy Me Love*), her mother (Mary Frann, TV's *Newhart*) and best friend (Park-Lincoln). "I liked that film," she says. "However, when I first saw *Fatal Charm*, it had been edited quite a bit. In fact, my character, Sandy, ended up murdered! A surprise to me, but it must have been needed. My cast mates were really easy to get along with. It was a fun movie."

Following guest spots on TV's *Space: Above and Beyond* and *Beverly Hills 90210*, tragedy struck and the actress returned to her home state of Texas, where she remains today. "I took a break from L.A. when my husband passed away from cancer, leaving me with two very young children," she says. "I'm originally from Texas and needed wide open spaces. I have a marketing business, which I started while I was still heavily involved in acting. It's called Park-Lincoln & Croyle Marketing, Inc., based out of Los Angeles. We find great inventions and place them on shopping channels and infomercials all over the world! I've done the shows live on the QVC Channel consistently since *Knots Landing* ended."

So is she through with the film industry? "I'm just now starting to actively search for roles in hopes of returning to the screen. It's my passion and love," she affirms.

In the meantime, she's glad to be known for opposing Jason Voorhees and winning the battle. "Today's films have so many more effects and techniques," she theorizes, "but the *Friday the 13th* films were the start of a certain type of genre, which will always be watched. It was definitely a plus for my career. I can see how for many it could be a deterrent, but for me it was great fun, and I followed it with many years of other work. I've been lucky to have great agents, managers and casting directors who remembered me even if I wasn't right for a certain role. I have always been treated with respect in this business and never felt any pressure to accept roles I didn't want to do."

Kari Keegan

Not many actresses can say they've had the honor of battling one of cinema's most vicious— and gruesomely creative — mass murderers. In fact, their group only numbers ten (keeping in mind one of them bit the dust via ice pick in the second round of mayhem). Still, out of their heroic club, only one can say she defeated her uncle Jason Voorhees.

In *Jason Goes to Hell: The Final Friday* (1993), Kari Keegan's character, Jessica Kimble, is the sole surviving lady (well, her daughter too) to have a blood relation to the hockey masked marauder. Of course, the subtitle of *Friday the 13th*'s ninth installment is the second false promise to the series conclusion, but it was a wise marketing ploy (lifted from 1991's *Freddy's Dead: The Final Nightmare*), which nicely wrapped up both the series and scored at the box office to the tune of over $15 million, making *Jason Goes to Hell* the most successful horror film of the year.

Keegan, an actress commonly seen in commercials who also appeared in *Jerry Maguire* (1999) and the thriller *Mind Games* (2003), admits, "I had no idea how popular the *Friday the 13th* series was. I'm embarrassed to say I didn't like horror films. When *Carrie* [1976] came out I was too young to see it, so I didn't until I was in college and it just freaked me out. I just don't like to be scared. When I saw *What Lies Beneath* [2000] I just kept letting out these screams and it's embarrassing! I can't see these things in theaters because I'm always grabbing people and annoying everyone! [However], when I got the role I immediately rented the first four and was subsequently horrified. I'd have to say I like the first one the best. It's my favorite.

"I was too young to see the original *Friday the 13th* [1980] when it came out, so I was completely unaware, and unprepared, for its huge cult following. It's amazing.

I mean, they're great movies and many of them are scary, but it surprises me that [ten] years later I'm still getting fan letters asking me questions about the movie."

Today the actress, still vibrant and youthful, is seated at the Coffee Bean and Tea Leaf, directly across from the Directors Guild of America offices in West Hollywood, California. Only days earlier, she discovered she's pregnant with her first child (she already has stepchildren with her husband). She talks about her love of being a mother, and reveals why it was easy for her to portray one on-screen, even before she had any.

"It was actually really easy because I was a nanny in college. Plus, I have three sisters who've had children. I think just being a woman gave me innate maternal instincts. Plus, being chased by a monster with a real baby in your arms, even though you're on a movie set, made it much easier to express those instincts," she concurs.

Actress Kari Keegan today (photograph courtesy Kari Keegan).

Keegan's Jessica wasn't an average *Friday the 13th* heroine. Sure, she was pretty and blonde, and quite capable of shrieking while finding mutilated bodies, but the actress expresses why she didn't mold her character after others. "Jessica wasn't a teenager, and she was a mother. She had to care for a baby, so instead I studied Linda Hamilton in *Terminator 2* [1991] and Sigourney Weaver in *Aliens* [1986]. They were strong women who had to care for children. Those were the guidelines I sought."

"I'm also not naked in this movie, which is the first question my mother asked. 'Do [you] get naked? Do [you] die?' and 'Do [you] cuss?' The interesting thing is, I did swear, and though I didn't have sex on screen, the fact that I had a child — out of wedlock, no less— meant I wasn't a virgin ... yet I *was* the heroine. I think being a mother brought in a new dynamic to the rules [though Tracie Savage's pregnant teen character got offed in 1982's *Friday the 13th, Part III* for the same reason].

Much like the challenge Lisa Wilcox faced in bringing the perils of young motherhood to the attention of a teenage market in *A Nightmare on Elm Street 5: The Dream Child* (1989), Keegan had to tread a thin line which would keep her appealing to an audience whose main concerns were shopping at the mall and attending parties. After all, the touchy topic was largely blamed for the beginning of the end of Molly Ringwald's teen-idol career with *For Keeps* (1987). While Wilcox admitted to worrying about the issue, Keegan says, "I really didn't think about it. I was more just in the moment of what was going on around me. I was in my early twenties, so I was still in that 'young person' mode. I was still able to connect and understand teenagers. I didn't feel too separated from teenagers at that point."

Jessica (Kari Keegan) is attacked in a police sation sequence which returned the *Friday the 13th* series to its gruesome beginnings (photograph by Mark Fellman, copyright 1992 New Line Cinema).

What did concern her was what the audience would think of the film. The late 1980s and early 1990s had found genre films bombarded with the sharp scissors of the Motion Picture Association of America (MPAA). *Friday the 13th* movies, in particular, seemed to have been directly targeted by the board, and if you were to watch the series today, you'll notice the kills get progressively dryer with each chapter. *Jason Goes to Hell* somehow managed to sneak in under the radar, perhaps the result of a new presidency which allowed Americans to be a bit less sensitive to the topic of gore and violence. Director Adam Marcus deliberately made the film gorier than intended, anticipating that the MPAA would force them to cut away unnecessary gore footage anyway, and everyone was surprised when the film was able to show possibly more graphic kills than the original film (the disintegrating man is quite juicy and a perfect example).

Reviews and fan opinions have been mixed for years, but Keegan only saw the positive aspects both on screen and within the audiences. "I really liked it," she says. "It stayed true to the script, tried to do something different and interesting with the series, and we had some really good actors. The characters Joey B. [Rusty Schwimmer of 1996's *Twister*] and Shelby [Leslie Jordan of TV's *Will & Grace*], the diner own-

ers, were really funny, and are an example of how much humor was in *Jason Goes to Hell* ... it really pokes fun at itself. We didn't usually do really stupid things like go into the dark house, at least not without the characters commenting they knew it was a stupid thing to do. It was very self-aware and never took itself too seriously."

From what Keegan saw first hand "by sneaking into Mann's Chinese Theater in Hollywood, California," audiences seemed to approve. "I saw it three days after the premiere. It was so much *more* fun to see it with a public audience, because at the premiere you're with your parents and worried about what everyone is thinking of you and the film, and you point out all the mistakes you made. When you see it with a real audience, though, you get more genuine reactions."

Lead actors Kari Keegan and John D. LeMay received real wounds in addition to their applied ones during the filming of *Jason Goes to Hell: The Final Friday* (photograph by Mark Fellman, copyright 1992 New Line Cinema)

She laughs and confesses, "I didn't even watch the movie. I watched people's reactions to it, which is the best treat for an actor. It was also a relief because they screamed in the right places, laughed at the right times, yelled at the screen. They seemed to really like it. Plus, I'd never seen a horror movie in a theater before, so I had no idea people actually yell at the screen. It was so great to hear people yell at my character about certain stupid things I did, like jumping over the table with the baby in my hands. 'What mother would do something like that?!' It was great! It was probably my favorite thing of the entire *Jason Goes to Hell* experience."

Keegan managed to sneak out of the showing with only two patrons recognizing her. "My hair looked different, so most people didn't realize it was me. The two who did just said hello, which was really cool, because it was the first time it had ever happened. Then as the summer went on and more people were seeing it, I was getting recognized all the time, which again is really fun when you're first experiencing it."

Ten years later, the frequent recognition has slowed, but the actress is amused at how often she still receives fan letters. "I haven't gotten anything really bad or bizarre," she confirms. "The one question people ask me most is about Kane Hodder [Mr. Voorhees himself], because he appears out of makeup in the movie and many of them are unsure of which character he plays. [He's FBI Agent #2 during the first massacre at the morgue.] I actually never give them a straight answer. I'll tell them he's one of three different characters and give them several clues, then let them try to figure it out. Most of the fans are really great. Luckily, I haven't gotten any wackos or stalkers."

One of her favorite people on set was Hodder, who portrayed the silent killer from 1988's *Friday the 13th, Part VII: The New Blood* through 2002's *Jason X*. Of the stunt man, Keegan announces, "Love! Absolute love. When he had the mask on, he'd become a completely different person. I videotaped some on set stuff where he's cracking jokes and is just a big teddy bear, but the minute that mask goes on he doesn't talk to anyone. He stays in character. Otherwise he was just the nicest man in the world. I'm sure the fans will hate to hear that, but he really was nice."

Even though Hodder was in charge of the stunt work, it didn't save the actress from receiving more than just bumps and bruises. Keegan, who did most of her own stunts, reports that, "because of the way it was shot, there were a lot of closeups, so you had to see my face. On the second day, we shot the scene in my garage where I'm carrying this big industrial flashlight. I dropped it on my foot and broke [my foot]! So when I'm being pulled out of the house and Stephen [John D. LeMay] throws me over his shoulder and runs to the car, it's because I couldn't run. It was kind of funny because we had to do that take about 15 times and John isn't much bigger than me. So for him to keep throwing me over his shoulder and run a good 20 yards with me kicking, screaming and hitting him, he wasn't able to walk much the next day either.

"So, in general, I did most of my own stunts, and it was scary. I also broke a rib, which I didn't realize until then is really easy to do. We were doing a stunt where I grab onto Kane and he swings me around. Then there was another scene where I got thrown into a tree trunk and I injured my neck. I got lots and lots of bruises. Lots of jumping over tables, getting thrown into things, getting my head slammed into lockers… Yeah, it was fun. I got a really good workout, and the makeup people had a great time trying to cover up bruises which weren't there the day before. Even though I was jumping down 20-foot holes, with Kane as the stunt coordinator I always felt I was in really good hands."

Accidents didn't only happen to the actress. Many were deemed so amusing they remained in the film's final cut. "There's a scene where I run back into the diner to get the baby and I have an argument with Rusty about her giving me the baby. I pick up the napkin dispenser and hit her with it, but I really came too close to her face and almost really hit her with it and said, 'Oh! Sorry!' Well, they ended up using that in the film! They thought it was funny, so when I saw it in the theater I was like, 'Hey! That wasn't supposed to be there.'"

Yet another flub occurred during the scene "where Stephen [LeMay] and Randy [Kipp Marcus] are fighting by the cop car and they each have guns and one says, 'I have a gun,' and the other says, 'Fuck that… I have a gun!' One of them wasn't supposed to have a gun. It was a mistake, and they just went with it. Everyone on set was just roaring. It was so funny they kept it in the movie."

A bit of the dark humor laced throughout *Jason Goes to Hell* even managed to follow Keegan home one evening. Excitement mixes with giggles. She recalls, "I had just moved to L.A. when I got the job, and really didn't know my way around the city. One night after shooting I was so exhausted I didn't even have the energy to wash my face. I just wanted to get home and didn't realize there was blood splattered across my face and a bloody hand print on my throat.

"So got lost as I was driving home and saw a Holiday Inn. At this point it's five A.M., so I pulled in and asked a kid who worked there for directions and he just stares at me. He slowly lifted his arm and pointed in the direction I needed to go, and as I turned away I saw a glimpse of myself in the mirror and realized what he was freaking out over. So I thought, 'If I try to explain, it'll get me into a 20-minute discussion I'm really not up for right now.' So I just got in my car and left, and as I pulled away I saw him copy down my license plate number and run back inside. The entire way home I expected at any moment to be pulled over by police. That's my favorite *Jason Goes to Hell* story. That poor kid still probably thinks I'd just bumped somebody off."

On the set, says Keegan, "I was scared all the time! Just the mere thought that at any moment something was going to grab me. Kane was really great at walking up behind you quietly and screaming really loud. He'd scare me so bad I'd think I was going to pass out! He wasn't even in costume."

"There's a scene where Jason bursts up through the floor and we had rehearsed it several times with where it was going to happen, but when we shot it we were walking through the room and there was this huge crash and bang behind us instead, so the reaction you see in the film is our real reactions," Keegan explains. "It was also horrible because we used real babies for a lot of those scenes and they'd get scared, so they'd have to bring in a new baby and all I could think was these children were going to grow up and hate me!"

Keegan shakes her head and laughs, "We're scaring them to death at nine months. Obviously for the really dangerous stunts we used sandbags, but there was a lot of tension around set because we were shooting at night in these really creepy places. I mean, Jason's house really was scary inside. They didn't dress that house. It was in the middle of this really beautiful complex and here was this old house right in the middle with dead trees and dead grass."

The film, and its precursors, were accused of being responsible for desensitizing youth to violence. Keegan has mixed feelings on the debate. "It's a really tough call. I've thought a lot about that issue regarding all violent movies, but horror films are in such a different class, because more often than not, they're obviously not real. I mean, Jason dies and comes back and dies again. It's just not plausible, and I think most people know that. I do think movie makers have to be careful and aware they're playing to an audience which typically is very young, susceptible and vulnerable. It's tough, because the news is far more violent and offers more negative images. I mean, car chases have become a cool thing to do because you'll be on the news.

"I'm all for having my rights and lack of censorship. We live in a society where it's tough to promulgate parents knowing where their children are and what they're doing. It's easy to say just change the channel, but when Billy's doing it then they all want to do it, so I hate to throw all the responsibility in parents' laps. We do need to encourage parents to take a more active role in their children's lives, and be aware of how much violence is in a movie our child is watching. *Jurassic Park* may be PG-13, but it's still a really scary movie for someone that young. If a movie is rated R, then make sure your child is of the recommended age before they can see it. My kids haven't seen *Jason Goes to Hell*, and won't until they're at the appropriate age. Maybe fifteen or sixteen. Kids are kids for such a short time, there's no need to desensitize them before it happens naturally."

Freddy vs. Jason hit theaters in the fall of 2003 to the tune of $80 million. Yet do today's youth find Jason Voorhees intimidating, much less scary, especially after the dismal performance of *Jason X* in April 2002?

"You know, I don't know. It's been ten years since *Jason Goes to Hell* and even in just that short amount of time we've become really advanced in technology and finicky about what kind of scares we like," Keegan thinks. "Look at *Harry Potter* and how advanced all those FX have gotten. I think if the script is good and the acting is good, and there's a great plot with some really good scares, people will like [*Freddy vs. Jason*].

"I think *Scream* [1996] basically did the same thing as *Jason Goes to Hell*, only they took it to the next level. I think [any new *Friday the 13th* movies] will have to maintain a certain level of sophistication audiences have come to know. You'll also have the hard-core fans who'll see it for no other reason than it's a *Friday the 13th* film. If Jason's got his mask on ... they're there."

Jason Goes to Hell, which found Jason's spirit jumping from one host body to another after his natural body is destroyed, received mixed reviews from fans for trying to deviate from the format of horny teens dying. Ironically, it's the same reason the film is one of the few chapters to receive positive reviews from critics, though some have cited a similarity to New Line's hit 1987 sci-fi flick *The Hidden*.

"I think anything new is always good. I mean, he'd been killed so many times, we had to come up with something unique. It was a clever idea, albeit way out there," Keegan laughs. "I think it worked. It benefited and made it great fun."

True, but what did she think of the infamous ending? "Well, everyone was just so excited it was the actual glove they'd used in the *A Nightmare on Elm Street* movies," she laughs again. "Everyone was trying it on. I though it was a clever twist and made people wonder where it was going to lead. Obviously it worked, because here we are a decade later and people are still talking about *Freddy vs. Jason*. It's led to a consistent buzz."

Agreed, but what was the audience reaction? "At the premiere, everyone was like, 'Ugh,' but the public audience was like, 'Oh! Cool!' There was lots of chatter and people were already discussing plot lines and practically writing scripts as they were walking out of the theater!"

Attempting to understand the franchise's fan base, Keegan eventually managed to catch up on the rest of the series when "my friends and I used to have *Friday the 13th* parties around Halloween every year. We'd watch them two at a time. Of course I wouldn't let them see *Jason Goes to Hell* because they'd just rag me for weeks afterwards. I think they're great. It's not my cup of tea because I don't like horror films, but they stand on their own. Obviously they're great or people wouldn't still be talking about them. They're exactly what a lot of people like … at some twisted level," she chuckles.

She finds it a bit more difficult to compare her installment to the previous ones because… "even though there are some connecting elements, I think each sequel is really its own film. *Jason Goes to Hell* stands out because it was so self-aware and made fun of itself."

While much of this element likely resulted from scripter Dean Lorey and director Adam Marcus, Keegan believes producer and original *Friday the 13th* helmer Sean S. Cunningham may have made some of those decisions as well. She says of Cunningham's involvement, "In the beginning not too much, which was kind of sad, because I absolutely adore him. There were times when we'd have multiple setups being done and Sean would sort of pseudo-direct a couple of scenes. He was an absolute pleasure and joy to work with. He was a very hands-on producer. This was Adam Marcus' first film, so Sean was in the background, but had a nice strong hand in the picture. I don't [know why he didn't direct]. I asked him once and he turned and told me to go do something else, so I never really got a straight answer. I know he was in the middle of pulling several other projects together at the same time, so I think it would have just been too much for him. His interests would have been too divided."

The actress was additionally thrilled to have an opportunity to work with some of her cast mates. "I adore Allison Smith," she exclaims. "Absolutely adore. She plays my best friend and is just this little spitfire. I was just gushing for the longest time because I didn't realize until I got on set she was the actress who played Annie on Broadway the longest. She's fabulous! I see her on *The West Wing* all the time now. She made me laugh all the time.

"Erin Gray [*Buck Rodgers*] was really sweet and wonderful, but we never had a scene together! It actually wasn't until after we'd wrapped that the producers realized they never established us as mother and daughter. So they went back and filmed a scene where we're on the phone together in a split screen. We were on set at the same time once in a while, though, and she is the most charming, mesmerizing woman. Erin and I did a short film together for Sean called *What Goes Around* [2000]. I played a very pregnant waitress and Erin leaves me a $500 tip. We still run into each other from time to time."

When queried about whether or not she'd be willing to return to Crystal Lake, or even the horror genre in general, Keegan hesitates, then smiles. "Uh, why not? Sure. Of course I would," she laughs. "Definitely if Sean was involved."

One thing she promises is to always keep her clothes on, no matter what genre she's seen in. She bites her lip when asked if she was ever approached with the request to go nude during filming. "Well, there were issues... I think they would've liked very much if I would've done it in the shower scene, but I don't do nudity. Period."

Deciding to be known for her talents over her body is a decision Keegan reached early on. In fact, acting has been pretty much her main desire in life since "oh, I was five at least, maybe earlier. I was a storyteller as a little kid. It's funny that I don't like to be scared, because when I was a kid I would come home from school and, if say Suzie wasn't in school that day, I'd tell my mother, 'Did you hear? Suzie ... run down by a car... So tragic.'"

Keegan laughs mischievously, "Everyone was either run down or kidnapped. Not that they were sick at home with an ear ache. So my mother knew early on I was [theatrical]. I would gather the neighbor kids and write plays and direct everyone, but of course I would also have to star in them. The scripts were always changing. One day it would be in a castle, the next on a farm, and then the next day it was in outer space...."

"My mother was kind enough to put me in acting classes when I was about eight years old, which I just adored. Of course, she started using that as a bribing point, because if I wasn't good she threatened to not let me go. Then in my sophomore year of high school I got a scholarship to go to the Pennsylvania Governor's School, which was a scholarship program where they gather all these kids from across the state of Pennsylvania and send them to Bucknell University for six weeks of training in all the arts: acting, jewelry making, dancing, playwriting, singing ... everything. After that I went to the High School for Performing Arts in Pittsburgh. Then I went on to college, so it's always been a part of my life. Of course I had the usual struggles actors go through, but I've been very lucky to work as much as I do."

In the years since battling Jason Voorhees, Keegan concentrated mostly on commercial work and married Dr. Craig Smith. "My husband is a transplant surgeon at UCLA. He's head of the Pancreatic Department and transplants kidneys. It's kind of gruesome, but I also thinks it's incredibly cool," she reports.

She smiles with pride and giggles at her how her best-known film makes her occasionally queasy from its gore-quotient, yet she'd readily love an opportunity to watch her spouse at work. As for her own career: "I do a lot of commercials, but I really kind of dropped out after *Jason Goes to Hell*. I didn't know what I wanted to do with my career or myself. I got married. Got a family..."

She did appear in a number of dramas, including *I Play with Broken Dolls*, *Chemical People*, *The Prince of Pennsylvania* and the popular Tom Cruise vehicle *Jerry Maguire*. "I was one of the bitter girlfriends who appear in this video montage," she says. "I just [completed] a film called *Mind Games*. It's a thriller in which I play a book editor whose client writes a best-selling book, then gets amnesia and wakes up married to some guy she doesn't know. The movie is just off and running from that point."

With a new movie and a new baby, Kari Keegan couldn't be happier. Her knowledge is something she's happy to pass along to those who hope to follow, to some degree, in her footsteps. "I got some great advice from Bill Murray," she smiles. "He said this was a game of monkeys. The more people you help, the more people will help you. So if you have an agent and your friend doesn't, try to set up some appointments for them. Someone else said, 'Don't give up five minutes before the miracle happens.' It's not an easy or fair business. A lot of times it's not even about talent. It's about being at the right place at the right time. The most important thing is to just be you. Don't be what you think other people want. Don't try to be Julia Roberts or Sandra Bullock. We already have them. Just be who you really are, and you'll be successful."

Where Did All the *Friday* Girls Go?

"Adrienne really appreciates your offer and thanks you for your support and interest, but she's trying to go down a different path now with her career…"

Hmmm. Another one. Well, at least I got a response … and thank goodness the voice was pleasant, unlike most of the *Halloween* actress' agents.

Well, that's strike six. Ms. King has politely refused the offer for an interview; Amy Steel (*Friday the 13th, Part 2*) never returned a single phone call. Dana Kimmell (*Part 3*), Kimberly Beck (*Part IV: The Final Chapter*), Melanie Kinnaman (*Part V: A New Beginning*) and Jennifer Cooke (*Part VI: Jason Lives*) are all missing in action. Wait a moment … yes! Lar Park-Lincoln (*Part VII: The New Blood*), Jensen Daggett (*Part VIII: Jason Takes Manhattan*) and Kari Keegan (*Part IX: Jason Goes to Hell*) are not only active, they've all agreed to interviews!

Well, happiness was achieved for a moment. Park-Lincoln and Keegan did go through with the interviews, and were beyond delightful, but Daggett, who was nine months pregnant, never returned phone calls or e-mails following our initial conversations. Contacting the *Nightmare on Elm Street* girls were so much easier…

Looking back over cinematic history, hugely popular and successful horror films have seldom been kind to a fledgling actress' career. Marilyn Burns (*The Texas Chainsaw Massacre*), Judith O'Dea (*Night of the Living Dead*), Lorraine Gary (*Jaws*), Heather Langenkamp (*A Nightmare on Elm Street*), Beverly Randolph (*The Return of the Living Dead*), Lori Cardille (*Day of the Dead*) and Jill Schoelen (*The Stepfather*) all suffered the curse, though admittedly many of them did continue to work, albeit mostly in lower budgeted horror. Only Mia Farrow (*Rosemary's Baby*), Janet Leigh (*Psycho*), Sissy Spacek (*Carrie*), Catherine Hicks (*Child's Play*), Virginia Madsen (*Candyman*), JoBeth Williams (*Poltergeist*) and Jamie Leigh Curtis (*Halloween*) had their careers flourish outside the horror genres (Farrow, Hicks and Leigh were already established stars). Even in post-modern times, the curse appears to be continuing … when was Neve's last non-horror hit? Oh, right. There wasn't one.

The *Friday the 13th* films did help launch a couple of already burgeoning careers, but it was never the leads. Kevin Bacon (*Apollo 13*), Corey Feldman (*The Goonies*), Crispin Glover (*Charlie's Angels*) and Rusty Schwimmer (*Twister*) all went on to suc-

The original *Friday the 13th* heroine, Adrienne King, has been trying to distance herself from the series for personal reasons.

cessful theatrical careers. Other supporting players (Lauren Marie Taylor, Peter Barton, Renee Jones, Kevin Blair-Spirtas and Scott Reeves) became high profile in the world of soap operas. In fact, supporting cast members tended to find more work in their post-victim careers. Marta Kober, Judie Aronson, Juliette Cummins, Miguel Nunez, Elizabeth Kaitan, Diana Barton and Darcy DeMoss found exploitation to be their niche.

Is it possible some of the *Friday the 13th* actresses may just be too embarrassed about intermingling with Jason Voorhees and his decapitated mother (Betsy Palmer, 1999's *The Fear 2: Halloween Night*)? *Friday the 13th*, and those associated with the series of nubile teens who do all the "bad" things teenagers aren't supposed to do, and as a result get slaughtered to varying degrees of gruesomeness, have always been looked down upon. Daggett once reported going to an audition for Oliver Stone, who looked at her résumé and said, "Oh ... you were in one of *those* movies." The industry, and even general mainstream audiences, have always guffawed every time trailers for a new installment appeared. What's more amazing is that, in spite of all the ridicule, *Friday the 13th* films always made money.

Sample: *Friday the 13th* (1980): $37 million; *Part 2* (1981): $19m; *Part 3* in 3-D (1982): $36m; *Part IV* (1984): $32m; *Part V* (1985): $21m; *Part VI* (1986): $19m; *Part VII* (1988): $19m; *Part VIII* (1989): $14m; *Part IX* (1993): $16m; *Part X* (2002): $11m. Not exactly humiliating numbers for U.S. box office alone, especially back when ticket prices in middle America averaged $4. Still, even distributor Paramount tried to disassociate itself from the franchise. As a result of the backlash, perhaps many of the ladies simply didn't want to be found.

Before you ask, "Did you really search hard enough?," examine the routes taken which led to dead ends. The Screen Actors Guild, which makes sure members continue to receive residuals, had agents listed for Beck and Cooke. When called, both agencies were disconnected phone numbers. Surf the web? Yep. Results: Nada. No fan clubs, no agent listings ... nothing. Even tried chat rooms to see if any fellow horror geeks had contacted them. No luck. Did I try the companies that produced the films? Sure did ... they don't keep records "that far back." Even had a well-connected casting agent place an ad in one of the industry's most popular papers. A little but of luck, as I managed to locate King and Park-Lincoln, plus Judith O'Dea as a bonus. Others turned up zilch. As did contacting former co-stars. In the end, Kimmell, Beck, Kinnaman and Cooke were definite losses.

Then came the e-mail from author Peter Bracke. Seems he's in the process of compiling the surprisingly untackled topic of the history of the *Friday the 13th* films and its vets in a book titled *Crystal Lake Memories* (due in 2004). He knew of my *Femme Fatales* articles with some former *Friday* actresses and needed contacts for those whom he couldn't find. My curiosity: "Who *had* he located ... and interviewed?" I was shocked by his reply.

"It is really a misconception that so many from the series have not continued to work actively," Bracke began. "I would estimate only 10 percent ... are not still involved in the industry in some respect. Many went on to successful careers behind the camera, or pursued other creative endeavors, from design to music to writing."

Bracke likewise found little success with SAG, and relied heavily on researching hundreds of Internet documents and relying on each new cast member he located to lead him to the next. "For example," he explains, "Adrienne King ... only came about after interviewing Joseph Zito [director of *The Final Chapter*], who had remained in touch with her over the years. Peter Barton [also of *The Final Chapter*] graciously offered a recommendation to Kimberly Beck. Without his generosity, it's doubtful she would have had the confidence in me to consent to an interview."

Well, sure, he found Ms. King, but so had I. However, he *got* the interview, and many others to boot. "The first reaction is usually incredulity someone is actually writing a book on [the series]," he says. "Then it is followed by a mixture of emotions, from excitement to intrigue to bemused gratitude. Aside from those who may have said no due to possible negative feelings towards the series (of which there were a mere six out of 90 contacted!), I have yet to encounter anyone who was genuinely ashamed or discouraging.

"Perhaps the most interesting aspect was ... I noticed a sort-of disconnect with how the audience views the work, and the actor's own feelings about the experience. Making a film demands a very, very different type of engagement from watching one. What for the actor was a minor blip in their career would become something almost fetishized by the fans, who often pore over every single line of dialogue. Many of the actors professed amazement at the longevity of the series and the passion the fans hold for their work. It also serves as a potent metaphor for Hollywood itself, which often thrives on the disparity between the illusion of movie making and how unglamorous the production process really is.

"Adrienne King decided to lessen her visibility after a difficult situation with a stalker who became obsessed with her after the first film came out," Bracke reveals. "Like so many, she found personal and professional happiness, and is now married and pursuing other creative endeavors, including voice overs and art. Ms. King, like so many other [actors], looks back with great fondness on [Friday the 13th] and how much pleasure it brings to fans. It's perhaps a forgone conclusion that many will continue to get the wrong impression about those who chose to lead a more private life, confusing it with negative feelings about their involvement in the series."

Bracke adds, "Ms. King's story proves there is more to life than acting, fame and Hollywood. People don't look beyond the surface and realize that those who leave a profession, which endears such notoriety, often do so by choice, and with better options ahead. Adrienne [taught me] you have to love for the process, not the outcome…"

In addition to promoting French coffee for much of the 1990s, Amy Steel, "who looks back fondly on her *Part 2* experience, if with a bemused grin," continued to work in pics like *April Fool's Day* (1986), *Walk Like a Man* (1987) and *Tycus* (2000). She has also guest-starred on TV hits *JAG*, *Chicago Hope* and *Home Improvement*. She, too, started a family and pursues other creative interests.

According to the Internet Movie Database (*www.imdb.com*), Dana Kimmell stopped working after 1990's *Night Angel*, but resurfaced as child killer Susan Smith in the 2001 TV movie *Sins of the Mother*. Like Laurie Bartram of the original film, Kimmell, who frequently appeared on sitcoms like *The Facts of Life* in her early career, is rumored now to be a born-again Christian who refuses to work in projects which shouldn't be viewed by children. She has also made it apparent in previously published articles that she does not approve of *Part 3*. Though Bracke has attempted to make contact with Kimmell through e-mail and phone calls, she has yet to respond.

Bracke found *The Final Chapter* heroine Kimberly Beck, who made her screen debut in 1964's *Marnie*, to be "tremendously witty and open about her experience. Another mistaken assumption about the *Friday the 13th* performers is that they were all newcomers [with no] prior experience. Ms. Beck would be a case in point, as she [began] acting as a child, and would go on to a very successful career throughout the 1970s and '80s. This included a chart-topping pop single in Australia." Though semi-retired today, Beck has a long and healthy list of features throughout the 1990s, including *Independence Day* (1996) and *The Secret Life of Girls* (1999).

Beyond surviving *Part V*, Melanie Kinnaman made one other film, 1985's *Thunder Alley*, and has since simply vanished. The same had been thought about *Part VI*'s Jennifer Cooke, though with a stroke of luck Bracke unexpectedly received an e-mail from the now married and retired actress' husband, which read, "Ms. Cooke has decided to move on. She's grateful for her experiences and the continued interest, but no longer wishes to do any interviews."

Part VII's Lar Park-Lincoln was an easier catch, and one I was actually able to connect Bracke with, as I'd already interviewed her in 2002. Bracke reports that Park-Lincoln "felt she had to keep her marriage a secret during the production of *The New Blood*, due to the difficulty in trying to land roles in an industry which can't separate an actress' personal life from the role she plays. [However], she was nothing but proud to have been a part of the series and movie history, and is the lone leading lady currently looking to get back into the business."

Jensen Daggett's career seems to have grown the most; she's appeared in everything from TV shows like *Will & Grace* and *Melrose Place* to lead roles in the movies *Major League III: Back to the Minors* [1998]. Initially positive about her *Part VIII* work, the actress seems to have taken a rest from the industry since early 2002 when she was due to have her first child. She, like Kimmell, has not returned phone calls or e-mails.

Jason Goes to Hell star Kari Keegan worked in commercials over the past decade, had a cameo in *Jerry Maguire* (1996) and landed the lead in *Mind Games* (2004). In the years since battling Jason Voorhees, Keegan married Dr. Craig Smith.

Can the most recent heroines, Lexa Doig and Lisa Ryde, of *Jason X* (a.k.a. *Friday the 13th, Part X*), break beyond the horror genre, or will they forever bear the same Crystal Lake Curse? Bracke, who hosts the audio commentary for Warner Bros. special edition *Friday the 13th* DVD (for the overseas market only), maintains that since most of the lead actresses left the business of their own free will, no curse really exists … except, perhaps, the curse of Hollywood.

"It's no secret how profitable these types of pictures really are," he states. "The *Friday the 13th* films, like so many others, helped to fund more 'respected' works, the kind which wouldn't have been made without 'popcorn' profits. Hollywood considers [B pictures] less than respectable. Yet [those films] afforded filmmakers the opportunity to really explore and take chances, albeit within set parameters. It's too bad more filmmakers of any stature don't make more genre pictures; I think going to the movies would be a lot more interesting of an experience."

Bracke, whose *Ultimate DVD* guide will be released by Putnam in 2004, concludes of the franchise, its leading ladies and scads of victims, "Not a single person I interviewed tried to do anything less but make the best movie possible with what they were given. Such commitment and dedication should be praised, not ridiculed. That, to me, is the real lesson of *Friday the 13th*."

Dreaming of A Nightmare on Elm Street

Lisa Wilcox

"I was a *huge* fan of the first *A Nightmare on Elm Street*. It was *soooo* scary. That first scene with [Amanda Wyss] on the ceiling was terrifying. I was already a fan of horror movies like *Dracula* and novels by Dean Koontz and Stephen King," Lisa Wilcox enthuses.

Her hair is a soft blonde, pulled back into a long, curly pony tail. Her face is fresh, eyes sparkling ... in all, she's stunning. Odd, since she appears to be the antithesis of Alice Johnson, the mousy, red-haired geek who was among Freddy's more emotionally diverse foes once she found her own inner beauty and strengths.

It's been 15 years since she starred in the box office hit *A Nightmare on Elm Street 4: The Dream Master*, but Wilcox, who repeated duties in the following year's *The Dream Child*, knows she'll never be able to outdo the sharp gleam Krueger's glove left on her career. "I still get recognized, especially if I'm wearing a pony tail," she laughs, unaware the couple at a nearby table in DuPar's Restaurant in West Hollywood, California has already realized who she is.

Should it be a surprise she's still getting fan letters and constant e-mail requests wanting to know about *Freddy vs. Jason*? When you consider *A Nightmare on Elm Street 4* was the fourth highest grossing horror film of the 1980s (raking in over $49 million domestically), peaked Freddy Mania (with masks, video games, comic books and costumes), brought new visual and makeup technologies into the mainstream, and even spawned a television series ... probably not.

What is surprising is the self-avowed fan of the series—even before she was a part of it—had no idea how big the franchise following had grown at the time she made the film. *A Nightmare on Elm Street 3: Dream Warriors* had pulled in huge tallies of $44 million in 1987, while the box office numbers of 1985's *A Nightmare on Elm Street 2: Freddy's Revenge* ($29 million) and the 1984 classic original ($26 million) weren't shabby either. Still, Wilcox maintains, "I knew the films and was a fan, but I had no idea how *big* it was. I never dreamed [15] years later I'd be getting interviewed for a retrospective. I was very fortunate as a young actress to get that role. The series is very respected, even beyond the horror genre. Just look at the box office receipts. People who weren't horror fans went to see them. They're darned good movies."

Amusingly, Wilcox says she almost didn't get the role. "I knew it was an *Elm Street* movie and really wanted to audition for it," she begins. "My agent submitted my information and I didn't hear anything, so I called him a few weeks later. He said the casting directors didn't want to see me because I looked too much like a cheerleader. I said, 'Don't they understand I can change my look?,' but we just let it go. A month later my agent called and said, 'You're never going to believe this. They saw hundreds of girls and couldn't find one they liked, so now they want you to read for the role!'"

She leans forward, her hands expressive, as though she were reliving the experience. The way she won the role was similar to the way Sissy Spacek landed the part of Carrie White 12 years earlier. Wilcox reveals, "I went in wearing no makeup and just looked like a wallflower ... well, actually, I was young and just couldn't wear *no* makeup, so I wore a *little* bit. Then I got a call back, but they said to wear *no* make up. So I did as they asked, and also hadn't washed my hair for several days...the whole thing. I did a screen test with Tuesday Knight, who'd already been cast as Kristen Parker. We did the scene where we're sitting outside the school talking about having matching luggage. Then I did another screen test with Brooke Theiss. That was on Friday, I got married on Sunday, flew off to Hawaii and learned on my honeymoon I'd gotten the part. So I flew back early and did a makeup and costume fitting immediately."

Wilcox had snagged the role with her heartfelt performance, but the production felt it was still necessary to make some adjustments to her dowdy look. "They wanted to put a rinse in my hair to make me look mousier," she says, shaking her head. "I said, 'I have naturally virgin blonde hair ... I don't know if you should do that...,' but they insisted, so every single day I'd get a rinse and they'd put oil in my hair, pasty makeup on my face, white out my eyebrows ... the whole thing. What I didn't know was blonde hair is very coarse and soaks in anything you put on it, so my hair never went back to its original color."

This was only a minor annoyance in a shoot Wilcox refers to as "fantastic! What a great group of people. The movie had such great one-liners and special FX and I think there was really good chemistry between the actors.

"Renny Harlin was a great director," she points out. "He was always very calm and had a dry sense of humor. He'd always find ways to add more layers to the film. There was a lot of openness to ideas on set. In one scene I was supposed to polish forks in the diner, and the way the light hit them made a shadow on the wall like Freddy's glove. I called Renny over and showed him. He gave me knives instead and we put it in the film. It was completely by accident, but it worked. Renny was like that — everybody was — just a lot of openness to ideas from everyone who wanted to make the film good and create something together."

She says playing the role actually turned into a form of therapy for her personal life. "I played [Alice] the way she was written," Wilcox says. "When I read the script for the first time, it affected me quite a bit. It was like reading about myself in fourth, fifth and sixth grades. I wasn't popular, I was a day-dreamer, I read all the time ... I lived in a fantasy world ... I was just a very mousy little girl. So Alice really was me growing up.

"It did bring up a lot from grade school. It was interesting, because in my mind it was such a hard time in my life. We moved from Missouri to California ... and I decided I wanted to become an actress. I wanted to be up on the silver screen and prove I could become somebody to all those people who had kicked me down. So it was a very powerful sensation when it happened. The funny and odd thing is people from [grade school] really did write me letters after the movie came out."

In addition to dealing with personal demons, the actress, who had already appeared in a number of television shows and movies, also had to comply with the new groundbreaking technologies in both computer imaging and special makeup FX.

Blue screens were in heavy use throughout the making of the sequel, a style used mainly in music videos and the earlier *Nightmare* films. Combined with extensive makeup FX by Screaming Mad George, Steve Johnson and John Carl Buechler, among others, it would all seem a bit overwhelming. Wilcox didn't think so.

"I wouldn't say it was difficult. You had to really listen and understand exactly what they were trying to recapture from something they'd filmed three weeks earlier. Plus, you have to imagine things are around you which really aren't. For instance, I'm in the theater holding onto the railing, then the stunt double comes in and does the actual flying through the air. Then we the shot outside the Crave Inn where the wind is blowing and Renny tells me I've just flown in through a movie screen ... then I back into the restaurant and I'm looking out the door at all of my dead friends in the theater, who, of course, weren't really

Lisa Wilcox as Alice in *A Nightmare on Elm Street 4: The Dream Master.* It remains the most successful entry in the franchise, and was the fourth highest grossing horror film of the 1980s (photograph by Rory Flynn, copyright 1988 New Line Cinema Corporation).

there when we were filming it, because I was looking at a blue screen. You really have to depend on your director to lead you through those scenes. Renny did a really good job. Everyone really believed in him and his vision."

"I love the theater scene," she adds. "How brilliant was that? She's in a theater and flies through a movie screen into the restaurant ... the popcorn is flying and her shoe flies off into the screen. It lent the story an element of *Cinderella*. Her one shoe flies off and she's walking around with only one shoe for a while. Then there was Alice in the Looking Glass, as she's looking at herself in the mirror, then flies through it to save Dan [Danny Hassel]. A lot of fairy tale elements. It made for a great film."

Since *A Nightmare on Elm Street 4* also had a number of action and fight sequences, the heat was also occasionally on Wilcox to perform a couple of her own stunts. "They sent me to karate school for a day of intense training," she recalls. "The front shots were obviously of me, but the back shots were a stunt double. They just wanted me to be able to lead off the stunts from the front. I also lead off the scene where I do a bunch of cartwheels, but a stunt girl took over the intense shots. We had some amazing stunt people. Some of them were Olympic gymnasts."

There was one instance, however, when Wilcox almost got the brunt of an effect gone awry. "The only time I almost got hurt was when I stood in front of the mirror before I jump through it," she divulges. "A stunt girl was going to go through the glass, but they needed to set up the shot and said the glass would break apart when I made contact with it. When they said 'Action!,' the glass exploded and knocked me off my stand. Thank God someone was standing behind me because I probably would have wound up with stitches. I had fake glass in my hair and was really shaken up by it. It was very powerful. It turned out what they used to make the glass break was turned up to a more powerful level than they'd thought. I think they sent me home early that day..."

She shakes her head a moment, then adds, "Otherwise, I really didn't have to do anything. There were some things which made me nervous, like the shower scene in *A Nightmare on Elm Street 5*. They had built this shower which was really just a room, and filled it with water. They had all the lights hanging around it, which made me nervous. You really put your life in the hands of the crew and have to trust them."

With her first foray into Freddy's world considered a social phenomenon, it was clear why Wilcox found herself back on the movie set of *A Nightmare on Elm Street 5: The Dream Child* (1989) just a few short months later. This time around, Elm Street is a much darker place. Not only was the Gothic visual look of the film soaked in black, orange and blue hues, but the storyline focused on social commentary about teen pregnancy, abortion, a young mother's rights, bulimia and drunk driving. Director Stephen Hopkins turned the landscape into an actual nightmare, where there are few of the bright red and green lights of the previous chapter or the cartoony, cutaway kills. Alice, now pregnant with Dan's child, must face not only adulthood, but the possibility Freddy may be possessing the dreams of her unborn child.

"I was happy with the film itself," Wilcox begins, "but I wasn't thrilled with the nudity. I had a clause in my contract about no nudity and having a body double. I've always said I would never do nudity. It's just a personal choice I made. I've had people try to convince me, 'It's for the film! It'll make it so much more realistic,' to which I say, 'Well, if I were playing a cocaine addict I wouldn't actually snort cocaine for the movie.' It's the same thing. There are ways around it."

Wilcox pauses a moment, adding, "I don't look down at other people who do it. I'm fine with my own sexuality, but I always knew I was going to have kids someday and didn't want them to go to school and get teased by other kids saying, 'I saw your mom naked in a movie.' That would be just horrifying to me as a child. Overall, though, I was happy with the final outcome of *Nightmare 5*. Performances were great and it looked wonderful. Kelly Jo Minter [who played Alice's best friend Yvonne] was lovely, and Stephen Hopkins was a wonderful artist at doing the sets and getting all the visual details perfect."

Was it difficult for Wilcox, who at the time had no children, to portray a teen mother? "Well, there's certainly a nurturing part of me," she smiles. "I've always loved children and animals, so that part was pretty easy to draw on. What's interesting is when she's pregnant in the real world, and not having to deal with Freddy, she's very hesitant about being pregnant and dealing with Jacob [Whitby Hertford], which really lent a strong sense to what the storyline was about."

Lisa Wilcox in an October 2001 photograph by Ward Boult (copyright/courtesy Ward Boult).

Putting such a hefty dilemma into the lap of a well-liked heroine was a risky one, but Wilcox feels the character was able to remain appealing to teens. "I think it still came off as a positive portrayal because of her father's [Nick Mele] reaction. He wasn't thrilled, but he didn't kick her out of the house and dealt with the situation in an honorable fashion. Their relationship grew stronger. He knew she had made a mistake, just by being a human being with raging hormones, so it kept those characters and the storyline appealing," she explains.

This time around box office numbers were a "mere" $22 million; could the more adult oriented storyline and darker images have turned away the public which had embraced the earlier chapters? "There's two ways to look at it," Wilcox assesses. "First, *Nightmare 5* didn't have nearly the same amount of success as *Nightmare 4*. It is a very dark film in both story and look. It deals with issues of teen sex, pregnancy, abortion, and what rights a teen mother has when Dan's parents [Burr DeBenning and Valorie Armstrong] want to adopt the baby and raise it as their own. So it definitely has some political themes. I think ultimately it has some good messages for both teens and parents. I also think part of the reason for the lower box office was that it was too much too soon. They released *Parts 3, 4* and *5* within less than a year of each other. It may have been overkill. If they had waited maybe 18 months or longer between each film, there may have been more anticipation for the fifth one. But *Nightmare 4* did so well they wanted to get it out immediately."

She continues, "It's also more violent. Especially the motorcycle sequence. There were some protests in Westwood, California, because the film was so violent. I was concerned about the violence as well, because it was so much more graphic than *Nightmare 4*. It was also censored more by the MPAA. Still, I think *Nightmare 5* is a good film. I think *1, 3* and *4* are the strongest. The storylines were more clear and they flowed much better."

Throughout both films, Wilcox knew she had a companion in her on-screen nemesis. "Robert Englund was a hoot," she exclaims. "First of all, for him to sit in that chair for three hours every day getting that makeup done ... I really felt sorry for him, especially after I had the makeup done on me for *Nightmare 5* and had to walk around in it all day. It's so horrible, [yet] he was lovely, patient and special."

Wilcox indeed found herself "Freddy-ized" during the film's climax, when Freddy possesses her body, turning her face into his burnt flesh and eventually tearing their combined bodies apart. "They ended up using puppets [glimpsed in an opening scene in 1994's *Wes Craven's New Nightmare*] for a lot of it, but I did have to wear the makeup for one day," she grimaces. "It was just nasty. You feel like a monster. It's very claustrophobic. I kept looking at my watch the entire day. It wasn't fun. For Robert to be able to do it again and again during all these movies and keep up his energy and enthusiasm is amazing. My hat goes off to him."

Wilcox says she was never approached to appear in *Freddy's Dead: The Final Nightmare* (1991) (which features *Nightmare 1*'s Johnny Depp in a cameo) or *Wes Craven's New Nightmare* (which featured cameos by *Nightmare 1*'s Nick Corri and *Nightmare 4*'s Tuesday Knight). "I was married and having babies at the time anyway," she shines. "Doing the films was great for my career. They opened a lot of doors for me. I got a lot of great opportunities and auditions. Unfortunately I get really nervous in auditions..."

Her discomfort during auditions certainly didn't keep her from having a long career both before and after her *Nightmare* days. She debuted in the 1984 comedy *Gimmie an 'F'* (now a staple of the USA Network), which was originally titled *T&A Academy 2* (!) and followed a group of misbehaving cheerleaders at camp. "I was a Demon Dance Squad member," she snickers, rolling her eyes with a tinge of embarrassment. "I actually took a semester off of college to make that work of art. It's one of those good T&A movies which used to be around all the time. Whatever happened to those? Fortunately I didn't do any of the T&A. We were supposed to be the cheer-leaders, but spent most of our time smoking and making out with the guys. It was my very first movie and I actually worked about six weeks on it."

She hangs her head a bit and continues to giggle. Also on her résumé are more impressive stints on popular '80s television series like *Hardcastle and McCormick*, *MacGyver*, *Valerie* (a.k.a. *Valerie's Family*, *The Hogan Family* and, ultimately, *The Hogans*), *Something Is Out There*, *It's a Living*, *Hotel*, *Star Trek: The Next Generation* and a year-long stint on *General Hospital*. Of those appearances, *Valerie* left the strongest impression.

"It was the first or second episode of the third season," Wilcox explains. "I did a guest star role as the new girl in town who everyone thought was easy because one of Valerie's sons [Jason Bateman] spread rumors about her. So, as usual, I get picked on. Then the show airs and when I see it Sandy Duncan is suddenly playing the role of their aunt and Valerie Harper's character has been killed off!

"Apparently she had been fired from the show and there was a court situation where she was going to sue them," Wilcox recalls. "Valerie told me later she was going to bring me in as a witness to prove there was no friction on set and that she did everything she was supposed to do. It was just weird because I filmed the episode with Valerie and they went back and refilmed all of her scenes with Sandy instead."

Wilcox continued her television appearances with the 1988 TV movie *Bring Me the Head of Dobie Gillis* and a season run as computer extrordinaire Ellen on the primetime soap *Knots Landing* (1989). The 1990's followed with a succession of guest roles on *Bodies of Evidence*, *Boy Meets World*, *Murder, She Wrote*, *Pacific Blue*, *Walker: Texas Ranger* and *Chicago Hope*.

She was also a series regular on the half-season run of *Bill & Ted's Excellent Adventures* as Missy Preston, Bill's two-years-older stepmother. Wilcox additionally appeared in the films *The Wedding Band* (1990) with Fran Drescher and William Katt, the Will Ferrell comedy *Men Seeking Women* (1997) and *Watchers Reborn* (1998) with Mark Hamill.

"I love Mark," she squeals. "He's a doll. The first day of filming, I was so nervous! I couldn't help it. I love *Star Wars* ... he's Luke Skywalker ... I was *so* nervous, and of course the first scene we shoot is this huge monologue where I have to walk and talk at the same time ... God forbid. I was so nervous, I kept flubbing my lines. I was so embarrassed. Then I finally relaxed and had the best time. I brought my kids down to the set so they could meet him and he invited us all over to his house so we could meet *his* children. He's such a warm, neat guy."

Watchers Reborn tells the same story of the previous *Watchers* chapters as a group of scientists experiment on a dog and its monster-like brethren. As usual, both escape and carnage ensues. Wilcox is Grace, the scientist responsible for both super-smart animals, who attempts to correct her own wrongs, while Hamill is the detective try-ing to end the murder spree. For the fourth film in a series which is neither horrible nor overwhelmingly necessary of being a franchise, this installment is surprisingly well-done with some genuinely tense moments and enjoyable characters.

"It really was a wonderful experience. We all had so much fun. One day my son was on set and the special FX guy showed him all the fake blood and props and taught him a lot ... he even let him help apply the FX! It was just a great group of people.

John Carl Buechler [*Friday the 13th, Part VII: The New Blood*] directed and was so easy going. He did the pizza and chest FX for *Nightmare 4*, so it was great to work with him again."

Could Wilcox have landed the role simply by knowing Buechler from their previous involvement? "Well, I had to go through the regular paces. Maybe John suggested me to the casting director, but I had to audition and do the screen test just like everyone else. Ironically, I read the novel *Watchers* on the set of *Nightmare 4* because [makeup artist] Howard Berger told me how good it was. *Watchers Reborn* is more closely related to the novel than any of the other installments, so it was quite a thrill to play a character from one of my favorite novels. Apparently 4 is my number," she laughs.

Her most notorious appearance of late was the FOX TV movie *Unauthorized Brady Bunch: The Final Days*, in which she played a sweet Florence

Lisa Wilcox today (courtesy Lisa Wilcox).

Henderson, flip and all. "Being on that set ... talk about 'Whoa!' I'm talking to Marsha Brady as her mother! It was pretty wild. Of course, everybody says I was too young to play the part, to which I have to say, 'Thank you!' I think they wanted a sexy Carol Brady. "It was kind of a rushed production, so I really didn't have time to do a lot of research."

She also starred in the Oscar-nominated short *The New Adventures of Chastity Blade* (2000), which is currently performing dual service as a possible television pilot. Once again, the actress found her ties to the *Nightmare* series enduring. "It was shot in Paris through a film school. I got a call from my agent saying there was this film student doing his final project who wanted me to be in it. I was like, 'A student film? Are you kidding me?' But the guy sent me the script and I *loved* it! It was excellent. I knew I had to do it.

"At the same time I was freaking out a little because I'd learned he was a fan of mine from seeing *Nightmare 4* and *5* as a teenager, and now he's grown up to become a director. So while I'm happy with the script, I'm also thinking *Boxing Helena* [in which an obsessed fan of a beautiful woman abducts her and cuts off her limbs to keep her from escaping]. So I made sure all the addresses were correct and everything was legitimate. He turned out to be a very lovely man."

It also seemed fate had destined them to work together. One day as Wilcox was packing to head to Paris, she moved a box in her home "and a letter fell out. When I picked it up it was from him! He had written it back in 1988! Here it is in my hand, and now I'm heading off to Paris to film his project.

"I play Maggie Hansen, a bored suburban housewife who loves to fantasize — here we go again into that theme," Wilcox smiles. "She dreams of becoming Chastity Blade, a character in a novel she's reading. Through an accident she's turned into Chastity with the whole cat suit thing, fighting crime, etc. It's really fun."

After *Chastity* was completed, LeFemif, the sponsoring film school, submitted the short to the Motion Picture Academy and it was nominated for Best Student Foreign Film. Delighted with the outcome, Wilcox has taken on the role of producer to try and get it produced as a television series in the States.

Meanwhile, Wilcox has joined business forces with her *Nightmare 4* alum Tuesday Knight and built an ever-growing enterprise of toe jewelry called Toe Brights. Available over the Internet (www.toebrights.com), the toe rings were a creation of Knight and her previous business partner. One fateful day the girls realized they needed each other to get through some personal difficulties.

"Tuesday and I had run into one another occasionally over the years, but we were never friends," Wilcox admits. "Even when we were shooting *Nightmare 4*, we really didn't connect. We didn't dislike each other, but just never hung out. We laugh about it now, because it was that stupid jealousy thing you have when you're in your twenties. We ran into each other at Staples Office Supply, got to talking and discovered we were each going through really rough periods in our lives. So we were in Staples for about an hour and a half crying and laughing. We became great friends and have talked to each other every single day since then."

Knight's business partner was splitting from their creation, so Knight asked Wilcox if she'd like to become her new associate. "So I did," Wilcox gleams. "Now [two] years later we've merged with another company called Destiny Marketing and have a facility for manufacturing, and keep doing bigger and bigger numbers. It's growing really fast. We have representatives, over 200 accounts, and are going international. It's just phenomenal. I do the marketing and designing and bring in more business, and Tuesday creates the designs."

With successful dual careers, plus motherhood a part of her life, would Lisa Wilcox ever consider returning to Elm Street? "Most definitely," she enthusiastically insists. "I want to see how they kill Alice! What would be fitting? I'm very curious, because each death pertains to each character's fear. I really wanted to do *Freddy vs. Jason*. I get e-mails all the time. People in the Midwest are writing scripts all the time. People really want to see it … but nobody from New Line has ever approached me about doing another sequel. So I don't have the answers, but I certainly hope they make me a part of it when it does get made."

Do today's post–*Scream* audience still find Freddy appealing or effective? "Not the exact same films," she theorizes. "The one-liners are out of date, just like the language. I think the *A Nightmare on Elm Street* films are moving into the 'classic' age. They're becoming dated. New films would obviously need a more modern approach. I think universally some characters, like Alice, will always be effective. She was really just the *Carrie* character: The underdog and quiet girl who finds her strength, wins and succeeds ... that concept will always continue." Visit Wilcox's website, www.lisawilcoxstar.com.

Tuesday Knight

"I really don't care about the glamourous side of the business any more. I find myself stepping back from that end of it. I'm tired of fake people. What I do enjoy is going to horror conventions and meeting these really cool people. Horror fans are so devoted..."

Tuesday Knight's smile is inviting, her aura vibrant. As she enters Jennifer's Coffee in North Hollywood, California, all heads turn. A burst of energy seems to have filled the normally quiet shop. Upon first notice, actress and signer Knight looks healthier and more glamourous than ever ... though she's quick to deny it. It's also surprising to note that, after a career known for chameleon-like alterations in her appearance, from the chain-smoking teenager of *A Nightmare on Elm Street 4: The Dream Master* to the overweight, back-stabbing agent of TV's short-lived *2000 Malibu Road*, Knight is still frequently recognized ... by her voice.

Though her résumé is a collection of over 30 well-known TV shows and movies, she decides, "*A Nightmare on Elm Street 4* is the one most people approach me on, but I'm thinking, 'What about that movie I did with Robert DeNiro?' [1996's *The Fan*]. I was thrilled to do [*Nightmare 4*]. I'll admit I was a bit nervous too, because I was replacing Patricia Arquette [as amiable heroine Kristin Parker from *Nightmare 3*], and I know her. When I went to the audition I thought, 'Don't do this to me,' because I knew I was going to have to live up to her. I [wanted the creators] to just give [my character] a new name."

It can be stressful, and controversial, when a new actress steps into the role of a popular character from a previous film (just recall the debate surrounding Julianne Moore replacing Jodie Foster in 2001's *Hannibal*). *A Nightmare on Elm Street 3: Dream Warriors* had earned over $44 million at the 1987 box office and made both Freddy Krueger and his teen counterparts horror icons. Though most of the cast ultimately found themselves forever attached to the genre, or jobless, Patricia Arquette reportedly fought the label, turning down a hefty offer to reprise her heroine role, instead favoring more dramatic roles and becoming a respected thespian in the Hollywood community. (Ironically, however, her most successful starring vehicle since then was 1999's $50 million–grossing possession flick *Stigmata*.)

Feeling it necessary to bring the character of Kristin Parker back to the fourth chapter with most of the other surviving characters, casting directors searched for a worthy replacement. Knight won the role, but knew the pressure would be heavy.

"There's a lot of expectations from both the audience and the producers when you're taking over a role created by someone else, especially that of a popular character. [However], when I got it I ran screaming down the street because I was so excited. It was my first feature film, and the original *A Nightmare on Elm Street* [1984] was my favorite movie. I *love* horror movies. Especially supernatural stuff which isn't too gory."

Winning the role was a test of the actress's talents, as she reports, "I went in for a regular audition like everyone else, then had a call back to audition for [director] Renny Harlin. He told me to go home and really watch *A Nightmare on Elm Street 3* and pay attention to how Patricia had portrayed Kristin. So I made myself up to look like her and went in and got the job. Once I started shooting *Nightmare 4*, I didn't think of [Patricia's performance] again. I only imitated her to get the role. I made Kristin my own. I heard later [Patricia] liked my performance, which made me happy.

"I guess I could say I *love* the craft of acting, more than anything. Once I'm on set I'm happy, but I *hate* the business end. It's sucky. I hate being judged every day and told I'm too skinny, too fat, too short, too tall, not the right hair … it just sucks," she scowls. "There's nothing else like this [Hollywood] world. There's all this glamour and you love being a part of it, but it's also so emotionally depleting. It really lowers your self-esteem. You're basing who you are on what *they* think of you. I remember in past years I was only 'okay' if I *got* a role. It meant I looked good. I would position my life all around the acting. Now I'm the complete opposite."

A fan of the *Nightmare* series, Knight was well aware of its ever-growing pop culture status. Still, she wasn't prepared for its repercussions on set. "When we started shooting the beach sequence, there were what seemed like six million kids trying to get into the trailer where Robert [Englund] and I were sitting. It felt like they were going to knock it over. It was kind of scary," she confesses. "It was one of those things where they love you so much they'll accidentally kill you. I asked Robert what was going on and he just said, 'Oh, nothing. It's what they do. No big deal.' He was so funny."

She speaks a bit more of her affections for her finger-bladed co-star, whose alter ego would ultimately chuck her head first into a fire and water-filled boiler, then talks of the real on-set traumas of making a feature loaded with special FX and multiple action sequences and stunts. "The only thing I didn't like about making *Nightmare 4* was that I got hurt a lot of times. I was even in the hospital once. They wanted me to do some things which should have been performed by a stunt double."

One of those instances was the frequently shown beach sequence, broadcast on nightly news programs when the film shot to #1 at the box office. Though she giggles about the sequence itself, filming it was another story. "They wanted me to be the one who sunk into the sand and I didn't want to do it," she states. "They used me up to the part where I'm screaming and [Freddy] pushes me down into the sand. Then the rest is a stunt double. They gave me these little goggles which didn't do crap. All these grains of sand got in and scratched my eye, which is how I got sick … threw up, the whole nine yards. So some other girl actually went under the sand. All the stunts and FX were groundbreaking at the time, but it absolutely made the shoot more uncomfortable and difficult than I'd expected."

Attempting back-to-back jobs didn't help matters either. Knight was already a permanent fixture on the daytime soap *General Hospital*, playing troublesome teenager Val, when she received the role in *Nightmare 4*. Rather than take time off the TV show, which can run up to 16-hour days, Knight soon realized her ambitious nature was being challenged too severely. "I exhausted myself by doing both at the same time," she readily admits. "I collapsed on [the *General Hospital*] set from exhaustion. It made all the papers. I was so glad to have two jobs, but was foolish because I was getting no sleep. So they wrote me out of the show. It was terrible. I lost the job because of it. It's a shame, because I really enjoyed doing [it]."

Knight remained satisfied with her decision to film *Nightmare 4*, because it changed her life and brought her singing abilities to the attention of a national public. As the film opens, a soft, feminine voice fills the room, whispering a deliciously dark and sweet love ballad to Freddy. The song was written and performed by Knight on a lark.

"I was working with my writing partner [Michael Egizi] doing some other tunes because I was recording my [first] album at CBS. We wrote and recorded the theme song in one day, ran it over to New Line, had Renny Harlin [*Die Hard 2*] and [producer] Rachel Talalay [1993's *Ghost in the Machine*] come down to the car to listen to it, and they took it right then! They didn't even know I was going to do it. Then when I found out it was going to be the title song I was blown away, because it was the first thing I'd ever had released like that. It was really a thrill sitting in a theater and seeing that New Line logo come up as my song played. Unfortunately it's not on the soundtrack album because I was really young at the time and they screwed me. People still write me endlessly because they can't find the song [now available on her website www.emote.org/tuesdayknight]."

Juggling acting and music (an inspiration she says came from her film composer father, Baker Knight) has always been troublesome for Knight, as one always seems to get in the way of the other. "My first record deal was with CBS, but I was doing *Nightmare 4* at the same time and really wanted to pursue other acting jobs [don't forget her drive to include *General Hospital* in the equation]. I got a second record deal with Epic and cut an album which did really well, but again I wanted to pursue acting, which is my first love. With music you have to go out on tour and put acting on the side. I didn't want to do that."

Knight continues to keep music alive in her life and career. "I just worked on a CD for Paul McCartney, which was great. I just started doing music again for me. I seem to get compared to Sheryl Crow and the Bangles. My music is very Beatles-esque. Paul said my music is reminiscent of the *Abbey Road* era. So that was *really* cool! I might do another CD of just my own music to satisfy myself, but right now I do a lot of music for soundtracks. This sweet girl, Kristine Pierson, created this wonderful website [www.tuesdayknight.com] for me through which the public can buy some of my music."

She returns to how *Nightmare 4* helped launched her career, which technically began with a stint on the TV show *Fame* and the 1988 TV movie *Promised a Miracle*. After seeing *Nightmare 4*, Knight claims, "I liked it. I thought it was really great. Not just because I was in it, but because I truly feel it was a great movie, which blew most of the others away. *Nightmare 1* is by far the best. *2* sucked. *3* was really good. *4* was great. *5* was … 'eh.' *6* is okay, and *New Nightmare* is great too."

Is it a coincidence she approves of 1994's extremely underrated *Wes Craven's New Nightmare* (a.k.a. *A Nightmare on Elm Street 7*), when she was one of the few series actors to make a cameo, alongside *Nightmare 1*'s Nick Corri, during the funeral sequence of Heather Langenkamp's on-screen husband? She insists, "Not at all. I loved the concept of everyone playing themselves. Wes Craven called me up and asked me to be in it. I'd never met him before, so I have no idea why he asked me, but none of the others. I wasn't crazy about the end of the movie, after Heather falls into Freddy Hell, but I really enjoy the rest of it."

Knight, who coincidentally is good friends with *Freddy's Dead* star Lezlie Deane and her *Nightmare 4* co-star Lisa Wilcox, begins to laugh as she addresses a 15-year-old rumor, extremely well-known in Hollywood, and even public circles, which she didn't hear until recently. "Lisa Wilcox is the one who told me everyone thinks I had an affair with Renny Harlin," she divulges. "I mean *everybody*! I never knew this! I was actually going out with Andras [Jones]! We were together during the entire shoot. Renny was kind of a womanizer. He wanted all my outfits to be the size of Band-Aids, like the Hawaiian bikini I wore [in the beach sequence]. It was basically one string up my ass. I'm like, 'So you expect me to shave everywhere in order to wear this?' It was awful. I made them attach a skirt."

Knight thinks she knows when and how the rumor began, saying, "Probably because Renny and I were very chummy on set. I'd sit on his lap and be affectionate. We were kind of flirtatious as a sort of fun thing. I guess everybody got the wrong idea, which is probably why Andras didn't get along with him very well."

In fact, some other tensions were prevalent on the set. While she has remained in contact with Wilcox and Jones, even sporting a long friendship with Toy Newkirk [Sheila], Knight believes, "Rodney Eastman [Joey] hated me ... absolutely hated me. I think he was really resentful I took [Patricia Arquette's] place. I think he came onto the project with a bit of an attitude because he'd been in *Nightmare 3* and felt it was his territory. On the other hand, Ken Sagoes [Kincaid], who was also in *Nightmare 3*, was so great."

When queried if nudity was ever an issue during the making of the film, she laughs a little louder. "Not really," she begins. "There was one sequence which never wound up in the film. They made a prosthetic of my chest and were going to have something weird happen with the nipples, but they never used it..."

Ultimately it was only Hope Marie Carlton (1994's *The Stand*) who received some topless time in the film, which doesn't bother Knight, whose only real concern was how the film would turn out in the end. When it raked in $49 million, becoming the fourth highest grossing horror film of the 1980s (behind *Aliens*, *Poltergeist* and *Pet Sematary*), Knight found herself inundated with horror film offers. She took none of them.

"I just wanted to do stuff which could show my talents. I didn't want to only be associated with horror movies. Now, if they asked me to do more *Nightmare* movies, I would. *Candyman 2: Farewell to the Flesh* was the only horror film I turned down which I wish I hadn't. Otherwise, I have deliberately shied away from horror. Well, actually, I did an episode of *The X-Files* ["Trevor," episode 6.17], if you want to classify that as horror. I did *Nightmare 4* because it's part of a really credible horror film [series], where as so many other horror films are just crappy. *Nightmare 4* was an honor to be in as far as I'm concerned."

In fact, in the years following the success of *Nightmare 4*, she acted in a number of comedies and dramas on large and small screens. Her TV guest appearances include *Matlock*, *They Came from Outer Space*, *Law & Order*, and *Profiler*. Her mixture of theatrical and made-for-television movies is a grab bag of hits and cult favorites. Among them, *The Preppie Murder* (1989), *Mistress, Who Killed the Baby Jesus, The Prom* (1992), *Calendar Girl, Cover Story* (1993), *Cool and the Crazy* (1994), *The Babysitter, Star Witness* (1995), *The Fan, Hindsight, The Cottonwood* (1996), *Telling Lies in America, The Perfect Mother* (1997), *Brother* (2000), *The Theory of the Leisure Class* (2001), *Daddy and Them* (2002) and *Small Souled Men* (2003). Still, she says if the right script came her way, she would consider appearing in another horror film, "as long as it had a really strong storyline."

Knight breaks off into a discussion of the weight-obsessed politics of Hollywood, referencing her regular days of obesity as Joy Rule on the Aaron Spelling-produced nighttime melodrama *2000 Malibu Road*. The show, which hoped to ride Drew Barrymore's career rebirth following her scandalous return in *Poison Ivy* (1992), registered huge numbers for its pilot episode. In one of TV's biggest nose-dives, however, the numbers plummeted to less than half the following week. The show was gone only a few episodes later. Still, Knight left such an indelible impression on both national audiences and casting directors, she's found the show's image of her remains strong a decade later ... and not always in a good way.

"When I did [the show], they asked me to physically gain a lot of weight, but [instead] I started losing weight because I had to wear the fat suit and was sweating all the time," she laughs. "The funny thing is because of the show, everybody thinks I'm a huge girl. [She's actually very petite.] People honestly think I put on 80 pounds to play Joy. My manager told me I wasn't getting auditions after the show ended because everyone in the industry thought I was fat. I had to go [to casting sessions] and prove I wasn't. I actually went in to this one [casting director's] office looking like Marilyn Monroe, sat on his desk and said, 'Do you get the picture now?' I'm known for outrageous auditions. When people recognize me, they compliment me for losing all the weight, but I have to let them down and tell them I was never fat to begin with."

The thin-girl-in-fat-suit image did catch on with a few knowing insiders, some of whom worked at *Playboy* magazine and offered the actress a chance to reveal her entire body, in its true form, to the world. It was an opportunity Knight jumped at, but she then reneged after considering the consequences. "They wanted to show I wasn't really the fat girl," she recalls. "I did the shoot, but decided afterwards I didn't want to do it. I didn't want to go down that road. I didn't want to be just another naked blonde actress in *Playboy*. So the photos were never published. I use a couple of them for publicity. The shoot itself was fine. I felt very comfortable doing them."

Another outrageous audition almost landed her an opportunity to portray the Material Girl ... by the legend herself. "Madonna hired me to portray her in the biography she was going to produce several years ago. Meeting her was amazing. We even did something together on the E! channel. It's funny, because when I first moved [to L.A.], I didn't want to look like her, but all the casting agents thought I did. So I changed my hair and look all the time, and, go figure, she wants to hire me years later. Then she decided not to do it. I think she felt it was just the wrong time. Then when FOX did their TV movie, *they* wanted me to play her, but you don't do a Madonna movie unless Madonna is involved. If I have her there telling me what to do, then it's credible. I'm not going to do something about her life which doesn't involve truth."

In person, she found the legend to be "strong and great. As long as you're right up there with her, she's with you. I think people are afraid of her, even though they like her. Robert DeNiro is the same way. People were so afraid to go up to him, it made *him* nervous and seem standoffish because he thinks people don't like him. So [on the set of *The Fan*] I just walked up to him and said, 'Hey Bob, how ya doin'?' and we got along great! When I met Madonna for the very first time at Warner Bros., she was hilarious! She started fake masturbating in front of me in the office and I just did it back to her. I was like, 'You don't scare me....' So we hit it off. Then she said something like, 'I'd love to fuck you because it would be like fucking myself....' It was really funny."

Her enthusiasm escalates even further with discussion of acting alongside Billy Bob Thornton (*A Simple Plan*), Kelly Preston (*Secret Admirer*), Ben Affleck (*Daredevil*) and the legendary Andy Griffith. "*Daddy and Them* is about a dysfunctional white-trash Southern family," she recalls. "Billy Bob was *wonderful*. I *loved* him. I play his sister, who's an upper white-trash, Delta Burke on *Designing Women* kind of character. Andy Griffith [is] such a genius. I would just sit back and study him. I learned so much by working with him. I wouldn't leave him alone. Billy had to keep coming over to tell me to leave him alone."

Knight claps her hands together with delight. Since she learned a great deal from Griffith, is there any advice she has for actors attempting to dive into the Hollywood culture? After serious thought, she offers, "Hold onto yourself. Don't believe your own hype. Be careful. Don't take your bouts with success too seriously. I've had them. When you do the photoshoots and magazine covers and appear alongside Drew Barrymore, you can get caught up in it. Then when you're *not* doing them, you start to feel doubtful of yourself. You need to remember and know who you are, and what you were *before* you came into the business. Otherwise you'll only start to believe what other people are saying about you, and you'll wind up committing suicide. The business tends to take control of you, and you need to be in control of it."

Tuesday Knight admits she's still flabbergasted by the enduring appeal of Freddy Krueger and her installment all these years later, though she's unsure of how today's teen market would react to the series which first terrified a generation, then made them laugh. "The new generation of younger audiences probably don't find Freddy frightening any more," she assumes. "I think people my age still do. I can still watch them and get creeped out. I saw *A Nightmare on Elm Street* at the theater, so I had that experience which has always stuck with me. I think it's an age thing. I did go see *Nightmare 4* in the theater and it was cool because people were screaming and laughing, then afterwards they were just looking at me funny."

She chuckles again and reflects, "I didn't know [*Nightmare 4*] was going to be a groundbreaking movie when we did it. I knew it was going to be something good, but I certainly didn't know it was going to be the most successful one. It was crazy to see the nightly news and have them showing my beach scene while they reported it was the #1 movie in America. I liked that! I was very proud of it."

Kelly Jo Minter

"People hardly ever recognize me by my face, because I'm always changing my look, but as soon as they hear my voice they know who I am. So people are always saying, 'You're that girl from Freddy Krueger!' It's a trip," Kelly Jo Minter smiles, sitting back at Chin-Chin's restaurant in Beverly Hills, California. As for her voice … you *would* know her the second she starts speaking. A bit of gravel and husk, mixed with a lot of street smarts, and as sprightly as one of the many rambunctious teenagers she portrayed throughout the 1980s and '90s, Minter is the kind of actress you'd swear you knew personally.

Minter admits she never imagined she'd be discussing her film and television career almost two decades after a chance meeting on the Universal back lot in 1984 began her career. Why would the actress, with 12 box office hits, nine highly rated TV movies, appearances on shows (*ER, Hill Street Blues, A Different World, Father Dowling Mysteries, Providence, Strong Medicine*), plus a hefty number of indie films among her credits, be shocked that she's still successful in the industry? For starters, she never planned to become an actress. Second, she's never spent a day in acting class…

"Actually, I was walking with a friend on the Universal lot and they were casting for the [drama] *Mask* [1985]. [My friend] kept trying to get me to go in and meet these people, and I finally did. So I auditioned for a role, not even knowing how the hell to do it, and I got the part [as Lorrie, the kind-hearted hooker Cher brings home to deformed son Eric Stoltz]. It was my first movie. It's always been like that. I didn't know what I was doing, but I've worked ever since and wouldn't change a thing."

She shouldn't. Among her impressive list of popular movies: *Summer School, The Principal, The Lost Boys* (1987), *Miracle Mile, A Nightmare on Elm Street 5: The Dream Child, Cat Chaser* (1989), *House Party* (1990), *Popcorn, New Jack City, Doc Hollywood, The People Under the Stairs* (1991), *Sunset Grill* (1993), *The Rich Man's Wife* (1996) and *Dead Men Can't Dance* (1997).

Her collection of well-received TV movies is almost as long: *The Pilot* (1984), *Badge of the Assassin* (1985), *Sharing Richard* (1988), *Murder Without Motive: The Edmund Perry Story* (1992), *Cosmic Slop* (1994), *A Face to Die For* (1996) and the high-rated drama *Stranger Inside* (2001), about a mother and daughter simultaneously in prison, which was produced by R.E.M. lead man Michael Stipes. Then of course there's *Tapped Out*, the indie urban drama she's spent the last year producing and starring in, on top of becoming a mother.

"The last three years have been a blur," she says, raising her hands to her temples. "I had my twins, produced *Tapped Out*, recently did a lot of episodic television … I'm always busy."

Though it's difficult for her to single out which of her films is the best, or even most popular, she concedes that her visit to Elm Street still receives frequent recognition from teens and adults. She shakes her head, a bit embarrassed, and confesses, "I really wasn't aware of how popular the *Nightmare on Elm Street* series was at the time I shot *Part 5*. I really don't watch those kinds of movies, so I had to go out and rent them. I knew who Freddy was, but I had no idea it was an actual phenomenon at the time." She soon found out.

Though the fifth film came in much lower than was expected ($22 million — still an impressive number for a horror film by 1980s standards), "Freddy Mania" was still reaping revenue in the form of board and video games, costumes, dolls,

Kelly Jo Minter with James Belushi in *The Principal* (copyright 1987, Tri-Star Pictures).

comic books and novels and more. Many factors have been blamed for the drop in box office numbers, including the dark tone of the film, both visually and plot-wise. The adult storyline of teen pregnancy, abortion, a mother's rights, plus excessive gore and violence, gave the MPAA a field day and resulted in protests outside some theaters. Interestingly, many critics cited those same reasons for why it should possibly be considered the *best* of the franchise.

"[*A Nightmare on Elm Street 5*] is a wild ride filled with gruesome makeup effects and mind-blowing visuals," wrote critics Mick Martin and Marsha Porter, giving the film a three-star review. A *Fangoria* critic was a bit more mixed: "New Line Cinema's never-ending story makes encouraging signs that new ideas can still be kicked out of this old 'mare... The film is at its best during some nicely disturbing confrontations between Alice (Lisa Wilcox) and her future son (Whitby Hertford), but whenever the script or direction manage to touch a meaningful psychological nerve, the editing begins to tap dance and the screen is spritzed with neon icing... Even with these formulaic limitations, the film works more often than not.... [The cinematography distinguishes] between lucidness and lugubriousness [which] makes this by far the best looking of the *Nightmare on Elm Street* movies."

"There were pros and cons to it," points out Minter, who plays headstrong and at-first disbelieving Yvonne. "People were used to one formula for the series. The [teenage] audience who had started with the series when the first film came out were starting to grow up. It was also very surreal, and I think a lot of those people liked [those elements]. I don't think the younger ones did ... and they're the group the film was marketed towards."

(*Left to right*) Yvonne (Kelly Jo Minter), Alice (Lisa Wilcox) and her dad (Nick Mele) welcome the new generation in *A Nightmare on Elm Street 5: The Dream Child* (photograph by Michael Leshnov, 1989 New Line Cinema).

A Nightmare on Elm Street 3: Dream Warriors (1987) and *4: The Dream Master* (1988) laid the humor on heavy and made the kills almost *fun*. One critic even referred to *Nightmare 4* as "lighter Freddy." The teens who had turned those films into blockbusters may not have expected, nor understood, director Stephen Hopkins' Cronenberg-like approach with an "Escherian climax." Minter, for one, remains behind Hopkins' vision.

"He was absolutely cool," she affirms. "He was really relaxed and never freaked out. There was a lot of waiting around because of all the special FX and so many other technical aspects, so it was a lot of 'Hurry up and wait.' It wasn't like Yvonne was a really deep character, where I had to do research. I basically performed her the way they wanted me to. Hell, I was getting paid to give them what they wrote, so that's what I gave. That was my motivation. The role was pretty much a no-brainer, and Stephen [knew what he was doing], so I trusted him to make me look good."

Her castmates (Lisa Wilcox, Erika Anderson, Danny Hassel, Nick Mele, Whitby Hertford, Joe Seeley, Matt Borlenghi and, of course, Robert Englund, among others) made the two-month shoot a breeze for the actress. "I really haven't seen most of them for a long time, but every once in a while we'll bump into one another. They were a good group of people. No egos. Everyone was just there to work and have fun. Even Robert Englund, who could have had the biggest ego, was so laid back and super-nice. I've worked on a lot of sets and they made it one of the easiest jobs I've ever had."

Though on-set memories are pleasant, she does acknowledge the controversy surrounding the film by parents groups deploring the excessive violence. "Films do have a lot of shock value, but kids can go out on the street and see crazier things ... especially today. I mean, the World Trade Center attacks ... that's reality. Freddy isn't. Does it glorify horror? Yes, but some people find that to be a form of escape. Would I let my own kids watch violent movies? When they're little, *no*. But when they get to a certain age, I'll decide which ones are appropriate, and which ones aren't."

"It's up to the parents," she continues. "Whether it's violence or simply something provocative, each individual parent has to decide what's right for their own child. If your child can't handle it, then don't let them watch it. Very simple. It's like creative licensing. It's the same with music. If you don't think what your child listens to is appropriate, take it away. Be a parent. I'm totally against censorship. You may not be able to hide the sexy billboards on the street, but you can control what happens in your own home. Parent your own kids, not others."

She reflects a moment on the film itself. "I thought it was good. Now that I'm actually making films myself, I understand how much it takes to get a project done. I know the *Nightmare* fans are all critics and everyone has a different view of the movie, but I just look at it and say, 'Man, they actually finished it. That's an amazing accomplishment.' I've done movies which have had trouble getting distribution, so I'm just glad people got to see it," she explains.

What they got to see a lot of in *Nightmare 5* was more elaborate special makeup FX, stunts and visuals than the previous chapters had shown. At one point, Minter's Yvonne almost takes a lethal jump from a diving board which has come to life. However, she admits, "All they had me do was run back and forth on the diving board in front of a blue screen. They added in the claws afterwards, and the stunt double did the actual dive."

Minter adds that the majority of the action sequences in *Nightmare 5* were performed by a double. "They had a stunt woman, who I keep looking for so I can use her on other films because she was really good. I couldn't have done the things they were making her do. I have done stunts in the past on foreign films where they don't require you to have a double. 'You want me to jump out of a helicopter? Okay....' I did a film where they really wanted me to do that. Another actress, Shawnee Smith [1988's *The Blob*], actually got hurt. She cut her face and they had to fly her back to the States for surgery. The whole production was dangerous. Even the stunt coordinator walked off. The movie was called *Dead Men Can't Dance*, with Michael Biehn, Adrian Paul, Kathleen York ... some cool people, but just out of control. Nothing like *Nightmare 5*.

"I wish I had one percent of [the series profits]," she laughs when asked what she thinks of the *Nightmare* franchise. "They have their niche. Everybody may not like them, but they have a huge cult following. Not every movie series, or actor, can say they've been a part of something *that* big.

"What was really cool about *Nightmare 5* was for once the black girl didn't get killed! That's what really made it stand out," Minter observes. Seldom within the horror genre does any character of ethnicity survive to the closing reel. Even so-called "hip" movies of the post-modern era like *Scream 2*, which make comments on this fact, manage to off the black kids by the third act. Interestingly, in the few horror films where a black cast member does come out a survivor, that character seems to have been portrayed by Minter!

"Bring me back like Pam Grier," the actress exclaims. "I don't really know why I always got to survive. It's not like the parts were just handed to me. I had to audition along with a lot of other actresses for those roles. I think I just project a 'kick-ass chick' attitude onto the characters, and that's pretty much who I am."

Minter chuckles and adds, "They also seem to have a certain vulnerability to them. I just wish [the film industry] would stop segregating the movies. Why does a movie have to be all-black, all-white or all-Mexican? Why can't movies just have all kinds [of ethnicity]? It's almost kind of a joke. Represent all kinds of cultures. Just make a movie."

She continues, "With *Nightmare 5* , *The People Under the Stairs* and *Summer School*, I didn't really feel like the token black girl. I think I paved the way for a lot of black actresses just by doing those roles. It may not get me the props, but I was the one booking the jobs, and those weren't black films. They were white mainstream films, and I was just glad to be getting the work, opening the door, and glad those people had the flexibility and minds to do it. It's not like black actors have broken through to mainstream films. You have a small group of leads like Halle Berry, Vivica A. Fox, Will Smith and Denzel Washington, but they're a certain type. That's not me. I'm just very free-spirited and in your face. Whoopi Goldberg has her thing ... I have mine. You don't have to be the star, and you can still leave your imprint on the film. *That's* what I like to do.

"Sometimes I have to make my own stuff happen. I don't look *black* black. I tend to look Puerto Rican or other [nationalities]. Unfortunately, Hollywood has a tendency to pick a small group of black actors and use them until they burn out, then pick up another group. I don't want to be a black actress. I want to be a character actress. I just want to hold my own and not be categorized, and so far I've succeeded. I'm still working consistently. I did take some time off recently because I have a family now. I just had twins, so I'm spending time with them. My family is my priority now, but I bounced right back [into the business] and I'm still developing projects."

Indeed, she has, especially now that she can be found behind the camera as well. She recently produced *Tapped Out*, a film about "two guys growing up. One wants to get into the record industry and the other is into tech work. They invent this device which will allow them to listen to girls' conversations, but instead tap into two music executives' conversation and hear the music they're playing. So the guys reproduce the music and put it out themselves. They then discover the consequences of stealing someone else's music and claiming it as their own. Coolio's in it. It's a music-driven urban dramedy."

A look of delight crosses Minter's face as she discusses producing her first film. "*That's* been a nightmare. It's hard working with a really small budget, but what makes it great is the quality people who want to get down with you and go for the long haul. It's hard work. I've learned a lot from doing it."

In addition to producing the film, Minter took on a starring role as Angie, sister of Tony, the main character. She also narrates the movie. Taking the lead female role, however, wasn't something she felt she could do because "my body wasn't

Kelly Jo Minter (*right*) is one of the terrorized teens running a horror film festival in 1991's *Popcorn*.

happenin'. I'd just had twins and I wanted to do what was best for the project. I want to get the people who look good and put it down. So, although I do star in it, I'm not the lead."

Conversation briefly jumps to some of her other well-known efforts, and their continuing popularity with teen audiences today. "*House Party* was crazy fun," she laughs. "It was kind of like the birthing of honest urban black movies which were fun and used a lot of great music. I really enjoyed *The People Under the Stairs* too. Wes Craven is one of the most gentle, funny, witty, yet subdued people I've worked with. I would *love* to work with him again. I loved him.

"*Summer School* was another really cool experience," she adds. "Mark Harmon [as the immature teacher] is one of those gracious, really super-nice people. So many people from that movie are still doing so well. Courtney Thorne-Smith [the shy girl with the puppy-love for Harmon] did *Melrose Place*, *Ally McBeal* and now *Life with Jim*. Ken Olandt [the sleeping stripper] is producing and acting in movies over in Germany. Shawnee Smith [the pregnant teen] is on *Becker*, and Kirstie Alley had *Cheers* and *Veronica's Closet*. Plus Carl Reiner was such a fun director..."

With so many hit movies on her résumé, one has to wonder if Minter sought out the roles suspecting in advance they were commercially viable, or was she simply lucky. "I was just doing my job and glad to be working. Everything I do I enjoy and give it my best performance. I can't stand to hear people complain [in the industry]. It's the only job you can do in a short amount of time and make a lot of money ... next to selling drugs," she states point blank. "Give me a break. Give me *your* job. I'll do it."

Would Kelly Jo Minter make a return the horror genre some day? "Absolutely," she insists. "Especially another franchise. I'd love to do another Freddy film. The crazy thing is the *Nightmare on Elm Street* franchise may have cooled off, but it's still in the psyche of a whole generation of teenagers who have grown up and are now in the working world. Many of them are in the film industry. Just like the Baby Boomers who are doing remakes of *Planet of the Apes*, *The Flintstones* and other films they loved from their youth. They can still relate to [Freddy's impact]."

Lisa Zane

"I haven't noticed too much fanfare over the fact that I'm his daughter, but I take great comfort in it," Lisa Zane says slyly, her raven hair and solid brown eyes deep and alluring. Nothing at all like the "father" she refers to—his flesh burned, fedora hat a dirty brown, red- and green-striped sweater torn and blood-soaked. Of course she's not referring to her real father who, like her mother and brother, are fellow actors. The man she is talking about is none other than Freddy Krueger, the on-screen maniac who countered her role as the good-hearted "Maggie — his daughter."

Yes, Freddy had kin. A daughter who was taken from him after his initial murderous exploits prior to being burned to death by neighborhood parents. It was the major story arc in *Freddy's Dead: The Final Nightmare* (1991), the then-promised conclusion to the seven-year-old franchise. New Line had seen diminishing returns from the previous chapter, *A Nightmare on Elm Street 5: The Dream Child* (1989), and feared their anti-hero was falling out of favor with the important teenage demographic. Rather than run the series into the ground as so many other franchises had already done (to name them would take up too much paper, so just consider the *Howling* series a prime example), executive producer Robert Shaye and Co. made the wise decision to go out on top.

New Line Cinema (known as "The House That Freddy Built") decided to send out their horror icon with a huge bang by not only making his final foe his own child, but by filling the feature with a list of top notch cameos (Johnny Depp, Roseanne, Tom Arnold, Alice Cooper) and filming the climax in 3-D. "The 3-D wasn't difficult," Zane recalls. "You had to imagine what the audience would be seeing, so you just had to try to enhance the illusion."

As a fan, Zane was fully aware of the popularity of the *A Nightmare on Elm Street* series when she accepted the challenge of heading up the sixth installment. She admits to a moment of hesitation, but her final decision was made when "I called my best friend, Vanya, and said, 'What do you think? Should I do it?' She said, 'Lisa, you are being asked to be the avenger of all the orphans and abused children. You should do it.' She made it sound like fate had reached around the corner and handed me an edict. What could I do?"

Lisa Zane and Robert Englund on the set of 1991's *Freddy's Dead: The Final Nightmare,* in which she plays Freddy's long-lost daughter Maggie (courtesy Lisa Zane).

On-set, Zane got a workout by performing a number of stunts during her fight sequences with Krueger. "I wanted to do more of my own stunts," she sighs. "I really loved the whole fight sequence with Robert [Englund]. He's a master at making thin little girls appear to have the upper hand in strength. He can take an air punch better than anyone, or be flung across the room by the force of a puny bicep. I loved flinging knives at him, and wrestling with him. Robert was always up, always on, always there for you as an actor. Serious with a sense of play."

She also enjoyed working with her other co-stars. "Lezlie Deane [Tracy] and I got along really well. She became a singer, too [in the girl band *Fem2Fem*]! Roseanne and Tom Arnold were a glamourous duo at the time, very Liz and Dick. I remember Robert making the astute observation that they were punk. Since then, I've broadened my definition."

Performing has always been in Lisa Zane's blood. Her parents were influential, as their participation in the theater culture in Zane's home town of Chicago immersed the young starlet in the lifestyle. "Both of my parents performed in a lot of plays throughout my childhood," she says. "It just seemed like the thing to do. I cued them on their lines, they'd take me to their cast parties ... I even got a job ushering when I was 11." Spending the summer of her seventh grade year doing a musical revue directed by her aunt increased her interest in performing. "That summer, I was full of joy every day."

As a child, Zane's first love was singing. "My parents both had really beautiful voices, especially my mother. She taught me a lot of old laments, folk songs, ballads ... Listening to the great singers growing up daunted me. I was shy about calling myself a singer. Also, I smoked and smoked and could never take my voice seriously.

"Years later in Los Angeles, I found myself living across the street from a opera teacher. I knocked on her door and asked her to teach me all the arias from *Carmen*. Her name was Louise Caselotti, and I loved her as a teacher. She was radical. She claimed warming up the voice was pointless. One should be able to get out of bed and with the first breath of the morning, sing a perfect note."

Temporarily setting her singing ambitions aside, Zane ventured into all genres of film, the sixth *Nightmare* film being her most commercial vehicle. Zane enjoyed seeing the film with a public audience. "It was a different experience than seeing a straight drama, let's say, because the audience were really converts. I felt like the guest at a party they were throwing."

Now that over a decade has passed since its premiere, and teens have had their view of cinema "reality" forever altered by post-modern hits like *The Craft* and the *Scream* trilogy, would today's audience still find the premise of *A Nightmare on Elm Street* frightening? "Depends on your suspension of disbelief, and willingness to allow a movie to get to you," says Zane. "To me, the silhouette of Freddy in his hat and sweater, ambling at the gate, sends a combination of chills and titillation through me, and always will. The evening I met him was like that. It was an exterior night shoot and he came walking down a shadowed street towards me in his classic get-up, to meet me for the first time, and I was genuinely scared ... and excited. He's oddly sexy in that makeup."

Prior to her stint on Elm Street, Zane had already accumulated an impressive tally of credits, including *Heart of Dixie, Gross Anatomy* (1989), *Pucker Up and Bark Like a Dog, The Age of Insects* and *Bad Influence* (1990). After the $36 million success of *Freddy's Dead*, Zane found herself on a number of casting agents' lists and spent the next two years in the films *Babe Ruth, The Passion of Martin* and *Femme Fatale* (1991). In the last, "I was the title [character who was] a woman with multiple personality disorder who marries an Englishman [Colin Firth] and then skips out on him in the middle of the night," she recounts. "He doesn't know why, so he spends the rest of the movie tracking her down and discovering the truth."

Surprisingly, Zane admits that, even after her childhood experiences with family and theater, she never seriously considered acting as a career. She went to college to study literature and writing. Yet after dabbling further into the art, and experiencing "Broadway shows [on frequent trips] to New York, [they] finally galvanized me."

Once Zane hit the audition circuit, she quickly landed work, but admits her first day on set wasn't exactly smooth. "In my first professional film experience, I was playing the lead girl in a romantic comedy," she recalls. "My first day on set, when I heard the word 'Action,' I got dizzy and almost fainted. It was a crazy, involuntary reaction. By the end of the first week, though, I was bossing everyone around, rewriting my lines, wearing my own clothes, dating my leading man ... it's just a milieu like any other."

In the midst of increasing movie work, she set aside film in 1992 and '93 to spend a season on TV's *L.A. Law* as Melina Paros. Soon after, she stepped right into a number of movies on both screens, like *Natural Selection, XXX'S & OOO'S, Unveiled, Floundering, Terrified* (1994), *Her Deadly Rival* and *Baby Face Nelson* (1995), plus another TV series, this time a voice on Marvel's animated *Iron Man*.

It was her first season stint as the dominating Diane Leeds, opposite George Clooney on *ER* that she is best remembered for (next to *Freddy's Dead*). Additional work followed in a variety of genres, but none of them were full-on horror. She insists it was never a conscious decision.

"I never tried to stay away from horror," she states. "I love horror. I'm always hopeful a horror film will succeed because if it's good, that means we all get to be taken to a dark place safely. I always felt horror movies, however schlocky, attempt to reveal, investigate, illuminate, expose … the duality in human nature. They exorcise our violent tendencies. Scary movies are a necessary ritual, and I like playing in them."

Additional films filled her resumé, including *The Nurse, The Nervous Breakdown of Philip K. Kick* (1996), *A Table for One, The Lonely Leave, The Secret Pact, The Kidnapping of Chris Burden* (1999), *Stolen from the Heart, Missing Pieces* (2000), *Monkeybone* (2001) and the TV shows *Profit, The Outer Limits, The Incredible Hulk* (animated) and *Roar*. More recently, critics considered her the sole reason to watch the weekly series version of the hit TV movie *Dinotopia*. Thirteen episodes were filmed, but only four aired. Zane, however, remains confident the rest will be released at some point.

To her surprise, the little hobby to which she had never given much consideration suddenly offered her a chance to add an entirely new element to her career. In 1998, Zane was summoned by "a Frenchwoman who owns a very popular restaurant and night spot, [who] asked if I would sing there once a week. I chose seven songs from my strange

Lisa Zane today (courtesy Lisa Zane).

and checkered repertoire from childhood and travels, and people really went for it! Every Tuesday I would do seven new songs, and by the end of six months I had a huge repertoire and a huge audience and decided to go to New York City. I hadn't forsaken acting … it's what supported me. I continued to work, go on location, come back again, resume my gig.

"For me, singing is acting. It's a very good idiom for me as an artist, and I'm grateful for it. I perform in a style you might call cabaret; the song is acted as well as sung, and there is no limit to the style of music. However, in the past year I've written and recorded about a dozen songs. Now I sing mostly my own material."

A CD of those original songs will soon be available on her website www.lisa zane.com. She's also determined to continue to portray a wide array of characters in all genres of film. "I love playing the dualities of human nature. I loved my role in the series *Roar* where I played a sadomasochistic Roman queen named Diana, who had an ongoing love affair with an evil sorcerer," she says with a smile. "She'd cause mayhem, then all at once her heart would soften. I could have played her for a long time."

Though she has no opposition to horror, would she be willing to confront Freddy Krueger once again? Her reply, simple and with a shrug, "Sure, why not?"

Lisa Zane has emerged as a well-known talent from within the entertainment industry by relying on her beliefs. "You have to be patient," she insists. "Get into a habit of working even when you're not working. Listen to yourself, and no one else."

Lezlie Deane

It's a relatively calm day on the patio outside Jennifer's Coffee in North Hollywood, California, as I await the arrival of Lezlie Deane. Best known to fans of the horror genre for her role as teenage delinquent Tracy in *Freddy's Dead: The Final Nightmare* (1991), Deane also appeared in a flurry of genre-related pics like *976-EVIL* (1988), *Girlfriend from Hell*, *Midnight Run* (1990), *To Protect and Serve*, *Monie Madness*, *Almost Pregnant* (1992), *A Place to Be Loved* (1993) and the hysterical *Plump Fiction* (1997).

A Corsicana, Texas, native born Lezlie Denise Lonon, she's also built up an impressive list of television appearances. Among them: *The Bronx Zoo*, *Hunter*, *Night Court*, *Hardball*, *The Outsiders*, *Father Dowling Mysteries* and *Jake and the Fatman*. She even had an early brush with Krueger's finger blades in a 1989 episode of *Freddy's Nightmares*.

When the actress arrives, she's easy to spot. Her hair is longer, but still a light, silky blonde. She has a cool air about her. She is confident and her handshake is firm. She's about to tell me everything I want to hear, and she's most likely going to try and throw a few shockers in just to see if she can catch me off guard. To her credit … she frequently does.

Is *Freddy's Dead* what you're most recognized from?

Yep. And also *976-EVIL*, believe it or not … Robert Englund's directorial debut.

Do you think you got *Freddy's Dead* because of *976-EVIL*?

I think they knew me because of [*976-EVIL*]. I'd gone in for *A Nightmare on*

Actress and singer Lezlie Deane today (courtesy Lezlie Deane).

Elm Street 4 with Renny Harlin and we butted heads. I was kinda pissed because I wanted that role. Then when I went in for *Freddy's Dead*, I didn't think I was going to get it, but [director] Rachel Talalay and I really hit it off.

What were you up for in *Nightmare 4*?

Actually, I first went in for Jennifer Rubin's part [of junkie Taryn] in *A Nightmare on Elm Street 3*, then went in for Tuesday Knight's role in *Nightmare 4*. Third time's the charm, I guess. It's cool though, because I don't die in *Freddy's Dead*. I would have in the other roles. I actually got the best role, I think.

How did you get the role?

I sucked dick [*smiles*]. I went in and auditioned. Then I went in and had to do a fight sequence with this guy named Roger and I really fought him. I think it really freaked him out and Rachel liked that. I got to study with this gentleman who's pretty well known in the martial arts industry. I learned all these techniques and how to fight with chains. It was really great.

Did you do your own stunts?

Actually, I did. In the scene where we're in the kitchen and my dad [Peter Spellos, *Sorority House Massacre II*] turns into Freddy, we're fighting and he says something like, 'Back off, bitch' and hits me in the head. He really did hit me! I had to get a tetanus shot ... I even have a scar.

So you and Robert Englund already had a friendly relationship from your time on *976-EVIL*?

Oh, yeah. I was madly in love with him.

Did you model your role after anyone in particular?

I just pulled out my tough side and took it from there. I was about 98 percent of the character anyway [*laughs*]! That's probably why I got the role. I'm always the bad-ass with a heart of gold.

How was director Rachel Talalay?

Very intelligent. I loved her. She was afraid of flying like me, so we'd compare notes.

How did you like working with Lisa Zane [Maggie]?

She's really cool. I still run into her every once in a while. She was great to work with. I also loved working with Yaphet Kotto [1979's *Alien*] ... probably loved working with him the most. He's a great man and is so cool.

How about Roseanne and Tom Arnold?

She was so awesome! Everyone was like, "Eeeww! You had to work with her?!" I think she's a wonderful person. When they were getting their makeup on, we were preparing to do lines and she was on the phone trying to get help for some girl who was being abused by her family. The short time I spent with her I only saw a very caring person. Even when we were on set, she wanted to make sure everyone else was comfortable and was receiving the help they needed. I only have good things to say about her.

How about Breckin Meyer [*Clueless*]?

I see him all over TV now and I just want to punch his head in [*laughs*]. He was so cool. He made up some song about wanting me to touch his "peaches" and eat his "cream." I was always with him and Ricky Dean Logan and we had so much fun together. He was just a kid then ... like 15 or something. I'm so glad he's doing well. I kind of knew back then he was going to do really well.

Did all the visual FX and 3-D make the film more difficult to shoot?

Oh, it was such a breeze! It was a long, fun shoot. The 3-D really wasn't difficult at all. We just had to make sure we pointed our objects in the right direction and be really careful around the camera, because it was so expensive. It took us about 20 minutes to grasp the concept of how it worked, and what we needed to do.

Did you see *Freddy's Dead* with a public audience?

Of course! I had to go see it five or six times. I'd sit in the audience and see if anyone recognized me. We all do that when you're needy [*laughs*]! It was very cool. They loved it. They were laughing a lot, and in a good way! The people in the theaters seemed to pick up on [the intent] of the film and really went with it.

Had you seen the earlier chapters?

I had seen a couple of them. I think this one was more like a "mad hatter" caper ... it sort of sat between the boundaries. I felt it could have gone really far in the [comedy] direction or gone the other way [into horror], but it just kind of sat in the middle. I felt, if they were going to make it into a caper-comedy type of movie, they really should have pushed it all the way.

Are you a horror fan?

Oh yeah. I had to go to the psychologist when I was seven because I saw *The Exorcist* (1973) and it pretty much screwed my head up for the rest of my life. Yet now I'm really attracted to horror films. I'm just a morbid kind of person. I like the dark stuff.

How did you get the lead role of Suzie in *976-EVIL*?

Same thing. I went in and auditioned and they actually had us do an improv scene, which I'm pretty good at. I had to be an asshole and white trash.... I'm always really good at doing those roles [*laughs*].

How was Stephen Geoffries, who has since gone on to become an adult film actor?
Really bizarre. He's just as bizarre as the characters he plays.

Tell me about the spider sequence, where you're doused with the eight-legged critters....
When I got the role, I told them I have a huge spider phobia and they reassured me I wouldn't have to touch them or have them on me. So, of course, right at the end of the shoot, they pull me aside and say, "Okay, we're going to have to have a couple of them crawl on you," I'm screaming, "What the fuck are you talking about?! I can't have these mother fuckers crawling all over me!" They had me go talk to the spider

Lezlie Deane discovered truths about her own past while shooting scenes involving the topic of molestation for *Freddy's Dead: The Final Nightmare.*

wrangler to reassure me I'd be safe from the tarantulas they were going to use.

So I go over to [the wrangler] who's got crates of these things and is telling me they're very docile creatures and if one were to actually bite me it would just be like a bee sting ... which wasn't comforting me. So we had to go through aversion therapy, where I'd get as close as I could to them, and then I'd have to back away until I got the courage to get closer again. She had one really big silver one crawl on me, and I noticed it was actually very pretty in the way it moved, but then it didn't stop crawling and kept getting closer to my face and I'm screaming, "Get this motherfucker off of me!" I was too freaked out. So when it came time to shoot the scene, I just couldn't do it. The wrangler had thought ahead, and brought some freeze-dried ones. She placed them on me, so when you see me close up by the sink and brushing them off they're actually already dead.

Then of course there's the part where I pull the top of my TV dinner back and they jump out of it. They had drilled a hole under the table and attached a canister filled with the tarantulas under it. They had spent so much time lighting the scene after they'd already put them in the canister, they were suffocating, so when I pulled the top off the tray they came flying out at me. So the reaction you see on screen is my real reaction. I was just screaming. Then they wanted me to go back and film it again and I begged them not to make me do it again, but we had to do it. Everything actually went fine during the scene, but afterwards they discovered they'd lost one of the tarantulas in this home and I don't think they ever told the owners there was a loose tarantula crawling around somewhere!

How does your family react to your involvement in the entertainment industry?

Oh, please — they pushed me out here! My mom still tells people, "My little girl killed Freddy!" I'm like, "Mom, it was ten years ago! Let it go!" My parents went to see *976-EVIL* in the theater, and I'm just sitting there thinking, "Please, somebody cover my dad's eyes when I'm on top of Spike [Patrick O'Brien]."

You did *976-EVIL* and *Girlfriend from Hell*, which technically is a comedy, yet kind of falls into the horror category. Did you ever fear being labeled a "Scream Queen?"

You know, *Girlfriend* and *Freddy's Dead* fall into the same category. They're so similar. As far as the label is concerned, I didn't fear it at all. Actually, my old band did a song called "Scream Queen."

Are you more into music now?

Oh, yeah. I don't act any more. I was acting for a while, then my manager put this band together and we were on tour for four years, so I really didn't have the time to go on any auditions or do movies, etc. One of the last things I did was *Plump Fiction*, where I spoof [Jodie Foster] in *Nell*. I had such a blast doing that! [However], music is my first love, and now that I'm growing up, I look back at my acting career and see all the bad, unrealistic dialogue I spoke, which other people wrote, and I just can't put myself in that situation any more. If I'm ever going to get back into acting, it's going to have to be something I help write. Also, not to be a "woman," but comparative to what's written for men, there's so much crap. I just can't do it. I also don't have that need to be famous. Does that make sense? Basically, I sort of grew up. I did the Hollywood thing, and actually got my "fame" from being in the band, which kind of quenched my thirst at the shallow end of being an artist.

So even while you were acting, what you really hungered for was the music?

No, not at all. Music just sideswiped me. Tuesday Knight [*Nightmare 4*] and I have kind of swapped careers, because she was a singer before she became an actress, whereas I did the opposite.

Let's talk about your lesbian-themed band Fem2Fem, which had two successful albums, 1994's "Woman to Woman" and 1995's "Animus"...

It was one of those girl bands put together, which end up getting screwed and making no money. We were the original gay Spice Girls [*laughs*]. It was really bad dance music [*laughs again*]. We were a put-together lesbian-band and not all of us

Lezlie Deane (*center*) and her bandmates from the group Fem 2 Fem (courtesy Lezlie Deane).

were lesbians. It could've been something really good, but the manager's own character faults made it not happen. It was very cool though. The best thing I can say about it is one of my band members is still my best friend. We toured with Nine Inch Nails and Marilyn Manson. Our second album was turned into a Western musical in London and we went over there and starred in it. The group lasted from about 1993 to 1998. Then, after the musical ended, the whole band just [fell apart] because the manager, who had been clean and sober for 12 years, fell off the wagon in every possible way.

When did you first know you wanted to get into the entertainment industry?

When I was tiny. Just because I needed affection ... a simple fact [*laughs*]. My first official role was as Lola the hooker on *T.J. Hooker* ... I made a career out of playing hookers and assholes with hearts of gold [*laughs again*]. Then *976-EVIL* was my first film role which, I think movie-wise, is my favorite. I'm most proud of it, because it had an amazing director, the script was very quirky, and there was some reality to it. Working with Robert as a director was a dream. It's so great to work with a director who's also an actor, because they understand the level you're on. He let's you find real moments to breathe life into your character, whereas other directors simply want you to recite the lines on the page and think no further about it.

After *Freddy's Dead*, did you receive other horror movie offers?

No. Just a couple here and there, but I felt I'd already done the Academy Awards level within the genre by having been in a *Nightmare on Elm Street* movie and didn't want to take five steps backwards. Am I just being an asshole? [*Laughs*]

If someone offered you a role in a film, would you take it?

Yeah, but only if I didn't have to go through that horrible audition process. I do still love acting ... when you're in that moment and the moment is true, that's being an artist. I just can't take the bullshit end of it anymore. I can't go through being told I'm not pretty enough, or I don't have the right clothes on....

When you did *Freddy's Dead*, were there ever any issues with nudity or sexuality?

Technically, no. They never asked for anything sexy. However, I learned something about myself. The storyline to my character was about molestation, and in making the movie I learned I had been molested in real life. It wasn't by anyone in my family, but when I started doing those scenes I began having flashbacks and thinking to myself during the scenes, "This is so weird. It's so easy for me to [perform] these scenes." I didn't have to prepare for them at all. I could just "snap" on cue. It was all very apropos.

The *Nightmare on Elm Street* films have always been targeted for inciting youth violence. Do you agree?

If anything, I think the *Nightmare* movies, and many other horror films, show that if you confront what frightens you, you'll come out stronger. On the other hand, violence is violence, and people are going to interpret it however they want. If we're talking specifically about kids, I think it falls on the responsibility of parents, not taking our rights away, or telling us what we can see or create, and what we can't.

Do you think the *Nightmare* films still have the same effect on today's teens in our post–*Scream* culture?

I think my chapter does, because you can look at it as being very camp. It holds true to the current trend.

Tell me about your time shooting *Plump Fiction*.

It was so great. Such a hysterical movie. Julie Brown [*Clueless*] was just awesome! She was such a pleasure to work with, and was so funny. The director was [also] great. I'd never done comedy before, and he just kept reassuring me I was doing it right. He'd always say, "You're funny, you're funny … just keep going!" Jennifer Rubin is in the movie too, but we never worked together. However, we finally crossed paths recently. I had to tell her I was a really big fan. I actually had to tell her we were in *Plump Fiction* together, and she asked who I played. When I [performed the role] for her she said, "Oh my God, I loved you! You were so funny!" Our paths had actually crossed several times at auditions [like *Nightmare 3* and *Lethal Weapon 3*, for the Rene Russo role]. When I went in to audition for *Lethal Weapon 3*, I thought I did a great job, even though they kept telling me I was too young for the role, but the director [Dick Donner] said he might rewrite the role to fit me in. So I was feeling good and walked out of the audition and saw Jennifer Rubin sitting there and thought, "Oh great … Jennifer Rubin's going to go in there and kick my ass." [*Laughs*] Ultimately, it went to Rene Russo, so neither of us got it, but I just think Jennifer is a great actress. The *Plump Fiction* experience as a whole was just wonderful. With that cast, how could it not be? So many talented people!

So why was *Plump Fiction* your last film?

The last day of shooting, I was supposed to be heading off on tour with the band and was trying to get them to hurry so I could catch my plane. It all kind of culminated right around that time, where I realized I couldn't be doing both and had to focus all my attention on the band.

How long have you and Tuesday Knight known each other?

At least [15] years. She used to bully me all the time because I was younger. She thought she knew more than me. We're like sisters. We have this weird relationship. I've known her since *Nightmare 4* was shot.

What kind of advice would you give to actresses just getting started in the business?

Turn around and go home [*laughs*]. Persistence pays off. Never give up on what you're doing. If you keep at it you'll achieve some level of success. I'm not saying you'll become famous and make a ton of money, but you will achieve a certain level of success. I truly believe that.

How would you summarize your overall experience on *Freddy's Dead*?

Timeless … it was a wonderful thing to experience. I'd definitely do it again. It meant so many things to me, but it's never truly ended. It just keeps going. It'll be something that will probably follow me for the rest of my life. So, I guess timeless is the best way to describe it.

As our interview comes to a close, I've decided Lezlie Deane is probably one of the coolest actresses I've had the pleasure of spending time with. She didn't kiss my ass, and she didn't pretend to be a part of the Hollywood scene. In fact, she preferred to extend herself far away. Then, when I thought she couldn't come across any more diverse or kick-ass, she caught me off-guard one last time. As a result of a wonderful gesture, and some personal ties, later that evening I was first on the guest list at L.A.'s El Rey Theater to see, in a very intimate venue, performances by Lifehouse ("Hangin' by a Moment"), Michelle Branch ("Everywhere") and The Calling ("Wherever You Will Go"). Like those artists, Lezlie Deane rocks.

Halloween *Hotties*

Pamela Susan Shoop

At first glance you recognize her: chestnut hair, soft pink lips, smoldering green eyes and a smile so warm and welcoming you feel you've known her for years … and through the magic of television and film, you have. For over 30 years she's graced both screens, delivering performances ranging from the tortured heroine of the early 1970s soap opera *Return to Peyton Place*, to the giggly head cheerleader of 1979's *Dallas Cowboys Cheerleaders* and a not-so-naïve mistress in the 1977 camp favorite *Empire of the Ants*. She was even among Michael Meyer's most famous victims as she dipped into a deadly Jacuzzi in 1981's *Halloween II*.

For a generation of young men, Pamela Susan Shoop was the sweet girl-next-door-turned-vixen they adored. Born to a celebrated military pilot and Hollywood actress mother, Shoop grew up in the spotlight, among celebrities like Nancy and Ronald Reagan, Ann Miller (1948's *Easter Parade*), Sonja Henie (1936's *One in a Million*) and Art Linkletter (1946's *People Are Funny*). Fellow high school alumni included Richard Dreyfuss, Albert Brooks, Candice Bergen, Rob Reiner and Larry Bishop. Despite the illusion of glamour and royalty, however, Shoop never saw it as an outlandish way of life.

"It didn't faze me at all," Shoop insists, perched amongst the power-lunchers at Jerry's Famous Deli in Studio City, California. "It's just the way my life was from the time I was a baby. I didn't know anything else. Then, when I turned 19, I moved out and discovered a different way of life. I always knew there were people less fortunate than myself. My mother spent a lot of time working with charities, which I became involved with at a young age, and I still do them."

Shoop thanks her mother, Julie Bishop, for many of her life's best lessons, including her decision to become an actress. Bishop, who starred in 84 films alongside legends like John Wayne (*Sands of Iwo Jima* and *The High and the Mighty*), Humphrey Bogart (*Action in the North Atlantic*) and Errol Flynn (*Northern Pursuit*), was an inspiration to her daughter. (Bishop also starred in films like *Tarzan the Fearless* with Buster Crabbe, *The Black Cat* opposite Bela Lugosi and Boris Karloff and *The Bohemian Girl* alongside Laurel and Hardy under her given name of Jacqueline Wells.)

"She was doing a play when I was 15 called *Tunnel of Love* with Bob Cummings," Shoop says. "I would tour with her and had such great fun. I just fell in love with acting because of it."

The influence prompted Shoop into her first stage role as the only girl in an all-male cast (including Cummings) in *Generation*. She later studied her craft at the University of Southern California and Villa Mercede in Florence, Italy, and appeared in a variety of stage productions such as *Picnic* with Robert Horton, *A Good Look at Boney Kern* opposite Don Knotts and *Dinner and Drinks* with William Katt.

The actress also credits her late father, Major General Clarence A. Shoop, a two-star general who was the Vice President of Howard Hughes Aircraft Company and (as reconnaissance pilot during WWII) flew the first photographic mission over Normandy's Omaha Beach on D-Day. "I was brought up with a wonderful family," the younger Shoop begins. "I'm so grateful for a wonderful childhood. You think of a General as very cold and strict, but my father always had a smile on his face. The happiest, kindest man. Very vivacious. My parents brought me and my brother [former Cedars Sinai Medical Center Chief of General Surgery Stephen A. Shoop, who is now the medical director of spotlighthealth.com] up with a lot of love. There was discipline, but it was given with love and encouragement. I was [taught] I could accomplish anything I set my mind to. It's a wonderful thing to teach a child. I was very lucky."

Judging from her résumé of over 60 television and film credits, she heeded her parents' advice. Known in Hollywood circles as "the chameleon" for her ability to

run the gamut of personalities on screen, Shoop began her career in the 1973 Oscar-nominated short film *Frog Story*. "It was a wonderful fantasy piece about a frog who turns into me after she's been kissed," she recalls.

Shoop's first major exposure to American audiences, however, still garners her attention from fans. "[It] really amazes me," she exclaims. "I played Allison MacKenzie on the daytime soap *Return to Peyton Place* [1973–74] and people still recognize me."

The actress recalls that her character (originated by Mia Farrow in the 1960s primetime version) "cried ... and cried and cried. Five days a week. She was a very depressed girl," Shoop laughs. "She was like my own personal-

Shoop in *Buck Rogers in the 25th Century* (1997 Universal City Studios, Inc., photograph courtesy P. S. Shoop).

ity at that age. Very shy and sweet … very loyal. Family-oriented and honest. Always the good daughter."

Although she remembers the shooting schedule as "rough," she asserts, "I loved it and thought it was really good training. My character was one of the most prominent on the show, so I had to learn 30 pages of dialogue every night, five nights a week. There was a lot of exposition and I'd have to keep repeating the same dialogue over with slightly different variations every day for people who had missed it the day before. I had to figure out were my character was at each point in the story. Did this happen three days ago, or yesterday?"

Shoop insists it was "difficult in the beginning, but by the end of the series it was so easy to memorize lines. It really helped me in [future] auditions because I could pick up the [script], go in and give a performance, whereas a lot of other actors are just trying to read off dialogue."

Though asked to tackle other soap roles after the show's demise, the actress preferred to pursue other areas of the small screen. Her early list of starring guest spots on television shows plays like a retro '70s enthusiast's ultimate fantasy: *Night Gallery, The F.B.I., The Rookies, Mannix, The Mod Squad, Switch, Gemini Man, Emergency!, Wonder Woman, Keeper of the Wild, Code R, The Incredible Hulk, Kaz, Vega$, CHiPS* and *Buck Rogers in the 25th Century,* to name a few.

Among her favorites was time spent on Paradise Island alongside Lynda Carter, Debra Winger and Carolyn Jones in the two-part "Feminum Mystique" episodes of *Wonder Woman.* In the episode, Wonder Woman's (Carter) younger sister Drucilla (Winger) ventures off the Amazonian island and joins her elder sister in America. Upon learning how to turn herself into "Wonder Girl," Winger is taken hostage by Nazi's who mistake her for her sibling. Discovering her roots, they return to her homeland in an attempt to take over the Amazons (Shoop among them as Magda) and the queen (Jones) and gain control of the metal used to make the bullet-defying bracelets.

"Lynda Carter was very sweet and nice to everyone," Shoop recalls. "I didn't get to spend much time with her because she was typically needed in every scene, so she was always busy. Debra Winger was also nice. She was really young and just starting in the business, but she was very confident and professional."

It was the *Addams Family* matriarch Carolyn "Morticia" Jones, however, who left an indelible impression on the young thespian. "She was amazing," Shoop declares. "She told my fortune. She read my palm and everything she told me has come true! At the time I didn't believe anything she was saying, but she told me two very personal things which happened just as she said they would. She was very interesting, and such a lovely lady."

In the midst of her frequent television guest spots, Shoop ventured into the next medium, running for her life and keeping a straight face in the cult horror confection *Empire of the Ants* (1977). Directed by Bert I. Gordon, connoisseur of camp fests like *The Food of the Gods* (1976), *Picture Mommy Dead* (1966) and *Satan's Princess* (1989), the cult pic follows a group of real estate developers (Joan Collins, Jacqueline Scott, Robert Lansing and Robert Pine among them) who are stranded on an island where man-eating ants have grown to enormous proportions. Its legendary status as an *awful*-ly enjoyable movie is one Shoop (who played feisty heroine Coreen Bradford) finds easy to explain.

"The sound man had a fight with the director towards the end of the shoot and threw all of the audio tapes into the swamp. We lost everything! So the entire movie had to be looped ... every pant, every grunt, every scream. One day, John David Carson [1974's *Captain Kronos: Vampire Hunter*] and I were looping in the studio. I had been hyperventilating for so long I almost passed out! The sound and our voices and actions never mesh. Plus, all our voices sound higher pitched than they really were..."

Enduring unpleasant locales and a heap of dangerous situations didn't help to create any sort of fondness for the cast. "It was really windy and muggy," she says, with an unexpected smile on her face. "We'd have to run through these swamps and by the end of the day I'd have dirt caked between my toes. There were creepy crawlers everywhere. There's a picture of me leaning

Shoop and John David Carson faced horrors both on screen and off in her first genre film, *Empire of the Ants.*

against a tree covered in filth with rain pouring down, and that's pretty much how it was!

"When we were hired to do the movie we found out there were going to be crocodiles in the waters we'd be shooting scenes in," she chuckles, then throws her arms up in the air. "We were guaranteed there would be a ranger on set to shoot any crocodiles which came near us or tried to attack. The day we filmed the scenes in the water, the crew stood on a raft and fed donuts to them! So when we went to shoot the scene in the boat, the crocodiles kept coming over to the boat and swimming around us ... and there was *no* ranger to watch over us!"

Shoop merely laughs and continues, "Then they had us jump into the water when the boat tips over. Jacqueline Scott couldn't even swim! We should have gotten hazard pay. We all just jumped in and swam as fast as we could. We didn't think about it. We just did it. That's what actors do. They take risks just to get the shot done."

Her time away from the set was no vacation either. She continues, "There were gun shots at the motel we stayed at and weren't allowed to leave our rooms. The women weren't allowed to go down to the bars by themselves. It was a dangerous area. [Still], we shot over Thanksgiving and Christmas and became a very tight group of people."

Among her favorite cast members was the ageless Joan Collins (*Dynasty*), who bonded with and became one of Shoop's closest friends. "Joanie was hysterical," she chuckles. "They'd drag us in a boat 30 minutes up river from our base camp to shoot. We'd be out there for hours and she'd call to the director, 'Oh Bert! I have to go to the loo.' He'd tell her to wait for ten minutes, but it would be 20, then 40 ... he'd always want to get 'just one more shot.' By the time someone would finally take us back, it was two hours later. It was a half-hour each way, and they didn't want to waste the time. Joan was a great sport and didn't complain. She got along with everybody very well."

The actress followed her swampy ordeal with other feature films, like *Dead on Arrival* with Jack Palance and the 1978 drama *One Man Jury*. There were also made-for-television movies like *Harold Robbins' 79 Park Avenue* (1977) (as a call girl drug addict opposite Leslie Anne Warren) and *The Dallas Cowboy Cheerleaders* (1979).

Co-starring with TV staples Jane Seymour (*Dr. Quinn, Medicine Woman*) and Lauren Tewes (*The Love Boat*), Shoop portrayed fun-loving leader Betty Denton. The actress proudly says, "*The Dallas Cowboy Cheerleaders* was, at the time, the highest-rated movie-of-the-week ever, except for *Roots*. I had such a great time doing it. There were 49 cheerleaders and five main actresses for two months in Dallas. We were taught all of the routines by Texie Waterman, and before one of the real games we all went out onto the field of the Texas stadium and performed in front of the fans so they could get shots of us with the real audience." Shoop insists the shoot was fun, but admits "those pom pons were so heavy!"

This period also offered her all-time favorite role, as a pregnant woman who gives birth in the back of a truck on a snowy Christmas Eve in the "Silent Night, Unholy Night" episode of *BJ and the Bear*. Shoop's eyes ignite as she begins, "Ted Danson [*Cheers*] played my husband. However, my character, Alison Spencer, falls in love with BJ [Greg Evigan] throughout the course of the episode. I'm in this terrible car accident and BJ comes along and saves me and helps me deliver the baby. Eventually I choose to go back to my husband, but name the baby after BJ. It was such a beautiful story and character."

In addition to return visits to *BJ and the Bear*, Shoop also lent her talents to the likes of *Hawaii Five-O*, *CHiPS*, *Galactica 1980* (a.k.a. *Galactica III: Conquest of the Earth*), *Fitz and Bones*, *The Fall Guy*, *Fantasy Island* and *Magnum P.I.*. Return visits to shows weren't uncommon for Shoop, but she notes, "I would do two or three episodes, sometimes as the same character, other times as a completely new character. I did the [two-part] pilot episode of *Knight Rider* as the lead girl. Then a few years later I shot an episode in Chicago playing a completely new person. They just called me up and asked me to do it. Once I played a character on a show, I didn't have to audition again. Sometimes it was the same role, but other times they just liked my performance and would ask me back to do other roles."

Her success in the TV medium can be attributed to what Shoop calls "loyalty from producers at Universal. Glen Larson was one of them. He considered me his good luck charm. Whenever he would use someone else besides me in a pilot, the show wouldn't sell, but they always sold if I was in the pilot. There isn't one I did which didn't get picked up. So I became his superstition. He gave me the choice to guest star in the *Magnum P.I.* pilot, or have a recurring role in another planned series, but I chose *Magnum P.I.*. The other show never got picked up."

Shoop's ties to Universal proved invaluable in 1981, when she received the role of Nurse Karen in the box-office hit *Halloween II*. To her amazement, the film remains her most successful and recognized role. "Unbelievable," she exclaims. "I'd never seen the original *Halloween* [1978] and didn't want to do it because it was a horror movie. I figured I'd already done *Empire of the Ants*, so one horror credit was enough. My agent, however, insisted I do it, and lo and behold it's where I received my most loyal group of fans!"

Halloween II was in 1981 what *Scream 2* was in 1997: *the* movie with which to be associated. *Halloween* had earned an astounding amount of money and became (until 1996's *Scream*) the most successful independent film in history. Directed by Rick Rosenthal (*The Birds II: Land's End*), *Halloween II* picks up immediately after the events of the original film. Bogeyman Michael Myers creates a new bloody path en route to the hospital where Laurie Strode (Jamie Lee Curtis) is cared for by a bevy of beautiful nurses.

Critical reaction was split: "Respectable sequel ... a frightening follow-up," wrote one, while another said, "Slick but needlessly bloody sequel ... sharply photographed and featuring a better-than-average supporting cast, but awfully pointless ... Jamie Lee Curtis is wasted..." Regardless, the general public obviously welcomed the sequel, making it one of the biggest hits of the year.

Shoop points out, "It was a huge project, but I didn't understand it then. I thought I was just going on another audition. I really didn't want to do it because I wasn't a fan of the genre. Once I got involved, I realized how important the movie was being considered."

Even throughout production, Shoop insists she felt little pressure. "I really didn't know what *Halloween* was ... I'd never seen it. So Rick and [producer] Debra Hill set up a screening after I got hired and we watched it. Even throughout the shoot I still didn't realize it was going to be such a big success. Then after it came out, it hit me because all these great reviews started coming out and mentioning me! My agent called and said, 'See, I told you you needed to do this!' So then I decided to go see it in the theater and find out what all the hullabaloo was about."

The only controversy surrounding the film since its release has been the amount of control producer-writer John Carpenter took in re-directing Rosenthal's final cut. While Shoop confirms that Carpenter directed some scenes, she maintains that the majority of the picture is Rosenthal's work. "Rick handled just about everything until the very end when John came in. I don't know if he wasn't happy with the film, but he just wanted to reshoot a couple of scenes and add some extra scenes which weren't in the original script."

According to the actress, Debra Hill was the only one on set the entire time. "John Carpenter did direct me in a couple of scenes," she says, "like when you first see me walking through the parking lot [with *Prom Night*'s Eddie Benton — a.k.a. Anne-Marie Martin] and a few of the hospital scenes, but Rick directed most of my scenes."

Working with a cast of professionals added to Shoop's fondness for the follow-up. "Jamie Lee Curtis was great," she says with a smile. "Like everyone else, she was very nice and wonderful and supportive. It's very hard doing a shoot like that and she didn't have a lot of dialogue. She had to wear a wig because she'd already cut off her hair into this adorable short [hairdo], but she needed to look like she did in the first movie. Then she'd be crawling around in the cold parking lot at four A.M. with barely anything on and scraping her nails on the pavement. She was really put through a lot of tests. We all were. She was young and had a lot of

Known as "The Chameleon" in Hollywood, Pamela Susan Shoop (seen here in a late 1970s pose) was popular for her statuesque figure and ability to perform a wide range of characters on screen.

energy and was willing to do anything. She gave 100 percent and never complained. There wasn't anything they asked which she wouldn't do."

Shoop expresses an equal fondness for Leo Rossi [1989's *The Accused*] who portrayed Bud, her on-screen boyfriend. "Leo is such a wonderful actor," she says. "He's a great character actor who's made a fabulous career for himself. He's very impressive, and so underrated."

For the most part, Shoop recalls her time on the set of *Halloween II* with affection, though there were a few mishaps along the way—for example, her infamous death scene. She and Rossi take a dip in a steamy Jacuzzi, where he is strangled and she is drowned while having her face melted off in scalding water. "They would put latex on my face and place a needle filled with Vaseline under the latex and fill it up more

and more with each shot. My skin was fine when they pulled it off, but my hair was severely damaged."

Stroking her now-blonde locks, Shoop continues, "For some reason they shot my death scene first, then shot the 'beauty' part where I get into the hot tub. The Vaseline had gotten into my hair and they couldn't get it out. They tried dry-cleaning it and the [hair stylist] washed my hair over 13 times and still couldn't get it out. My hair was damaged for a really long time afterwards."

The actress also received a severe ear infection from the repeated dunking in the water, which she says was "cold and dirty. They were playing it off like the water was boiling, but it was absolutely freezing! Leo and I were so cold, our teeth were chattering!"

Shoop, who attests to a love for the first two films and 1998's *Halloween: H20*, confirms she still receives residual checks, "the bonus of being in a movie which is practically guaranteed to be shown annually. It always comes back to haunt me. I can't believe it's still such a popular film."

What she doesn't understand are the two alternate versions of the film's conclusion. "I always end up seeing the television version, which is different from the theatrical version," she comments. "In the original version, Laurie Strode is in the ambulance and Jimmy [Lance Guest of *Jaws: The Revenge*] sits up behind her with a sheet over him like a ghost. Then they drive off together, crying. In the television and video versions, she's alone in the ambulance. I don't know why they changed it, because in the cut version Jimmy passes out in the car where Laurie is hiding, then he's never seen again. It doesn't make sense."

Another situation also rests uneasy with the actress, both for the scene's purpose and her hesitant involvement. As Nurse Karen prepares to dip into the hot tub of death, she drops her towel, allowing for ample exposure of her breasts. Minutes later, during the gruesome melting phase of her death, her naked body is repeatedly pulled from the water and exposed for titillation and the contrast of her beautiful body vs. her horrifically mutilated face. Shoop doesn't buy into the latter half.

"I wanted Karen to be modest because she was a nurse on duty in a hospital and was supposed to be very intelligent," she begins, shaking her head. "In the original film, P.J. Soles' character [Lynda] was a free spirited teenager, so it was more acceptable. But Karen was supposed to be a professional adult who wouldn't so willingly jump into a hot tub."

Filming the scene proved to be the actress' most difficult on an emotional level. "We shot the nude scene in two days and it became increasingly uncomfortable for me," she divulges. "The second day I cried all the way to the set. I didn't want to do it again. At one point, Rick said to the crew they should all film the scene in their underwear to make me more comfortable, and all of the men flat-out refused. I said, 'See! It's not so easy!'

"Leo was wonderful because I had never done nudity before. He was so respectful and protective. He was actually more nervous about his own nudity than he was about mine [*laughs*]. Debra was very protective of us both. That's one of the advantages of having a female producer. At one point they wanted to take off all my clothes

Opposite: Theatrical art for Pamela Susan Shoop's most successful film, *Halloween II*.

and show me getting into the tub fully nude, which wasn't in my contract. I knew it would wind up in dailies somewhere and didn't want to do it, and she really stood up for me. I will always be grateful to her for [her support]."

Surprisingly, when asked if she would do the scene over given the opportunity, Shoop offers an interesting variation on the expected response. "There are two parts to that answer. If I was then who I am now, I'd deal with it a lot better. Back then I was very shy. It was hard for me on a lot of levels. One of the worst parts was that I'd asked for and been promised a closed set, but at one point I counted 19 people in the room!"

Shoop's eyes twinkle as she continues, "The second part of the answer is that I probably wouldn't do it now because of my husband ... who used to be a priest."

What makes Pamela Susan Shoop and Terrance A. Sweeney, her husband of over 15 years, stand out is their very public stance on their union. Sweeney, a five-time Emmy-winning writer and author of four books, including *A Church Divided: The Vatican vs. American Catholics, GOD &....* and *Streets of Anger, Streets of Hope: Youth Gangs in East L.A.,* had already been struggling with the historical issues of celibacy within the Church when he met the actress. After a large number of emotional conflicts were placed behind them and they were well on the path to proving to the world their love was real, Shoop picked up a pen and, with her husband, co-authored a 1993 best-seller based on their experiences, *What God Hath Joined.*

As Shoop recalls, "When he left the church to be with me, it was a scandal. Over 100,000 priests have left the church for the same reason. The scandal surrounding us, however, was due to how vocal Terry was about it. He became vocal to the public when he was told to either destroy his notes [11 years of research] about the celibacy laws throughout history, or leave the Jesuit Order after 24 years of service."

Sweeney refused, begetting one of three notable waves of controversy (the second focused on their wedding and the third resulting from publication of their book). The couple ultimately stood strong to face every challenge placed in front of them.

"On the day we married," Shoop proudly states, "we held a press conference. He said he loved me and he loved God and he loved the church, and there was no reason why all three couldn't be compatible. We started our own non-profit organization AMADEUM [translation: "Love God"] which helps priests and women in love."

The actress-turned-activist shakes her head as she continues, "On the day we met, a priest in Italy who'd been in love with a woman for over 20 years couldn't bear to hide it any more and hung himself outside his rectory door. Another priest in England threw himself under a train. I know two women who killed themselves for the same reasons. It's a really ugly side of the church which needs to be revealed, because there are a lot of people in pain."

Shoop offers many little-known facts surrounding the church and its secrets (it's easy to see why her book remained on the top of the charts for several weeks). "For over 700 years there were married priests! Over 40 married Popes! Even several of the apostles had wives! When the first Popes tried to enforce celibacy, there was a lot of bloodshed and chaos. A very dubious beginning. The church still won't acknowledge it, even though Terry's research has proven it's true. Our hope is to restore the right to marry to Roman-Catholic priests."

Don't think, however, their love story doesn't have at least one Hollywood twist.

Whether a divine act of God or merely coincidence, Sweeney partook in a bit of eerie irony. In 1983, Sweeney, still a dedicated Jesuit Catholic priest, became Richard Chamberlain's technical advisor on the controversial mini-series *The Thorn Birds*. In the ten-hour epic, Chamberlain portrays a priest who falls in love with a woman (Rachel Ward of *The Final Terror*) and must battle his demons over choosing his love for the church or his love for Ward. The end results are ultimately disastrous.

"Terry and I are always being compared to *The Thorn Birds*," Shoop admits. "We have newspaper articles from all over the world comparing us to that movie. Richard Chamberlain ended up becoming very good friends with my husband. We like to tell people we are *The Thorn Birds*, but with a happy ending."

While creating real-life drama of her own, Shoop continued to bring Hollywood drama into the homes of millions of Americans. With *Halloween II* a hit, the actress was in high demand, tackling new shows like *T.J. Hooker, Fame, Masquerade, Whiz Kids, I Had Three Wives* and *Scarecrow and Mrs. King*.

"You know, I've been in the business for 30 years and have to say there isn't anyone I didn't like, which is really rare. I've been very lucky. Some people were more difficult than others, but there was never anything negative directed towards me. There was never anything I couldn't work around or work with. I think it might be because I treated all of my jobs as just that … a job. I came in, did my work and went home."

Throughout the remainder of the 1980s and 1990s, the actress appeared in shows like *Murder, She Wrote, Tales of the Gold Monkey, Simon & Simon, The Law and Harry McGraw, The Highway Man, Dangerous Curves* and *Kung Fu: The Legend Continues* and telepics like *The Rousters* (with Mimi Rogers and the late Jim Varney).

With a résumé so extensive, one has to wonder why Shoop has been absent from both screens since 1996. Though some blame is placed on a leg-foot injury requiring multiple surgeries over the past few years, Shoop points a finger towards the youth-obsessed culture of Hollywood.

"I'm in a certain age range which typically doesn't work," she states very matter-of-factly. "I look at a lot of the people who were older than myself and were working when I was younger, and they're not working at all now. Most roles are for 20-year-olds, so it's a lot harder now. If I could work the rest of my life as an actress, I would because I love it so much. It's what I do."

Don't think she's wallowing in self-pity. "I've been in the age range where I'm too old to play a young character, but too young to play an older character. I'm not sure where I fit in now, but I'd love to go full circle and do a soap opera again. I also got into the writing with my husband, so I'm focused more there now too, and really enjoy it."

Shoop's husband is extremely proud and supportive of her career and the choices she's made, but one has to question if she'd return to the genres which depict violence and the seedier side of life. With so much negative attention focused on Hollywood since Columbine and other incidents of youth-related violence, Shoop has a view of her industry to which not many actors will admit.

"I do think [violence in society] is partially [Hollywood's] fault," she begins. "I think they capitalized on it, which isn't right. There's a way to portray violence and special FX in a way which is less harmful. I don't support violence which incites people

Pamela Susan Shoop today.

to commit violence ... and I do believe some of it does. Especially films which children see. Children emulate the 'heroes' they see in action films. I'd rather see more films like *Braveheart* [1995]. You can show violence with a hero who fights for causes ... fights for something right. Not a hero who fights just to rack up bodies and glorify the violence around him."

Tough talk for a woman who was chased by killer ants and nibbled on the bloodstained fingers of a mad slasher. Shoop, however, is quick to defend certain types of cinema violence, and why she would gladly do another horror feature.

"Horror films are more tongue-in-cheek," she says. "They're not real. *Halloween II* and *Empire of the Ants* are horror movies, but I truly don't think they caused any trouble. I mean, nobody's going to be a giant killer ant. As for Michael Myers, I don't see anyone trying to emulate him. [People] don't generally want to be Michael Myers. He's not portrayed in a positive way. Movies like *Natural Born Killers* [1994], however, do portray the violence and the [degenerate] characters as a good thing. That's where the problem and the differences lie."

Shoop continues to keep herself busy with not only writing, but also serves a number of charities and groups including Good Tidings, The National Charity League and A.R.C.S.: Achievement Rewards for College Scientists. She also offers a bit of advice to the ingenues swarming casting calls.

"Learn your job," she insists. "I've been told by casting directors there are two types of actresses in this town. The ones you want to hire for a role, and the ones you want to hire for a good time. I was always taken seriously from day one. If you ever want to make it in this town, don't start off playing games. You play a game once and that's it. Learn your craft; learn how to walk and talk at the same time and how to be a professional."

With a career spanning 30 years, Pamela Susan Shoop obviously followed her own advice. Visit her website, www.pamelasusanshoop.com.

Stacey Nelkin

"It was absolutely freakish to see my body double dressed identical to myself with her head missing and my head coming out of a hole with no body," Stacey Nelkin laughs. Now, 20 years after she took on the role of Jamie Lee Curtis's successor in *Halloween III: Season of the Witch*, Nelkin looks back at the controversial, Michael Myers–less entry with no less love than when she was on set.

The film, in which Nelkin plays assumed heroine Ellie Grimbridge, a lass seeking her father's killers in a town occupied by a warlock (Dan O'Herlihy) and his androids (including *Halloween II*'s Shape, Dick Warlock), has long been the subject of many debates. Rather than focus on the slashing and screaming of nubile teen victims, *Halloween III* uses the theme of the holiday and a truly unsettling, updated electronic score by Carpenter and Alan Howarth from the previous films. Here, attention is on the worldwide phenomenon surrounding a series of masks known as "The Halloween III"— get it?

An evil warlock has placed minuscule pieces of Stonehenge into computer chips inside the masks. As children around the world watch a heavily promoted "Big Giveaway" on All Hallow's Eve, their masks will simultaneously activate, melting the kids' heads off; the remnants exude hordes of bugs and snakes, which will in turn devour the adults. Ellie Grimbridge (Nelkin) and Dr. Daniel Challis (Tom Atkins) are on the hunt for the reason behind her father's skull crushing, and wander onto the sinister plot with only hours to stop it.

Halloween franchise purists have long disowned the film for its lack of storyline connection to the rest of the series, while others argue over its *Invasion of the Body Snatchers* motifs. The scenario is laced with homages to the earlier films (including a mask thrown over a security camera which "sees" through its eyes as Myers did in the original, plus a cameo by Nancy Loomis, now sporting the last name "Kyes"), but the production team's intent was to turn the franchise into a yearly anthology with each film following a new storyline. Public disinterest led to a much smaller box office than anticipated (though its $18 million haul isn't exactly insulting). An uncomfortable, nihilistic conclusion didn't help matters either.

Still, many critics praised producers John Carpenter, Debra Hill and director Tommy Lee Wallace for attempting something new with an established moneymaking series in the wake of the dying slasher subgenre. Additionally, viewing the movie as a stand-alone film, several serious critics agree that *Halloween III* is arguably fascinating and an underrated mix of science fiction and horror.

Nelkin never felt any anguish over the story direction or her leading lady status. "I left [the storyline decisions] to the 'Higher Powers' who were paid to have those concerns," Nelkin says with a smile, though still shaken by the then-recent events of September 11, 2001. "For me it was a worthwhile acting opportunity. Plus, [taking over Jamie Lee Curtis' lead] was an honor."

Nelkin adds she was "not aware of drastic differences" between the filmed script compared to the one which led to a dispute between Nigel Kneale (*Quatermass*) and

Carpenter. Kneale, who penned the original script for *Halloween III*, later requested his name be removed from the film after scores of rewrites severely altered his initial vision. She does admit that Carpenter's involvement in the film "was pretty much 'in name only,' but his name carries a lot of weight."

If there was any turbulence on set, Nelkin claims she never knew of it. "The shoot as a whole was fun, smooth and a great group of people to work with. Tommy Lee Wallace was incredibly helpful and open to discussion on dialogue or character issues. I loved him." In fact, her only moments of tension were with her nude love scene with Scream King Tom Atkins (*Creepshow*).

As a woman (Garn Stephens) in the motel room next door is having her face zapped off by a laser gone awry in a Hal-

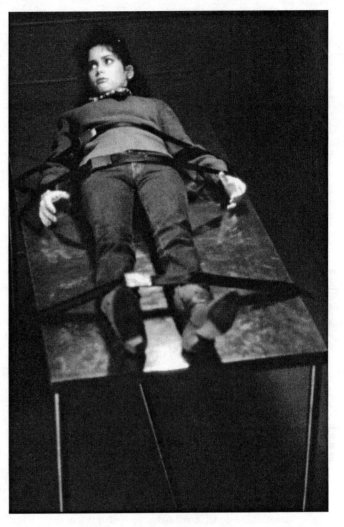

Ellie (Stacey Nelkin) is prepared to experience the doomsday device in *Halloween III: Season of the Witch.*

loween mask (only to have beetles crawl from her gaping jaw moments later), Nelkin and Atkins are engaging in some illicit sex. Though nude for only a few moments, the actress confesses, "I was a little nervous, but it was tastefully done. Doing nude scenes, by the way, is very technical, not titillating … no pun intended."

She recalls a fondness for the character she portrayed, a tough little cookie exuding a deceitful innocence backed by a lot of determination. "Ellie was very spunky and strong-minded. Although I like to think of myself as having these traits, she was written that way in the script."

Though she admits "I was never a groupie for the horror genre," she does acknowledge being fully aware of the extreme popularity of the first two films. "After a makeup artist friend of mine was hired to work on *Halloween III*, he told me about it. I [auditioned] and landed the role."

Certain something is wrong, Ellie (Stacey Nelkin) and Challis (Tom Atkins) go to her murdered father's store where they discover the gruesome *Halloween III* masks.

Seems like a fairly simple story for a thespian who "fell in love with acting at the age of 9, got an agent by 14, was flown out to California at 18 to do the film *California Dreaming* [1979] and just continued from there." The comedy, about a goofy Chicago dude trying to fit into L.A.'s beach community (which also starred Tanya Roberts and Dennis Christopher) unveiled Nelkin to the public, but more attention was brought to the ingenue in the unflattering form of major tabloid controversy throughout the late 1970s.

Rumors persisted the young actress had a love affair with Woody Allen, a relationship put on display in the critically acclaimed 1979 hit *Manhattan*. Nelkin is ready to let the stories die. "There's been a lot written about [our involvement]," she says, "most of which lacks accuracy. Enough said."

With attention to her private life fading in following years, the actress was able to focus on her career both on stage and in front of the cameras. "I started out doing theater and have done it throughout my career," she says, contentedly. She has, however, some dismay over the role she *almost* played as "The Sixth Replicant," a dying android in the science fiction classic *Blade Runner* (1982).

"Mary was a fantastic part," she says with a sigh. "The [creators] were dealing with a writers strike, and the film was already way above budget. So they decided it was cheaper to cut the extra story point. Originally it was between me and Daryl Hannah [*Splash*] for her role, but they thought I was too physically small to convincingly take on Harrison Ford. So they offered me the part of Mary."

Nelkin forged ahead with a steady stream of work in television and film throughout the 1980s and '90s. She had already surfaced on television episodes of *Eight Is Enough* ("a total kick!") and *CHiPS*, plus the TV movies *Like Mom, Like Me*, *The Triangle Factory Fire Scandal*, *The Last Convertible* and *The Chisholms* (which led to a 1980 series). Additional goofball comedies filling her résumé include *Up the Academy*, *Serial* and *Going Ape!*

She snapped up the lead in *Halloween III* and also landed the role of Cora Spencer in the 1982 TV movie *The Adventures of Pollyanna*. Her later TV appearances included *Simon & Simon*, *Finder of Lost Loves*, *The A-Team*, *The Fall Guy*, *Murder, She Wrote*, *Crazy Like a Fox*, *The New Twilight Zone*, *First & Ten* and *Hunter*. Nelkin found herself a hot property following the release of *Halloween III* and acted in a number of non-genre films: *Yellowbeard*, *Get Crazy*, *Sunset Limousine*, *Group Madness* and *The Jerk, Too*.

Towards the end of the decade she found herself in daytime drama as Christy Russell on the short-lived soap *Generations*. The early '90s continued her string of work, in a succession of indie dramas like *Distant Cousins*, *Ride with the Wind*, *Basic Values* and the Oscar-nominated *Bullets Over Broadway*. She says of her character in *Bullets*, "Rita was a sensual Bohemian of the 1920s. Unfortunately, not all of [my scenes] wound up on screen. I only worked directly with Mary-Louise Parker, John Cusack and Rob Reiner, [who] were all terrific."

Halloween III isn't the only film fans remember her for. "*Up the Academy* still gets me a lot of recognition, while for other types of fans it's *Bullets Over Broadway*." Of all her work, she says, "*The Triangle Factory Fire Scandal* is one of my favorites. *Going Ape!* was a lot of fun to do as well, and will be fun for my kids to watch..."

Her latest foray was the lesbian drama *Everything Relative* (1996). The film, about a group of college friends gathering again after fifteen years, was a critical hit. Mick Martin and Marsha Porter wrote of the feature, "You won't find a better or more relevant film about lesbians than this striking independent effort that features top-notch production values, a thoughtful and witty script, plus outstanding performances." Nelkin has bittersweet feelings towards the project.

Portraying her character, Katie Kelser, was an enjoyable opportunity. "She was a strong, opinionated, fun, terrific Jewish lesbian," Nelkin says, then offers, "I would say more positive things had I and the rest of the cast been fully paid."

The experience soured her, and coupled with the start of a family, Nelkin temporarily stepped away from acting. She returned to her native Manhattan and settled down with her family because "it was time to come home. My husband and kids are my love and hobbies. Offer me the right part and I'd consider getting back into the [film] industry, but I'm a full time mom and loving every minute of it. Besides," she adds, "the industry is even more cutthroat now [than when she began]."

So what would the one-time screamer offer in the way of advice to today's ingenues? "Go to college," she suggests. "Get a degree to fall back on. If you go for [a film career], let it be your all-consuming passion. Study with the best people you can and try not to take rejection too personally."

Sleepaway Camp *Cut-Up*

Felissa Rose

"Crazy how paths continue to cross in life, eh?" Felissa Rose begins, referring to our first meeting (August 1998) in an L.A. book store where I worked. Little did I know my entire day ... well, actually, my next two *weeks* would find me floating around the store exclaiming to anyone who would listen, "I met Angela!"

To a generation of slasher aficionados, the image of her beautiful, soft face atop a hairy, naked male body had been seared into our psyche. When she came up to me and asked for assistance, I was almost positive it was her, but hesitant to ask. Then she spoke in her thick Brooklyn accent, and my instincts proved correct. Like a five-year-old child about to ask Santa if he's real, I blurted out, "Are you Felissa Rose?"

Her eyes grew wide with bewilderment and her mouth hung open. I added, "You were in the movie *Sleepaway Camp*, right?" A scream of sheer horror came from her mouth and she ran from the store. As a dozen shoppers stared at me, I figured I'd made her a bit uncomfortable. I've met actors and actresses who want to forget their screen pasts, but this was a bit extreme.

Thirty seconds later she returned. With an embarrassed laughter, she begged, "Who put you up to this?" She looked back and forth for the hidden TV camera. I insisted I was merely a horror geek with love of slasher femmes. She ran from the store a second time.

Another minute passed. She returned with just as much gusto, pointing to two gentlemen and another lovely lady who, until now, I hadn't noticed were staring at me. She asked, "They put you up to this, didn't they?" I insisted they hadn't, and to prove it I gave her a quick rundown of her character's murderous exploits back in 1983. She was determined not to believe this wasn't a prank and ran from the store a third time. Her friends followed.

I went on with my routine, my manager now ready to speak with me about harassing customers. Just in the nick of time, Felissa returned. She was a bit more laid back, but questioned one last time if I had truly recognized her, or if I had been paid to embarrass her by her company. It turned out that she and her friends had just been to dinner where she informed them she had been in a "little" movie called *Sleepaway Camp* and two of them didn't really believe her. She thought this was too much of a coincidence. She also apparently had not been recognized for many years, and didn't think anyone had seen it. Kind of sarcastically I responded, "Are you kidding me? Everyone (my age at least) has seen *that* movie!"

How Felissa Rose could have gone so many years without being recognized is beyond me. Many years since our first meeting, she still maintains an eerie youth. Though now in her early thirties, the actress (who skipped out on 1988's *Sleepaway Camp II: Unhappy Campers* and 1989's *Sleepaway Camp III: Teenage Wasteland* because she was attending college) appears almost identical to the pretty, doe-eyed serial killer with a thick mane of jet black hair and a soft voice she portrayed 20 years ago.

Oddly, the actress and her film became bigger cult items in the few years between our meetings. Though she could not believe she had even one single fan at the time, today Rose and the cast of *Sleepaway Camp* are packing horror conventions. "About two years ago I received a letter from Jeff Hayes, who runs the wonderful website www.sleepawaycampmovies.com. [Suddenly] I saw people [talking about it] on the Internet and got a great thrill out of knowing people had heard of the movie," Rose recounts. "Now, once in a while, teenagers will approach me or friends will tell their own friends they know me, and they're shocked. It's a funny reaction!"

Shot over six weeks in Glen Falls, New York, by writer, director and executive producer Robert Hiltzik, *Sleepaway Camp* rode the coattails of the *Friday the 13th* craze by featuring nubile teens skinnydipping and getting hacked to bloody bits by

Angela (Felissa Rose) looks on as Meg (Katherine Kamhi) tries to convince Paul (Paul DeAngelo) that Angela is hiding a deadly secret in *Sleepaway Camp.*

a killer at Camp Arawak. To keep in the running with the scads of killer-in-the-woods slasher flicks inundating theaters at the time, Hiltzik threw in a couple nifty twists. First, the cast was made up of mostly children. Although characters ranged in age from about 12 to 15, they were still susceptible to the sharp end of a butcher knife.

Second, the kills were inventive. The nasty teens, and even nastier adults, met their ends by beehive, boiling water, a very effective arrow in the throat and a hot curling iron up, *ahem*, a sensitive area. Hiltzik made you want to see these people perish. Most of them were incredibly unpleasant. The more beautiful they were, the meaner they acted and the more horrible their deaths. Adding to the quease factor was an uncomfortable sense of perversion elicited by a creepy cook (Owen Hughes), who referred to the film's 12-year-old girls as "baldies."

There was also a risky homosexual subplot which, though never actually addressed, is obvious throughout the film, from images of Angela's father in the arms of another man to the frequent disrobing of the teen boys. "I'm sure they were intentional. I mean, Angela's dad was blatantly gay. Robert really wanted that out there. I was aware of it and I really think it adds to the story. Angela was used to seeing two men and had to figure out who she was sexually as a person, mainly because of her little (or big) secret."

Nifty Ed French makeup FX also make the film memorable. Snakes crawl out of mouths, heads are chopped off, flesh is boiled away. Then there's the infamous show-stopper finale for which *Sleepaway Camp* is most definitely known. After 20 years and up against the new technology of CGI, many of the FX still come off as fresh and realistic as they did in 1983.

Of her final stance on the beach with her, um, surprise, Rose recalls, "The last scene was supposed to be me wearing a 'prosthetic.' Isn't that funny? Robert spoke with me about it and I agreed. Instead, they had Ed French make a mold of my face [for a mask], which they put on a guy's body. The only problem was they had to find someone 18 or older because of the nudity, and they had to have my body shape. Hello! I was a 13-year-old girl! They had to fit the facial mold which was slim because I have a narrow face. It was a long and arduous process, but they found someone at Albany State College. He got paid well and got really drunk before they filmed the scene!"

Rose, who had only done some theater work and modeling for Dell Books before *Sleepaway Camp*, chuckles again. Her road to unexpected cult star began when she was sent on an audition after her managers heard about the casting call for a "wide-eyed, flat-chested, any ethnicity, 13-year-old girl. [My] managers were great, but they weren't sure if they could find work for a little ethnic girl. When they got word about Robert Hiltzik, they sent me to meet with him. The first audition was great because we hit it off and I got to do a lot of improvisation. I walked out feeling like I'd gotten the role. Then on the second call back I could tell I was going to be Angela. A month after the second audition, my manager said the role was mine if I wanted it."

Considering the very adult topics of murder, transvestites, homosexuality and molestation, one has to wonder what kind of effect the story had on Rose's mind, and why her mother allowed her to take on the role of the killer. "My mom is really cool and didn't mind the subject matter as long as I was safe and didn't have to do anything crazy myself," she explains. "Her only concern was about the killer's hands

Director Robert Hiltzik and star Felissa Rose in August 2002.

and Robert had already decided my hands were too feminine to use. So Jonathan Tierston (who played Angela's ticking time-bomb cousin Ricky) got to do all the killings, because of those oh-so-masculine hands."

"It's funny, because people always wonder if I was screwed up from playing this role and making this film, and the truth is I am…" Rose says with a giggle. "Just kidding! Making a movie is so different from what appears on screen, I didn't have time to realize what a fucked-up situation I'd gotten myself into. (Only joking, Robert!) For me, it was like I really did get to go to *Sleepaway Camp*. I had a great time!"

The actress attributes her ease through the production and her fond memories to "an incredible cast! We were all really close, so unfortunately I don't have any cat fight stories. Katherine Kamhi [Meg] and Karen Fields [Judy] were like my sisters."

She insists there was no age prejudice on set, as everyone treated her "like a little sister. They just wouldn't let me come to the parties in the motel rooms … for which I'll get them back this time around! I've remained in contact with John Dunn [snake-in-the-mouth Kenny] over the past 20 years. Within the past three years I've been close with Robert Hiltzik, Jonathan Tierston and Glenn Ford. Since the *Fangoria* Horror Convention [January 2001] I've been in touch with Loris Sallahian [beehive victim Billy], Tom Van Dell [Mike], Paul DeAngelo [head counselor Ronnie] and Desiree Gould [wacky Aunt Martha]. I'm so lucky to know all these great people again!"

She spent more time with them in fall 2003, as *Sleepaway Camp IV* finally went into production. Though plot details are scarce (Hiltzik is being secretive and has reportedly written four individual scripts, each with a different killer and only one of them involving the character of Angela), what is known is that Ed French returned to the FX department along with Jeffery S. Farley (*Kingdom of the Spiders*) and Christopher Bergschneider (*Final Stab*), while former cast members like Sallahian and Dunn participated in the crew (since their characters perished in the original). Although Tierston, Gould and DeAngelo returned to their roles, Rose acted as the long-overdue sequel's associate producer and casting agent. Does this mean she won't be in front of the camera?

"I can't say ... I really can't," Rose says wincing. "It depends on which script is used. I've always wanted to do the fourth one, so I was really excited when I realized the potential of it happening. I read the scripts for [*II* and *III*] and was asked by Jerry Silva [producer of the first trilogy] to do them, but I wanted to go to college. I had just been accepted into Tisch School of the Performing Arts, NYU, so I got my B.F.A. instead. I've seen the sequels and think they're great. Pamela Springsteen [who took over the role] is an awesome Angela. I'd love to meet her someday and exchange stories."

Will audiences be interested in a sequel to a 20-year-old franchise? "I think they will, because we're old school. It's always fun to see something you haven't seen in almost 20 years come back with a new twist. I think people will be shocked by this one," Rose assures. "It's Robert's twisted little mind at work again, messing with people's heads. The [original film] is still popular because it deals with teenagers and is kind of funny to laugh at because of how '80s it looks!"

(*Left to right*) Ellen Sandweiss (*The Evil Dead*), *Femme Fatales* editor Lisa Coduto and Felissa Rose (*Sleepaway Camp*) at Flashback Weekend Horror Convention, August 2002 (photograph by Jason Paul Collum).

Rose looks back on her *Sleepaway Camp* experience with complete fondness. "It was such a big part of my childhood," she smiles. "It's really hard to look at it objectively. On opening night I went to the theater with all my friends and watched it for the first time with a public audience. It was the best feeling! The energy in the theater was intense. People were really freaked out by the ending. I felt really good about the film."

Rose, who has done a string of independent films (1988's *Another Woman*, 1993's *The Night We Never Met*) and theater work over the years, agrees that the film was a plus for her career, even though she didn't take any major roles following its completion. "It's especially [rewarding] now that it's all come back around. I've been doing interviews, appeared at several conventions … it's been a strange and thrilling ride all these years later."

So why didn't she go after other horror roles once *Sleepaway Camp* started pulling in money at the box

Felissa Rose today.

office? "I didn't think I'd gotten any offers. The film came and went, and no one had called me in. Plus, I never really thought to ride the Scream Queen wave. I just went on with my life. Later I found out I *was* getting offers, but my [former] managers wouldn't send me on the auditions because they were for horror films. They felt it would've been a bad career move. They'd rather have a client who did nothing rather than one who only did horror. They never even told me the offers had come in. Now I have new management and I am going to take advantage of the renewed interest.

"I'd love to do more horror films, and recently got the chance in Dante Tomaselli's *Horror*," Rose says. She's since become the new indie film princess, having filmed *Under Surveillance*, about a madman hunting the residents of an apartment complex (including fellow *Sleepaway* alum Gould), the short horror-comedy cannibalism tale *Grandma's Secret Recipe* and other eye-catching titles like *Zombiegeddon*, *Scary Tales: The Return of Mr. Longfellow*, *Corpses Are Forever* and *Nikos*. She also recently co-starred with *The Evil Dead* alum Ellen Sandweiss in *Satan's Playground* and will reconnect with Tomaselli for an *Apparition*.

As Felissa Rose prepares to become a late-in-coming Scream Queen, she continues to reminisce about her days at *Sleepaway Camp* and confesses to an on-set romance with Tierston. "I had a little love affair with Jonathan, which was a lot for Robert to deal with," she chuckles. "Jonny and I are now best friends, so it's all water under the bridge, as Aunt Martha would say. The hormones were flowing and the age difference didn't help. Jonny was 17 and I was 13, so it ended pretty quickly, but it was a *big* crush for me."

Rose smiles softly and mentions the person who not only eased her through the production, but ultimately changed her life forever. "Robert is a really funny guy," she says. "He seems shy when you first meet him, but that's hardly the truth. I loved working with him. As a director, he was very supportive and thorough in helping the actors portray their characters. Any time I felt unsure of what was going on in a scene, he'd sit and talk about it and really identify what had to happen."

Felissa Rose still can't believe a film 20 years from her past continues to make such a huge impression on horror fans, and her own life. "I guess it's all timing," she evaluates. "Jeff Hayes really found everyone and decided to call Robert Hiltzik when he visited me in New York and from there everything started to come together. I am very thankful to everyone who has put their hearts into the great websites out there and I'm appreciative for them and the other fans for keeping *Sleepaway Camp* alive."

Screaming ... with Laughter

Elvira's Haunted Hills Busts Out

The sharp blade of the pendulum glistens in the moonlight as the shrieks of a nubile woman fill the night air. A deranged count has imprisoned the lass in his dungeon, and death is imminent ... unless the hero—who speaks English even though his mouth doesn't match the spoken words—can save her. "Is this the first of the new series of Hammer films?" you ask with bated breath? No, but it does resemble the Edgar Allan Poe–Vincent Price movies of years long ago. It also holds true to the tradition of exposing ample bosom, supplied enthusiastically by everyone's favorite Mistress of the Dark, Elvira.

It's been many unbearable years since our heroine of corny barroom jokes and knowing winks graced the silver screen. Thanks to determination and—gulp—her own retirement funds, Elvira has finally completed filming of her second motion picture, *Elvira's Haunted Hills*.

It's 1851 in the fictional village of Carpathia, Romania. Desperate to finance her dream of performing in a Paris can-can show, Elvira, broke as usual, and her maidservant Zou Zou (Mary Jo Smith) stop off at Castle Hellsubus for the night. Sure, the castle is creepy, but wait until you meet the residents. There's noise-sensitive Lord Vladimere Hellsubus (Richard O'Brien), his scowl-wearing second wife Ema (Mary Scheer) and his anemic daughter Roxanne (Heather Hopper), for whom fainting and vomiting are favorite pastimes.

All is not right in this world of fog, decaying castles and graveyards. Seems somebody wants Elvira dead because she "coincidentally" resembles Vladimere's dead wife, who "coincidentally" perished exactly ten years ago this very night. Not that the huge pit and pendulum in the basement had anything to do with it....

If this all sounds strikingly familiar ... well, it's supposed to. Scripted by Elvira's alter ego, Cassandra Peterson, and long-time writing partner John Paragon [1985's *Pee-Wee's Big Adventure*], the Mistress' new outing is fashioned after the Roger Corman and Hammer films of the 1950s and '60s. Peterson grew on up on the late-night chills enacted by Vincent Price, so making *Elvira's Haunted Hills* is her ode to childhood.

"I really wanted to get the look and feel of the old Corman movies," Peterson explains. "When I was a child, those were my absolute favorite movies. Vincent Price was my favorite star. I loved movies like *Pit and the Pendulum* [1961] and *The Tomb of Ligeia* [1964]. They scared the hell out of me. They're so old and dorky now, my six-year-old watches them and laughs ... but they were a sense of the time."

The cast of *Elvira's Haunted Hills* (photograph courtesy Queen "B" Productions, 2002).

Aiming to recapture the look of those gothic pics made Sam Irvin (1994's *Oblivion*) the premium choice for director. "It's a homage to so much of what was influential in my childhood," says the man who grew up at the theaters his father and grandfather owned. "I wrote letters to Vincent Price while I was growing up, and he always responded. He even sent compliments when *Guilty as Charged* [Irvin's 1990 directorial debut] came out. Vincent just seemed to be there in the room when we shot [*Elvira's Haunted Hills'*] pendulum scene."

Irvin calls the new Elvira feature his favorite among his own credits, which include co-producing 1998's Oscar-winning *Gods and Monsters*. "It's my dream come true," he says. "I grew up on those movies. This is such a fabulous homage to them."

Ironically, *Elvira's Haunted Hills* has caused the director's career to come full circle. "When *Guilty as Charged* came out, Cassandra was one of the few people to catch it in the theaters ... I think my mother was the other one [*laughs*]. "When I met Cassandra a few years later, she told me how much she loved it and that she'd been hoping to track me down to direct her next Elvira movie ... if it ever happened. I thought it was just cocktail party lip service, but all these years later [and her cameo in his 1993 thriller *Acting on Impulse*] here I am as the director. Cassandra's one of the few people in Hollywood to keep her promises."

With all the enthusiasm, why the long wait for a second Elvira movie? *Elvira, Mistress of the Dark* (1988) did an impressive turn at the box office, and its TV airings, which include a top-rated debut on NBC, continue to score high numbers. Additionally, video sales of Anchor Bay's video release have surpassed 75,000 units over just the past few years. Producer Mark Pierson, Peterson's manager and husband, thinks he can explain the delay.

"It wasn't for a lack of trying," he says. "New World Pictures [who bought the distribution rights from financier NBC] started having problems as we were making the [first] movie. They went bankrupt while *Mistress of the Dark* was in release. Therefore, after just three weeks in 300 theaters, where it had already made $8.5 million [a successful per-screen average by 1988 standards], the film got yanked. So it looked as though the film didn't do well, through no fault of our own. Since people [in Hollywood] don't look at the reason it left theaters early, it made a follow-up more difficult to sell."

As for the movie's subsequent video and television success, Peterson laughs, "I wish I had a nickel for every time it gets aired. Actually, that's about all I get." A curse seemed

Elvira (Cassandra Peterson) on TV's *The Fall Guy*, one of her 100 film-television appearances (photograph copyright 1984, 20th Century Fox).

to float over Peterson and Pierson's heads throughout most of the 1990s. A deal was made in 1991 with Carolco pictures to produce the second chapter, but the company folded just as the picture went into production. The year 1993 saw an opportunity for CBS and 20th Century Fox to launch a weekly Elvira sitcom; a pilot was shot, but never aired.

Peterson remains a bit steamed over the outcome. "It was called *The Elvira Show* and we were positive it was going to go," she reveals. "There was so much hype and publicity and excitement about it. All the network executives came to see it, which is unheard of, then an odd set of occurrences began. The head of the network was ill the week they were deciding which pilots to pick up, so they flew in another guy from New York. He took a look at the pilot and said, 'Who is this Elvira person? I've never heard of her. We can't show this kind of cleavage on national television!' And that was it. It was all over."

She points out that a short time later the family sitcom *Sabrina, the Teenage Witch* debuted with an almost identical plot. Peterson acknowledges that the Sabrina character is based on a comic book, but maintains the show has more in common with the Elvira pilot. "I was one of two wacky aunts along with Katherine Helmond," she says, "and we were trying to raise a teenage girl just discovering she was a witch. We even had a talking black cat voiced by John Paragon! These are things on the Sabrina show, but *not* in the comic book. So I'm a little bitter."

The actress, then speaks of attempts to get a new feature film made based on three individual scripts, including the much-mentioned *Elvira vs. the Vampire Women*. Ultimately, however, she and Pierson realized the fate of Elvira's next big-screen appearance rested in their hands, not Hollywood's. "My career does better outside of the Hollywood system," Peterson admits. "If I had to wait on decisions from executives, I'd be busing tables for money. That's why I'm glad we financed this new movie on our own…"

Peterson and Pierson dug into their own pockets—with some help from Pierson's folks—to get the movie made. They were simply tired of trying to convince executives and investors that Elvira was a lucrative commodity. She remains the best-received celebrity at Disneyland, has the best-selling Halloween costume of all time, performed to sold-out crowds at all of her Knott's Berry Farm shows, and her guest appearances on over 100 television shows earned them the highest ratings of each season. Let's not forget her own hit TV series *Movie Macabre*, which aired new episodes from 1981 to 1986 and continued in reruns until 1993.

Funding the feature themselves allowed the couple to take complete creative control. "We had to create and organize a little mom and pop business to get it done. It's great, because nobody tells us what to do. The movie is entirely our own. That's why I like this one better. John and I wrote this exactly as we wanted." Referring back to *Mistress of the Dark*, she adds, "Everything we'd write, someone would tell us to change. 'Take these characters out … put these in.' They forced me to add those teenagers to the script, because they believed no teens would come to see it otherwise. Yeah … just like when they didn't see *Alien* because there weren't any teens in it, right?"

She felt *Mistress of the Dark*'s script was watered down, yet insists she's relatively happy with it. Still, she feels *Elvira's Haunted Hills* is more true to the character. "It's pure Elvira … with no executive input."

Determination—and money—in place, Peterson joined Paragon in completing a script after "many hours of rewatching old Gothic horror films." They made sure to fill the script with knowing winks to fans, yet keep the jokes comprehensible to younger audiences unaware of the subgenre.

They also relied on a little superstition. "Cassandra, John and I went to The Groundlings [the LA-based theater troupe where Peterson got her start] for Phil Hartman's memorial," Pierson recalls. "Phil's brothers had placed his ashes in some Magic 8 Balls and gave them to his closest friends. That night, John had a dream about making the movie, and when he woke up he asked the 8 Ball if we should do it and the message read 'Definitely Yes.' So we did."

To save money, Pierson says that "we reverted to Horror Movie Making 101: Set the movie in one location [a castle]. Then we changed our state of minds from telling others 'We're trying to make a movie' to 'We are making a movie.'"

Pierson and Peterson flew to Italy in the summer of 2000 to scout locations, but discovered every place they liked was unaffordable. Luckily, Pierson's brother-in-law Robert Dornhelm (director of ABC's *Anne Frank* mini-series) was from Romania and knew how cheaply a movie could be made in the impoverished country, which offered low rates in an attempt to build up a local film culture. Pleased with their findings, Pierson and Peterson returned to the U.S. with a preliminary budget (around $1.5 million).

The couple initially planned to hand the directing reins to writer Paragon, but a scheduling conflict forced the writer to bow out. Dornhelm was subsequently considered, but was already connected to *Anne Frank*. Then they recalled the cocktail party conversation with Sam Irvin. "I called Sam to ask him about shooting in Romania, because he'd done *Oblivion 1* and *2* there," Pierson recalls. "We liked Sam's sensibilities and knew he would be right."

Peterson concurs "He was a dream come true. He had so much of the same mindset. He *knew* these old movies. He recited *Pit and the Pendulum* to me word for word. He loves the genre and grew up with it. It was a blessing to have him direct. We never argued about anything; Sam totally saw my vision. He was open to any ideas and changes. We just kept thinking along the same lines."

Next came choosing the cast. With Lord Hellsubus modeled after Vincent Price and Christopher Lee, it seemed only natural to approach Lee to take on the role. "Because of how fast we were shooting and the extremely long hours, plus how physical the role was, age became a factor. I've met Christopher before and absolutely adore him, but we needed somebody younger because it was so demanding." Other actors, like Mick Jagger (!) and Richard Chamberlain (!!) were also approached, but the decision finally came down to hiring *The Rocky Horror Picture Show*'s Richard O'Brien. Peterson says, "He really nailed it. He was perfect."

Other roles were filled with comedic actors like Mary Scheer (*MAD TV*), Scott Atkinson, Mary Jo Smith and Heather Hopper (*Saved By the Bell*). Peterson found the cast to be hysterically talented. She notes of former child actress Hopper, "We had tons of girls coming in at the last minute to audition for the role of 'anorexic girl.' When Heather walked in, Sam and I looked at each other and thought, 'She's not really right for the role.' Then she wound up blowing us away with her performance. She's a real pro and a total professional. She brought so much more to the character than we thought there was going to be."

Peterson soon found the cast was more than willing to improvise on set. "All the actors are fine comedians," she enthuses. "They all had a great sense of timing, so most of their improv was through body language rather than dialogue. I appealed to them to [make changes]. Richard O'Brien improvised the most." She laughs a moment, admitting, "We had occasional head-butting when he'd change a line and I'd beg him not to, but ultimately everything came out great. He did a fantastic job and added things which were really funny."

Peterson wants to stress that *Elvira's Haunted Hills* does hew closely to the genre it simultaneously spoofs. "This is like a true Gothic horror movie classic," she exclaims in her best Valley Girl impersonation. "Yes! That's what I'm going to call it! I like that! The first film had a little bit of horror going on around Elvira. She was like a little fish out of water in Everytown, U.S.A. In this one, she's a little fishy in water. She's in her element. As a horror movie, this one will play better."

"I tried to make it look like an old Hammer movie," Irvin adds. "Everyone assumed we shot in Romania to use their castles, but it's not true. The Hammer films never used real castles. They were always these great matte paintings or optical shots and models. It gave them a fairy-tale quality.

"I didn't want to use a real castle," he continues. "A lot of them are in the middle of nowhere, and to light them at night is just a nightmare. Plus, from a budgetary standpoint, it's too expensive and requires too much labor. Thankfully we managed to make the [real] castle look a little fake … like it's out of *Grimm's Fairy Tales*. I wanted the fantasy."

Between August and November 2000, Irvin, Peterson and Pierson found the fantasy becoming a reality … quicker than they'd planned. The Internet played a key role in keeping the pre-production moving. "Radu Corciova and his wife Iyanna e-mailed photos of set designs on a daily basis," Pierson explains. "They had people working around the clock and it all came out fantastic. So communication was fine." Filmed entirely in Romania over five exhausting weeks of 12 to 14-hour days, the production wrapped just three days before Christmas.

Peterson is quick to acknowledge the dedication of those who worked with her. She also notes the positives and negatives of their location. "The craftsman take real pride in their work. They're not spoiled. They work twice as hard as people [in America], and without benefits like craft service. [Plus], financially, Romania made it easier. We never could have shot this movie in the U.S. So the price was right, but some of their equipment was old and their studios were under-equipped, with no heating, and many supplies just weren't available. It's just a very poor country. We ate cabbage and potatoes every day for breakfast, lunch and dinner. Plus, I'd have to apply my makeup with barely any lighting." Ultimately, the old tungsten fixtures did prove somewhat of a blessing in her eyes. "They gave our film that wonderful old-fashioned look," she claims. "Still, it wasn't easy."

While everything was completed successfully, Peterson and company wanted to make sure their product would be accessible to all audiences. "There aren't as many risqué elements in this film as there were in the first," says Peterson. "We want it to be more appealing to younger audiences, like ten and up. Of course, there's plenty of boob jokes, which have to be there because she *is* Elvira, after all."

She laughs a moment, then admits, "We really wanted a PG rating. Even though she's sexy, Elvira really is a PG person. Well … maybe PG-13, but she'll never get into R-rated material. I don't want to make a movie parents won't let their children see. Still, we want to keep it fun for the adults. Probably the sexiest thing in the film is a little dance number, but it's nothing dirty."

With the tone slightly different from the sassier *Mistress of the Dark*, plus the lack of returning characters and a different period setting, *Elvira's Haunted Hills* isn't a true sequel. "It's really completely different," Peterson confirms. "I think of it as one in a series. Kind of like Jim Varney's *Ernest* movies. They were a series, but weren't related to each other."

Pierson explains that each new Elvira movie takes place in a different time period, so eventually all of the films will create the character's entire life story. "We're hoping the movie creates more of a myth for the character," he asserts. "Now we know she's existed at least since 1851 in Carpathia, not 1981 in a little L.A. television studio. It builds a whole extra dimension to the character."

Peterson is delighted by the idea, but admits, "I honestly don't know how many movies I have left in me. We could always have somebody else take over the character, just like they did with the *Batman* and James Bond movies. I'm still hoping to make at least another one or two before I retire." She chuckles, then adds, "Retirement is *much* further down the line. Besides, *Elvira's Haunted Hills* was made with the money Mark and I had saved for retirement, so we have to get it back. We've basically been working for free this whole past year."

The year 2001 marked the twentieth anniversary of the birth of Elvira: In late 1981, after Peterson was sent on an audition by a friend to become a hostess of trashy and cheesy late-night horror films, Elvira became an immediate cultural sensation, thanks in large part to her portrayer's then-whimsical idea to give her a Valley Girl attitude. So why has horror's version of Marilyn Monroe and Madonna endured for two decades?

"Tying yourself to a national holiday is really good way to go. I tried to horn in on Easter too," Peterson laughs. "Halloween comes around every year, and therefore, so does Elvira. I honestly thought it would last only a year or two. I figured I'd make some money (less than $350 weekly before taxes for the first several years), then get another gig. I'm just as surprised at her success as everyone else. She is one of those fortunate accidents."

Pierson, who has managed Peterson's career since the beginning and helped her obtain all of the rights to the character in place of raises from her original bosses, adds, "What's so appealing about Elvira is her personality. She says some really corny jokes at times, but she says them in a way people know she's 'going there.' Her attitude just gives the worst old jokes fresh life. Statistically, her numbers are strong across the board in every category: men, women, black, Hispanic, white, gay, straight, all religions and age brackets ... except for one. People with an annual income of $150,000 and above. We have a theory those are the executives who don't realize the market which is right in front of them."

Over 20 years, two full-length features, over 100 guest spots, a hit website (www. elvira.com), video games, thousands of personal appearances ... does Peterson ever tire of putting on the extreme makeup ("In the beginning I was so trampy! They had me do episodes of my show standing under a street light. You can imagine how that made me look!"), tight dress ("I became a little less trashy and my audience expanded. I guess I sold out, but what the hell!") and the beehive wig ("I can tell what year it was by how high my hair is! In 1987 I looked like Marge Simpson!")? "Yeah, when I was putting on make up at four A.M. with no lights," she says rolling her eyes. "Generally, I really like being Elvira. I don't get tired of the character. I love her.

"People tell me I should do other things, but I've made a living off of her and enjoyed it. Why would I do something else? I'd have to go on auditions and deal with all that crap again! Ugh! Forget it! I'm very comfortable with her, plus she gives me some sort of release ... being able to get my ya-yas out there. I can be this unique character and act the way I want and people give me their gratitude and love. It's a wonderful feeling!"

So exactly how long does she hope to continue playing Elvira? "What time is it now?" she says in jest. "It's hard to say, because every year I say I'm not going to do it within a year, then the year comes and goes, and I'm still doing it. I guess I'll continue as long as I don't look pathetic in my dress. I do hope I have a lot of years left, though the other day my daughter asked my husband, 'When mommy dies, can I be Elvira?,' and I'm thinking, 'Great. Now she's trying to bump me off ... probably poisoning my coffee or something.' Plotting already. Six years old and she already has her eyes on it."

The main reason Peterson, Pierson and Irvin brought *Elvira's Haunted Hills* to fruition? Pierson sums up, "If we were to retire this year without having done the movie, and didn't do anything further, I'd feel like we'd gone out with a whimper. I want Elvira to go out with a bang. There are still so many great ideas, plans and projects we want to accomplish. That's what really propelled us to put our retirement egg at risk to make this movie. We felt we owed it to Elvira, her legacy and her fans."

Elvira's Hills Are Still Haunted

It's amazing how quick a year can pass, especially when crazed with personal appearances and jetting around the nation to promote a feature. Such is the case for screamdom's Queen, the Mistress of the Dark herself, Elvira.

Actually, Elvira has had it fairly easy this year ... it's her alter ego, Cassandra Peterson, who's been doing all the leg work for the Mistress' second feature film, *Elvira's Haunted Hills*. "I've been to over 20 cities so far to promote the movie and have another 20 or so to go," Peterson begins, as she grabs a few moments of relaxation. "I attend all the film festivals, conventions, charity screenings, etc. I introduce the film, meet the fans and sign autographs. I also do tons of press in each city–TV, newspaper, radio and magazine interviews. I've had an incredibly busy schedule over the past few months. I have no idea what time zone I'm living in."

Peterson isn't doing this alone. Manager and husband Mark Pierson, who executive-produced the film, has been equally bogged down with travel, plus putting together screenings and personal appearances for his star, and, oh yeah, trying to get the film distributed....

"This was *not* the original plan," Pierson smirks, a tinge of disappointment, and disgust, in his voice. "In February 2001 we had screenings in Los Angeles for the distributors, both majors and minors, looking for a distribution deal. I went through this process being very wary, knowing what the deal is in this town. It's rigged against the filmmakers and investors. 'Points' mean nothing. I know the tricks they play in their accounting. I didn't want to fall victim to [it]. The first movie [1988's *Elvira, Mistress of the Dark*] [grossed] north of $20 million in home video alone, which we should have been entitled to a portion of, but we got nothing. That's normal. That's how it goes in Hollywood.

"I went and had these screenings and thought, 'Well, if I made this movie for $1 and can sell it to these distributors for $2, then I've made my profit. I've made my deal. That's a business.' What I learned is studios are used to paying about 20 cents on the dollar, so I would be losing right away. The game would be over. Now, had I taken one of those deals it may have gotten the movie onto 2,000 screens and had millions paid for advertising, but for me, it would be over. I would have lost a lot of money and never [received] anything else. So, not having the deep pockets other companies have, I figured we could start distributing the film with this grass roots campaign, to get word of mouth started."

A look of satisfaction crosses Pierson's face as he adds, "We started going out to sci-fi, horror and comic book conventions, film festivals, gay and lesbian film festivals, AIDS charities... We will have built a national campaign city by city going with the videotape and our suitcase and playing our movie. We've been getting good radio and TV play and print in newspapers, so it's built a lot of awareness while costing us very little money. However, this approach was never our original plan ... it just sort of evolved into this and took on a life of its own. I realized, as the investor, I'm the only one really standing to gain or lose anything. No one else is going to champion this movie for me and Cassandra."

As it turns out, Pierson and Peterson were both able to thumb their noses at Hollywood executives. Thanks in great part to a huge opening in L.A. over Fourth of July weekend 2002, followed by front page acknowledgments in the film industry's lead trade papers *Variety* and *The Hollywood Reporter*, *Elvira's Haunted Hills* has since expanded to regular theatrical screenings nationwide at least through Halloween and beyond its video-DVD debut in early October 2002.

"I need to be sure to give Cassandra just as much credit, because I

Elvira carries on the hysterical tradition of bad barroom jokes and offers homages to AIP horror films in her comedy *Elvira's Haunted Hills* (photograph courtesy Queen "B" Productions, 2002).

book 'em, but she's the one who goes everywhere and does the promotions," Pierson stresses. "I know we seem to be following the paths of people like William Castle [1958's *House on Haunted Hill*] who took their films and literally drove them from city to city to get them seen, but honestly we're not setting out to follow anyone's footsteps. We're just reinventing them as we go."

A Sam Irvin–directed ode to the Vincent Price–Edgar Allan Poe–based films of the 1960s, it finds Elvira–circa 1851– spending the night in a castle inhabited by the macabre Hellsubus clan, who love spending time with the Pit and the Pendulum in their secret dungeon. The horror-comedy is finally receiving its due, but Peterson isn't fully satisfied, feeling it has more of an audience to reach.

The actress says, "I still can't say for sure that it is a success ... we haven't seen any [money] yet. [However], from the response we've been getting at our various screenings around the country, I have a very good feeling about the film.

"It's definitely still a struggle. From now through early fall, we'll continue to screen it around the country. In October, the video and DVD come out and during that month I think we'll really get a good idea of how well it will do. However, next year there's the foreign market..."

Peterson rolls her eyes, aware that there's so much more work to do. It's the reaction from fans, however, which keeps the eternally perky and youthful comedienne trudging forward. "The fans really seem to love it," she shines. "They've been screaming and laughing very enthusiastically throughout the film. Audiences have begun clapping even before I bend over and they see 'Applause' written on my butt!"

She laughs, adding, "Traffic is way up on our Internet site (www.elvira.com). We're getting 40,000 unique visitors a week. Sales of merchandise have gone way up as well."

With the film clearly a hit in both the theatrical market and the film festival circuit, plus critical praise coming from audiences and critics, why the struggle to get Hollywood to pick up on it? "These days, major studios just aren't picking up small independent fare," Peterson divulges. "They're all geared toward the blockbuster. Have you seen any of the majors release a nice, little movie lately?"

Pierson concurs, "[The major studios] are just not built to operate that way any more. The big studios only want to release big movies. It's become franchise entertainment. There is no middle-budget movie business in Hollywood any more. It's completely gone."

Peterson continues to threaten to retire her black wig and form-fitting dress. Many began to speculate about her retirement more as a result of her frequent appearances out of costume while promoting the film, opting to expose her natural long red tresses instead, and stoked by the cancellation of her annual performances at Knott's Berry Farm throughout the Halloween 2002 season. The Marilyn Monroe of horror, however, reassures she's not quite through with cracking dumb barroom jokes and playing up juvenile humor.

"There are different reasons [I've appeared at parades and other appearances out of costume]. I'm appearing at screenings as myself because I'm not only the star, but the writer and co-financier of the film, so I feel when I'm out there promoting it, Cassandra can speak about the film with much more credibility than Elvira can. Elvira has a tendency to just crack jokes and act goofy.

"The parade was all about comfort. I did the Tournament of Roses Parade and nearly froze my chi-chis off in January. The last parade I did before the West Hollywood Gay Pride Parade was in the Palm Springs desert in the middle of the day. I was dressed as Elvira, and thought I would die from a heat stroke before the parade ended. I vowed that day never to do another parade in that get-up! I forced a poor drag queen–double to suffer ... she loved it," Peterson exclaims with a howl.

Regarding her Knott's vacancy, Peterson explains, "Two reasons: First and most importantly I need to be out there promoting *Elvira's Haunted Hills*, not stuck down in Orange County, California, for September and October.

"Second, theme parks in general have really been hurting since 9/11 and Knott's decided to cut back on their Halloween Haunt budget this year. One of the ways was by asking me to move to a smaller theater, which I declined. I can't say I blame them, but I didn't want it to seem like I couldn't fill the main theater. All the shows I've done at Knott's have always been well attended, and I felt like moving to a smaller venue would reflect badly on Elvira."

Peterson remains amazed at her creation's enduring popularity since she was "born" in 1981 as the hostess of *Movie Macabre*, a horror movie–themed show produced by an L.A. based indie television station. Pierson believes he knows why the character has remained a fan favorite, and why she has become a business entity unto herself.

"She's funny, witty, human, sexy, flirtatious, campy, self-deprecating, her own boss … what's not to like about her?" he questions with an admiring smile. "One thing I appreciate more and more is that her humor is dark, but it's very broad. She's plays it off as 'dumb,' but it's intelligently done. It appeals to children and adults.

"She's incorporated a lot of cinema history into her style. I can look at jokes and routines and realize, 'Hey, that's the Three Stooges,' or 'That's Jackie Gleason…' –all these influences and references she's studied and learned. She's constantly honed and built this character for over 23 years and just gets better at it. I really admire her professionalism. When [*Elvira, Mistress of the Dark*] appeared on television, she had to see it on TV. She wanted to see it with commercials so she could get a sense of the real time of it. With both Elvira movies, she had to see them with audiences [multiple times] so she could see what they liked about them, and how they responded to them. The character endures because of Cassandra and everything she's put into it."

Pierson acknowledges that Elvira's new feature has certainly had an added effect on her merchandising as well. "We've kept pushing her for the past year because of the movie, so we need to keep her visible … then, who knows?" he shrugs. "The industry is full of false retirements—Kiss, the Eagles, Frank Sinatra… Cassandra doesn't want to go down the path of appearing at supermarkets and little events. If *Elvira's Haunted Hills* does well enough where we've made our money back, and then some, so that we had a cushion and didn't have to mortgage our house [they did, and also spent most of their income plus some of their family's financing the Romanian-lensed feature and most of its publicity costs], then we'll consider going into a third movie."

A third Elvira romp? Could fans really be so lucky? Peterson breathes deep. "I just have to see if I can get through this one first! From inception to the foreign market, the whole thing will take at least three years to complete. I'd love to do more Elvira movies … perhaps a whole series. You know, *Elvira Goes to Prison*, *Elvira Goes to Hell*, etc., but I can't even stand to think about it at this point!"

Pierson adds, "It really depends on how much money this one makes. I wouldn't push myself this close to the edge again. I fell under a real time issue. It's no secret Cassandra just turned 50. When we started shooting this in 1999, she's telling me 'Look, I'm not getting into this costume any more after 50…' and I don't blame her. I support her in her decision. Like Marlene Dietrich, Greta Garbo, Cary Grant and other actors who bowed out early while they still looked beautiful, I think it's all right and appropriate, and it's certainly their right to choose. We want Elvira to go out with a bang. I couldn't live with myself if we didn't make this movie. I'm glad we made it.

"I don't have any regrets. I risked my health and my wife's health and our financial future and marriage. I put a lot of things on the line. So I feel we're entitled to whatever success this movie has…"

With the film heading towards a decent profit, *Elvira's Haunted Hills* remained in theatrical release beyond its video-DVD debut from Goodtimes Entertainment, which has helped back the duo's Queen B Productions with some of the financing for publicity. "We're hoping it'll become some sort of cult film like *The Rocky Horror Picture Show* [1975] or, more recently, *Hedwig and the Angry Inch* [2001]," Pierson says. "There is a market out there. Nothing would please me more than to have this continue to play theatrically, because I would love for people to have the opportu-

nity to see this film in a theater. I would love to see this play on 2000 screens simultaneously, if it didn't cost me giving up my copyright, having to bill me millions of dollars and gypping me out of millions more … that's what the average person doesn't know [about the deals which would have to be made with a major distributor]."

Peterson is aware that her duties are far from over, as *Elvira's Haunted Hills* have carried her into 2003. "The movie seems to be taking up most of my time and energy at this point, and I feel it will still be doing that well into next year. When I finally come up for air, I'd like to begin work on my autobiography, which I've been putting off for years because of lack of time."

In spite of headaches, Pierson insists he would do it again. "When Cassandra and I look at *Elvira's Haunted Hills*, we're pleased with it because, unlike the

Elvira's creator and alter ego, Cassandra Peterson, humors her *Elvira's Haunted Hills* director (Sam Irvin) in a 2001 photograph shot by Denice Duff (courtesy Denice Duff).

first movie, this one is ours," he confirms. "Everything which wound up on screen was what we wanted there. We [and director Irvin and co-screenwriter John Paragon] didn't have to deal with any outside influences. [It] is truly an Elvira movie."

As an added bonus, Peterson happily reports she has one less concern thanks to another hit movie of this past summer. It seems that the Mistress' princess, Sadie, was vying for her mother's throne at this time last year, having asked her father (reported in *Fangoria* #212), "Daddy, when mommy dies, can I be Elvira?" Peterson is relieved to announce the pressure is off. "Oh, no. She's over that," Peterson smiles. "This year she wants to be Spider-Man!"

Julie Brown

She's a woman of many disguises, displaying the best of her form in most every media format imaginable ... on television (MTV'S *Just Say Julie*, *Strip Mall*), in movies (*Clueless*, *Medusa: Dare to Be Truthful*) and even song ("The Homecoming Queen's Got a Gun," "'Cause I'm a Blonde"). They all end with the same result: immense, pain-inducing laughter.

For 20 years, Julie Brown, an adorably spunky self-described "henna head," has brandished one of the comedic medium's most recognizable, and scathingly funny personalities. Her targets: Usually among the most famous, or infamous of celebrities including Debra Winger ("Of course you're fan ... *shut up!*"), Tonya Harding ("I'm gonna go out there and kick her ass...") and, of course, Madonna ("Do you know how almost fired you are...?").

She's acted along side Elvira, Linda Blair, Lily Tomlin, Victoria Jackson, Jon Bon Jovi, Geena Davis, Jim Carrey, Jeff Goldblum, Sandra Bernhardt, Courtney Cox Arquette ... even Mrs. Brady's alter ego, Florence Henderson. Not bad for a true born-and-bred "valley girl" who, although her family's third generation of show business, never really knew she could use her tweaked sense of humor and talent towards a career.

"My great grandfather was a director and an actor, my grandfather was a film editor, my uncle was a prop guy and my parents met at NBC," she begins, seated at Peet's Coffee in Studio City, California. "It's pretty unusual to have so many generations in the business."

Brown says her sense of humor is indeed a family trait, but adds, "My brothers (one works in the industry as an assistant cameraman, the other has written for television shows like *The X-Files* and *Quantum Leap*) are really funny, but they're not performers. I think we all share in common being a little bit twisted and funny. I find them hilarious."

With so much family in the industry, it seems odd the actress never considered entering the field. "I always did it," she reminisces, "but I never knew I could do it for a career. I was always in the shows in high school and college. When I was really young I was in a Kodak commercial. [The producers] came to my school and discovered me."

This brief taste of stardom didn't last long. "My parents, because they'd been around show business so long, thought everyone who grew up in the business was so seriously damaged they wouldn't let me do it afterwards. They didn't want me to become Judy Garland," she giggles. She loved the experience, but understands her parents' motives.

Her first foray into creating her own material was in high school when "we did a rock version of *Alice in Wonderland* ... I wrote all the music and performed as well. I always did multiple things, but never thought I could do it with my life because my parents always told me I couldn't. So when I went to college, I was an anthropology major and was really into science."

She considered herself a good student during her time at Northridge College in California, but Brown's creative side was about to poke through the stacks of reading material. She finally realized, "It was *soooo* boring and hideous. I had to really study and wasn't into it at all. At the same time I was in a Readers Theater production of some play and was reading poetry. It had been two years since I'd been on stage and I just *loved* it! So I told my parents 'I *have* to do this! I don't care....' Once I told them, they were really cool with it. I think because they'd always been around it they were hesitant, but once they saw me getting into it they said, 'Go ahead.'"

Soon after shifting majors and schools, Brown was introduced to a fellow thespian who would forever change, and ultimately begin, her career as a comedienne. "I first met Charlie [Coffee — her long time friend and co-writer of much of her material] in acting school when I was performing with somebody else at a school function. Charlie had performed in a summer stock and I sat down to ask him advice on where this other guy and I could go perform, and Charlie and I hit if off," she says, beaming.

The friendship quickly blossomed and by coincidence, "the other guy ended up dropping out of school. So Charlie and I just started writing and performing together at school. Charlie was a year ahead of me and had this third year project. His was the first class at ACT [American Conservatory Theater] to take this particular program [two years was the average] and there were only six or eight students, so they each got to do their own show."

It was at this point that their on-stage charisma and antics paid off. Brown remembers, "Most people did these really literary and theatrical things, but Charlie and I did the most stupid comedy stuff and everybody went nuts. I did [skits] like [a woman] eating coffee-flavored douche who has an orgasm [a routine replicated on *Just Say Julie*] ... it was really out there."

The ingénue discovered that "people loved it and we got booked right then. I was so excited! We just started performing in nightclubs after that [event]. Then there was a point where Charlie just didn't want to do it any more, so I carried it on my own, but we remained writing partners. Acting is just not his thing he needs to do. He likes writing."

Though Coffee preferred to remain off-stage and behind the camera, he still manages to pop up on each of her projects if even just for a few moments. On *Just Say Julie* he frequently stepped into frame as her stage manager who, throughout the course of the show, manages to be physically assaulted in one way or another. He was also seen in Brown's *Medusa: Dare to Be Truthful* (1992), *Attack of the 5'2" Women* (1994) and came close to appearing on her comedy series *Strip Mall*. Brown sadly states, "We never got around to it because he was always too busy [as a writer-producer], which is a shame because he's a very funny performer."

Proving her own merits alone on stage, the stand-up comedienne found herself landing gigs in San Francisco, which Brown says "was all really experimental. I was just doing everything like making up songs and characters and sketches. It was really fun, especially in San Francisco, because as soon as I started performing I got a gay following." It was also during this period that Brown received her first true "big break" thanks to a certain famous audience member.

"The first acting job I got paid for was ... in one of those [educational] films about 'date rape.' I played the girl and was horrified," she laughs. "My first [Screen Actors Guild] job, however, was a role in *The Incredible Shrinking Woman* [1981] starring Lily Tomlin. She saw my act in San Francisco when I was performing with Charlie. I wrote her a letter [which] she gave to [*Batman Forever* director] Joel Schumacher and they had me come in."

Brown smiles as she recalls

Julie Brown's first on-screen role was in 1981's *The Incredible Shinking Woman* (photograph courtesy PLPR, Inc.).

Tomlin's determination to get her featured in the film, a comedic take on Richard Matheson's classic sci-fi novel *The Shrinking Man*. "I guess she told them they should give me a little part in the movie," Brown believes, "so they gave me a role as a housewife talking about laundry on a television set. It was only a couple lines, but it was so incredible! So, Lily Tomlin got me my SAG card! It's weird, because you normally think [stars] wouldn't pay attention to something like [a fan letter]. I worked with her again on an episode of *Murphy Brown* and she was really sweet. She's so talented and amazing."

Brown spent the next several years bouncing between her stand-up routines and small roles in films like the Clint Eastwood-Sandra Locke comedy *Any Which Way You Can* (1980), then picked up bigger roles in *Bloody Birthday* (1983), a slasher film of the era which found her as the eldest sister to a soulless ten-year-old girl, and the hit comedy *Police Academy 2: Their First Assignment* (1985). Then there were the guest spots on a number of popular television shows like *Laverne & Shirley, Happy Days, Cheers, Buffalo Bill, The Jeffersons* and *Newhart*. Then, one sunny afternoon, a thought came to the comedienne's mind which would launch her career into another unforeseen path ... music.

"It was really bizarre how it began," Brown laughs, still seemingly amazed by the initial thought and eventual transition. "I was doing stand-up by myself and was starting to get frustrated because I kept finding it had the same basic cynical attitude. A lot of the women doing stand-up were using self-deprecating humor and I thought it was so boring and not theatrical.

"After about six months I was going nuts and struggling to come up with something different. Then one day I was driving down the Hollywood Freeway and the song "The Homecoming Queen's Got A Gun" just popped into my head. I sat down and worked with Charlie and another music guy to get it done, then started performing it in my act. I just wanted to do something which was more than just some jokes."

The song became a hit on the comedy circuit, then, once produced as a single, escalated Brown to the next level of fame. Still expressing surprise that the song went national, Brown remembers, "It was the first thing I'd done where people really knew my name and it was a national thing. Rhino [Records] had started releasing it in certain areas of the country and it was becoming this cult hit. I'd already done episodes of [TV], but people don't know who you are from those kinds of parts. So the record was the first thing I'd done where I got a lot of attention for myself.

"The really interesting thing is because the songs were so theatrical, Warner Bros. asked me to come in and pitch them movie ideas! So I pitched them the idea for *Earth Girls Are Easy* because the song was on the album and everything the movie is about was in that song. And they bought it! All because of that first record."

The record in question was a five-song EP titled "Goddess in Progress" which also contained the catchy, equally hilarious tunes "I Like 'Em Big and Stupid," "Will I Make It Through the '80s?" and, perhaps the singer's best known hit, "'Cause I'm a Blonde." Warner Bros. went on to buy the rights to the album (several of the songs were re-released on the *Earth Girls* soundtrack) and gave her a new album deal but, as Brown recalls, "I still had to convince Seymour Stein of Sire Records [part of Warner Bros.] to do a whole second album, which was an entirely different episode of insanity."

The insanity came in the release of "Trapped in the Body of a White Girl." The sophomore effort reissued "Homecoming Queen" and "I Like 'Em Big and Stupid," but added eight new songs, including the title track. The songs were a mix of 1980s love ballads like "Time Slips Away" and "Callin' Your Heart," which were countered by the campy confections "Boys Are a Drug," "Every Boy's Got One," "Shut Up and Kiss Me" and the hilarious rock tune "Girl Fight Tonight."

Though "Trapped" was another hit, the comic actress turned unexpected cult hit singer never did a third official album. "I'm kind of horrified by the music business now," she laughs. "I've done songs since then, though, like in *Medusa* and other specials. "It's so weird because you couldn't tell somebody to do all this to get attention. You couldn't write it down, because in show business you can't map [success and fame] out at all. Everyone I know got into the business in completely different ways. There's no *one* way to do it. It's usually out of nowhere."

As her original songs brought her to the notice of Warner Bros., Brown got her first taste of the highs, lows and all-out chaos by taking on the role of screenwriter to pen (along with Charlie Coffee and then husband Terrence E. McNally) the sci-fi comedy *Earth Girls Are Easy*. The road from its mid–80s inception to its final theatrical release in 1989 proved taxing on the performer, who also starred in the film as outrageous, over-sexed hairdresser "Candy."

"It was a fucking nightmare," she exclaims and bursts into laughter, rolling her eyes. "It started off as a starring vehicle for me. I worked on it for two years ... 18

drafts ... and they kept saying 'Just one more draft ... one more and it will get made. We promise.' I'm working on this with Charlie and my ex-husband who is not a writer [but is part of the project] because he paid for part of the album to be produced and decided he should be involved in writing the script. So that was a nightmare in itself."

Getting the film — about a group of furry, rainbow-colored aliens (Jeff Goldblum, Jim Carrey, Daman Wayans) who crashland in Valley girl Geena Davis' swimming pool and run loose in the streets of Los Angeles — to maintain Brown's original vision proved just as taxing. "We finally attached a director, Julien Temple, who wanted to add so much to the film [that] the budget became so large Warner Bros. said I couldn't star in it," discloses Brown, who was supposed to play the lead role of Valerie ultimately given to Davis. "So I had to go into this huge showdown with my manager and the head honchos at Warner Bros. My manager said, 'Look, they're not going to make it with you, so you've got to figure out what you're going to do.'"

A clause in her contract ultimately helped the disgruntled creator. "I had the power to not let the movie get made, according to the contract," she reveals. "So this was a big deal. I could stop the whole movie. I realized what I had to do was rewrite another character [a gay male hairdresser] for myself. It was the only choice. So I went in with my proposal, and they were really nervous, because they realized they were taking the whole movie away from me. It was so depressing to have spent two years on this project you've put so much into and worked so many hours and experienced so much angst."

Unfortunately, Brown's stress wasn't allowed to subside following the meeting. "Then the guy I wrote all the music with held it up because he had the grand rights to it. So he got all the money from the grand rights because he's a jerk, and because my ex-husband didn't get him to sign the papers. There were so many things like that."

Brown is describing one of the worst situations of her career, yet maintains her humor and never stops smiling. "I remember when they told me they were going to get Geena Davis and Jeff Goldblum [then-married] to star. There was a party at Julien Temple's where I met them and I was just horrified because Geena is, like, 6'1" and the part was [meant] for this little Valley girl. "Geena's very nice, but it was just another shocking thing to deal with.

"It wouldn't affect me like this now, but at the time I was so attached to [it]. Everything was so important and such a big deal. Then, when we were finally making the movie, Julien Temple decided he would ban all the writers from the set for no particular reason, so I couldn't show up until I was actually [filming] my part. I thought it was really terrible."

To worsen matters, "In the middle of all this, I'd gotten separated from my husband. So I felt, 'This is terrible. We've all worked on this project so long and now he can't be on the set and when I get down there I'm going to tell Julien my ex-husband should be able to come down.'"

Brown quickly kicks back into humor mode. "When I finally got there, I realized how cool it was that my ex-husband had been banned from the set, and I finally started having a really good time!" She laughs and confesses, "So the actual filming was the most fun I'd had during the whole experience. Plus, by then I'd pretty much

Candy (Julie Brown) tries to lift Valerie's (Geena Davis) spirits with a makeover in *Earth Girls Are Easy* (Vestron).

let go of the part of Valerie. I had the really funny [dance] number in the beauty parlor, among others. So those moments were great.

"Then it was another two years before it got released, because the company which made it went bankrupt. Finally, Vestron acquired it. It was just the most psychotic experience ever."

The actress-screenwriter had decided that the hellacious delays and letdowns were worth it. "Even the process of going through the torture made me understand you can't be *that* attached to a project. It was the lesson of the whole experience, which is a great thing, because I've never gotten so attached to a project again ... ever. No project I've done since has caused me the amount of pain *Earth Girls Are Easy* did. "As time goes on it gets easier, in a lot of ways. I have my family now [a new husband and son] and my actual 'real' life is so great that a project is never going to derail me like *Earth Girls Are Easy* did."

She notes the cancellation of her three-season hit *Strip Mall* on Comedy Central. "When [it] got canceled, I was like, 'Okay ... time to move on to the next thing.' In a lot of ways it was a relief, because it was really hard in terms of time and energy. It was a cable show and there was a lot to it. I had to work all the time and I missed my family. As usual, I was doing too much. I was executive-producing and writing and starring in it. It was a lot of fun to do, but the moment it was over I just said, 'Okay, let's just do the next thing.'

"That's the great thing about *Earth Girls Are Easy*. It's actually a very cute movie.

Julie Brown with the cast of 1995's *Out There* (photograph courtesy Sam Irvin).

There's enough distance from it now where I can just look at it as this separate little thing and there's a lot about it which is really wonderful. So I don't regret it ... *now*. Along the way I was like, '*Ugh!*' Now, though, I think it's great."

Indeed, especially based on its cult following and consistent showing on Comedy Central. Though not a hit during its theatrical release, its subsequent success has even spawned ... a Broadway musical?

"Yeah," Brown chuckles. "There's a guy who's going through the torture now. It's really funny because he's calling all the time freaking out. He's dealing with this person for these rights and getting directors and losing directors and it's a total nightmare for him. My ex-husband still owns some of the rights and this guy had to get them from my ex who's fucking with him. He called me up and said my ex was being a nightmare and I'm like, '*Duh!*'"

As laughter ensues, Brown continues, "So, yes, there is a guy from Australia doing it. Charlie and I are contributing to the adaptation for Broadway. Maybe someday we'll be there, but right now we're just like, 'Good luck!' He's the sweetest, nicest guy and I really hope he pulls it off. I almost feel bad for him because he's so sweet and really didn't know what he was getting himself into."

Aside from a few contributions to the new script, Brown and Coffee are keeping a distance from the new incarnation. "No," Brown squeals. "I can not go there again! I've said everything I have to say about furry aliens."

In fact, the writing partners have mostly steered clear of major studios since their *Earth Girls Are Easy* experience. "Charlie and I wrote another movie which Disney was going to buy," Brown informs. "It was supposed to be another starring vehicle for me, but they wouldn't guarantee it. I just couldn't go through it again, so we didn't sell it to them. We've written movies for Showtime and HBO. It's just an amazingly frustrating process, especially when you're trying to create a vehicle for yourself to take through the studio system. It's just madness, which is why not that many people do it."

Brown continued to guest star on television shows like *Monsters* (the episode "Small Blessing," about a woman and her terror tyke) and *Quantum Leap* ("Maybe Baby — March 11, 1963," in which she tries to run off with a child she believes is rightfully hers). She also joined the ranks of a still burgeoning network, ultimately becoming one of a few number of pioneering comics to affect the original MTV generation. When her comedy sketch show, *Just Say Julie*, debuted in 1989, it immediately shot to the top of MTV's ratings.

The show, in which Brown basically portrayed a zanier extension of herself, generally had an outrageous theme for every episode wrapped around an average of three music videos. It was immediately clear the "hottest little henna head on MTV" didn't always get to choose the videos she played, making for ripe targets. Her frequent victims were singers like Samantha Fox, Sheena Easton, Paula Abdul, Debbie Gibson and the New Kids on the Block, whose videos she would often "jump into" (through the magic of blue screen) and make none-too-polite remarks.

The themes of her shows were also completely out of left field. Brown usually spoke directly into the camera (which often found its way into her ample cleavage) and at the MTV audience (often patronizing them by explaining complicated words and situations as if viewers were too brain-damaged from watching the network to understand). She also made her crew a part of the action. In one of her most hilarious episodes, her crew quits and walks out in mid-show because she's on a PMS rampage, leaving her to operate equipment on her own.

Other classic episodes found her (and guest Linda Blair) being terrorized by her faux-psycho sister Debbie, who's just escaped from a mental institution (Blair ends up lobotomized by the shows' end); another where she travels around the world to halt a plot designed to destroy MTV; and yet another attack of PMS which causes her to bloat to enormous proportions just as a swimsuit magazine spokesman (frequent player Stanley DeSantis) arrives. Her solution? She throws on a blonde wig and pretends to be Samantha Fox.

Just Say Julie frequently featured singers (Jon Bon Jovi, Kip Winger, Gene Simmons) and actors (Michael McKeon, Elvira) introducing their latest projects. It also had a series of regular players including Stacey Travis (*Hardware*), Paula Irvine (*Phantasm II*), Christy Dawson (*Medusa*), Jody Travis (*Attack of the 5'2" Women*) and Larry Poindexter (*Sorceress*). Other veejays like Downtown Julie Brown (known as "The Evil Julie Brown," as the red-headed Brown often referred to her) and Martha Quinn (as a cocaine addict with a violent personality) would pop in to parody themselves.

Brown's contribution to the growth of the network (from its music video days to where MTV is today (with very little music in its programming), was recognized in a Winter 2000 mini-documentary. Brown, however, doesn't seem too sure the network really understands her show's, or other comics shows (*Remote Control* and *The Big Picture*), involvement in its history.

"I do and don't know how important *Just Say Julie* was," Brown chuckles. "I don't know if MTV feels that way. The thing about MTV is, in general, when they go back, they really stick to their veejay thing. What I was doing was much weirder. What does make me mad is they have their MTV Awards, which was something I started on *Just Say Julie* which we'd air around Oscar-time. We did it two years in a row, then suddenly MTV is doing their own version, and they're using the same categories! So they kind of took them from me.

"I also started doing the bits where I'd jump into videos and make fun of them, then later *Pop Up Video* came along, and even *Beavis & Butthead*. So I was sort of a pioneer in that aspect, and it's kind of irritating because they took my ideas and didn't give me any credit for them!"

Brown laughs and shakes her head. "MTV is like its own little machinery," she decides. "They don't really care much about their own history. They're really just there in the moment and don't look back. The network is *sooo* young. It's always been very young (as in youth-oriented). It's hard for me to watch now. I think you have to be under 25 to watch it, or even twenty. It's like you're watching it, then suddenly, 'I can't follow it ... these songs don't mean anything to me.' MTV just passes you by really quick. My son is seven now and thinks Britney Spears and 'N SYNC are wonderful. I'm going, 'These people are so much closer to him than they are to me!' That's kind of scary!"

More frightening is the fact that the original MTV generation are now parents to the current generation of viewers. Does Brown think her show; the number-one rated on the network from 1989 to 1990 (which covers two seasons), would still work with today's MTVers?

"I don't know," she ponders. "I think I might be too old for them, but I think the sensibility would work, because it's kind of an immature concept, and the character was pretty immature. I don't know if I could pull it off any more, because I don't know if I still have the same spirit of being that immature. Even at the time I would sit there and think, 'I can't do this for very long.' Yet they liked it a lot. So I think the show itself would work if somebody else did it and they could recapture that sort of energy."

What post-modern singers would Brown set her sights on if *Just Say Julie* were to reappear with all new episodes? "I guess Britney and all those little singers who came out of *The Mickey Mouse Club*," she laughs. "'N SYNC, Christina Aguilera ... they are just like performing monkeys and don't have anything to say. They're like mini–Las Vegas people! They're so scary to me because they have even less content than Madonna."

Her comment about the Material Girl prompts another question. Why was Madonna's public image and "Blonde Ambition Tour" documentary *Madonna: Truth or Dare* (1991) scrutinized so frequently on *Just Say Julie* and famously in Brown's 1992 critical hit *Medusa: Dare to Be Truthful*? "She was such a huge performer, I think I identified with her in some weird ways. We both grew up Catholic and were trying to be outrageous. I was also extremely fascinated that she was creating such an impact and there wasn't much content. I found it absolutely amazing, much in the same way as Britney Spears is today. There's nothing that they're saying..."

"It's not like I think Madonna is bad, because she makes some perfect dance music. Look at her hit song, 'Music.' She says, 'Music brings people together…' Well, you know … *duh*! It's just so nothing. I think she's always gotten to me on that level. She's appealing to this mass audience and has nothing to say, yet I felt completely intrigued by her."

Brown herself had issues she wanted to express, and used her newfound popularity to promote what was, at the time, a still seldom-discussed issue … teenage sex. Appearing in one of television's first safe-sex and condom commercials, Brown remembers the controversy boiling more from within its own promoter's fears than the public's. "I thought it was really good to do that kind of stuff," she smiles. "At the time they asked me to be a part of those public service announcements, I thought it was good to use the fact that kids knew me, and to promote safe sex to them. It was the beginning of everyone starting to jump on board with those messages. There was some controversy, but it was because MTV wasn't going to air them at certain times. So it was internal controversy at MTV itself. It wasn't like there was an actual uproar against it, but as I remember, MTV was scared of one."

While promoting her beliefs and supporting MTV in making the commercials, Brown soon found MTV wasn't as supportive towards her needs to keep *Just Say Julie* moving forward. After the 1990 season, and with the show still number one in the ratings for the network, Brown tried to get her employers to cough up more cash for better production values for the third season. They refused, and to the shock of most, Brown pulled the plug on her own series. Only two seasons had been lensed, yet the show continued to air repeat episodes (which also got good ratings) until 1992.

It seemed the series has been lost to audiences who didn't think to record the episodes during their initial run. Happily, Brown reports, "I just got the rights to sell *Just Say Julie*. I have to sit down and edit them. I looked at the contract and realized nobody was doing anything with them, so I thought someone should be distributing them. I called up MTV and they said, 'Yeah. Go for it.' The way the contract reads, they're technically viewed as veejay segments, even though it was an entire show."

You won't find the series on store shelves for a while yet. While the actress has the rights to the skits, she doesn't have the rights to the music videos shown during each episode. This may put a temporary hold on their release, especially since the music videos owners may be less than happy with Brown's mocking. "I can try to get the rights to the videos and make deals, but it's a whole other project and I don't have the time right now. I will do it at some point. I really like the show. People still come up to me and tell me how much they enjoyed it."

The early 1990s saw Brown in a plethora of new comedy output, including a CBS special which was basically a toned-down version of *Just Say Julie*, minus the music videos. She had a TV guest spot on *Get a Life* (as Connie Bristol in the premiere episode) and lent her voice to the animated shows *Batman* and *Tiny Toon Adventures*, in which she spoofed her MTV success as "Julie Bruin," star of *Just Say Julie Bruin*, in an episode titled "Tiny Toon Music Television."

She later created and starred (alongside newcomer Jennifer Aniston) in the FOX network sketch comedy *The Edge*. Though the series only lasted one season, Brown was hardly out of work. She had cameos and supporting roles in a variety of features, including *Spirit of '76* (1991), an amusing cult item about celebration of July 4, 1976, which found the actress as a stripper representing Lady Liberty. To help recreate the era's personality, the film also starred David Cassidy, Barbara Bain, Moon Zappa, Tommy Chong, Devo, Rob Reiner, Leif Garrett, Don Novello, Olivia d'Abo and even Iron Eyes Cody (the crying American Indian from the anti-pollution ads).

Brown appeared as Judy alongside Bobcat Goldthwait, Paul Dooley and Florence Henderson (as a drunk) in 1991's *Shakes the Clown*. A story about a drunken, disorderly clown and his friends, the film created some very minor controversy when "real" circus clowns protested on tabloid shows (including *A Current Affair*) that the Goldthwait-directed comedy portrayed them in a non-funny light.

Coureney Cox, Arye Gross, Mitzi McCall and Kevin Pollak were among Brown's co-stars in the next year's *The Opposite Sex (And How to Live with Them)*, about a hormonal group of friends living in the same building. She also starred in *Nervous Ticks*, a comedy shot in "real time" about airline employee Bill Pullman, who tries to run off with Brown (as Nancy Rudman), a married woman.

Brown next had an uncredited cameo as a waitress in the 1992 action thriller *Timebomb*, in which amnesiac Michael Biehn (*The Terminator*) finds himself targeted for assassination. It was Brown's own homespun take on Madonna's critically acclaimed documentary, however, which put Brown in what she considers her biggest spotlight. *Medusa: Dare To Be Truthful* (1992) premiered on the Showtime network to enormous ratings and critical acclaim. The black-and-white "mockumentary" followed fictional pop diva Medusa (Brown) on her "Blonde Leading the Blonde Tour." Medusa was a manic-depressive pop sensation with an unrelenting ego and an insatiable sex drive, all curiously similar to the exploits of a certain other singer.

Take for example Madonna's infamous "fellatio with a water bottle" sequence in *Truth or Dare*. Brown ups the shock not with a larger bottle, but with a watermelon ... and sucks it flat! In another segment, Madonna is seen on stage dealing with faulty electrics and microphones. Brown's take? Medusa steps into a puddle on stage and gets electrocuted while her half-brained dancers think she's changed the routine and simply mock her convulsions; everyone later tells her it was her best performance ever. Not only does she become agreeable again after receiving these compliments, she decides to make her electrocution a permanent part of the show.

The searing impersonation became her most recognized performance. Even Madonna took notice and sent Brown a half-drunk bottle of warm champagne. "We have a mutual friend who's a choreographer and she was working with him on her tour. I was working on a video and he said, '*Madonna sent this to you*,' and handed [it] to me. I'm like, '*What does this mean?*' and he didn't know. So we just sat there laughing because we're thinking, 'Is this a nice gesture? Is she being a bitch?' Who knows? I didn't save it, which I should have ... I could have sold it on eBay...

"When I did *Medusa: Dare to Be Truthful*, her agent called my manager and said she really liked it. Then later I heard she didn't like certain parts of it, like when I rolled on the dog's grave, which was a take on her scene were she rolls on her mother's grave. Then when her dancers wound up suing her, which I made up, it turned out to be true. She didn't like that. I figured she would like it because I think she's hugely narcissistic. It was making fun of her, but was complimentary at the same time. It talks about how beautiful she is and being the biggest star in the world. That's why I think she liked it."

The performer found *Medusa: Dare to Be Truthful* her most successful project critically and emotionally. "I made the most money on *The Edge* and producing the TV show *Clueless*, which was a lot of fun, but I think people like *Medusa* the most. I got amazing reviews from everybody—*TV Guide, People, Entertainment Weekly*. People still talk to me more about that one movie than anything else I've done."

Furthermore, *Medusa* (which featured the spoofed songs "Vague," "Expose Yourself," and "Everybody, Be Excited") was emotionally satisfying. Brown affirms, "I think *Medusa* was really amazing because I was completely in charge. I was executive producer, starred in it, wrote the music … I controlled every aspect."

She sits back and smiles. "Showtime really didn't know what I was doing, so they never knew to get involved in it. It was this really strange moment where a network didn't know to be intrusive. It's the only thing I've done where I got to do everything I wanted and where nobody stopped me or got in my way. Then everybody liked it and I thought, 'Well, God, why can't this always happen?' But it doesn't. It's about the money. When people are putting money in or they have a title, they want their say and to have their input."

She shakes her head, "*Medusa* was just that magical moment where it's all mine and I felt like, 'I think I'm doing this right.' *Earth Girls Are Easy* had been devastating for me on so many levels, then here I am, completely in charge and the result came out wonderful."

Her next comedy *sliced* apart the sensationalized accounts of Lorena Bobbitt (who cut off her cheating husband's penis) and Tonya Harding (who arranged a "hit" on fellow ice skater Nancy Kerrigan). "Already on the next Showtime movie, *Attack of the 5'2" Women* [1994], which was a lot of fun to do, more studio people got involved because of the success of *Medusa*. They decided suddenly they needed to be there and get involved and have opinions and approve the casting…

"Maybe I just need to be more of a bitch. I just don't have the energy to be a ball-busting Hollywood bitch. I think I have a better life and people like working with me because of it, so I'm not going to be that way. It's not worth it."

Brown portrayed the infamous duo as overweight and insane women who, oddly, are adorably hateful. In fact, weight jokes and negative nods towards the Hollywood ideal of stick-thin women became a regular element of Brown's productions. "Um … it sucks," she protests. "It's really strange to me, because it's gotten to the point where the women are *really* skinny—like super, frighteningly skinny. I can't make myself that skinny any more. I exercise all the time and don't eat a lot of crap, but I can't be stick-thin and it's really irritating me because it's *sooo* fake! I think the only people who can achieve it are really young, or who have gone completely insane and won't eat anything. In *Strip Mall* I tried to *not* make everyone really skinny because it's such a bad image. It's really horrifying and wish it would end. I'd like to see [the trend] go back to women looking like Sophia Loren and Marilyn Monroe. I think in real life men don't want their women to be that skinny with nothing on them. I honestly don't think it's what they want, yet it's a media image. So, I hate it."

Drawing from life experiences, good and bad, has always been where Brown found inspiration for her humor. "My whole life … my childhood … being frustrated," she contemplates. "I think most artists use their frustrations. It's about getting attention and about people listening to you … about you not feeling attractive. All those things which are negative you turn into something interesting or funny. It sort of gives you a release. Even 'The Homecoming Queen's Got a Gun.' I was a homecoming princess at my high school. I was aware of how stupid it was, but also how exciting it was. What did it mean? How bizarre is it to put girls up on a box that way? [My song] kind of asks the question, and then this girl's got a gun and it shows there's much more craziness going on beneath the surface. So even in that image ... you're just trying to tell some sort of truth about your life ... about the stuff which stresses you out.

"I read this quote by William H. Macy [1996's *Fargo*] where he said, 'Nobody who had a happy childhood went into acting,' which I think is true. Most people in show business didn't grow up really happy and satisfied and fulfilled, which is why they need to express 'something.' So I think it's the torture of your childhood."

Brown laughs again (which, in case you hadn't noticed, she does *a lot*). What elements does it take to make the comedienne laugh? "Lots of things"— she laughs. "I think I laugh at things pretty easily. I think there are a lot of people who are funny. Lots of comedians and actors. My husband is funny ... and my son is *really* funny. He's hilarious.

"Things which are absurd and quirky. There's not much network comedy which is really funny to me. It's so manufactured and worked-out and deliberate. It's not quirky. They take the edges off. Things which come out of nowhere or are unusual make me laugh."

Following the success of *Attack of the 5'2" Women*, she again lent her voice to animated characters on television shows like *Aladdin*, *Animaniacs* and *A Goofy Movie* (1995). She also appeared in the mini-series *Band of Gold* and the comedy *Out There* (1995).

Directed by Sam Irvin (*Elvira's Haunted Hills*), who

Sam Irvin and Julie Brown, who worked together in 1995's *Out There* and her comedy *Strip Mall*, reunited in May 2001 for a photo shoot by Denice Duff (photograph courtesy Denice Duff).

also directed Brown in episodes of *Strip Mall*, *Out There* focused on a down-on-his-luck Nobel Prize–winning photographer (*The Rocketeer*'s Bill Campbell), who accidentally finds proof of aliens on earth. Brown portrays Joleen, a trailer park denizen obsessed with U.F.O.s. Though Campbell's character thinks she's insane, Joleen turns out to be more aware of the truth than expected.

The same year, Brown appeared in the box office smash hit *Clueless* opposite Alicia Silverstone (*The Crush*), Brittany Murphy (*Girl, Interrupted*) and Stacey Dash (*Mo' Money*). As uni-sex gym coach Ms. Stoeger, Brown bantered with Silverstone's Cher. The success led to a regular weekly sitcom replacing Silverstone with *The Rage: Carrie 2*'s Rachel Blanchard, but keeping most of the movie's cast (at least in a variety of guest appearances). Brown was not only among the cast of the series, but also acted as producer over its three-season run. She also appeared on episodes of *Goode Behavior* and reunited with Lily Tomlin for the "From the Terrace" episode of *Murphy Brown*.

Her next starring role came in the exceedingly funny yet overlooked comedy *Plump Fiction* (1997). As food-obsessed Mimi Hungary, Brown spoofed Uma Thurman's role in *Pulp Fiction* (1994). Other famous movies which took a beating in the comedy, which unraveled in *Pulp Fiction*'s multi-story manner, were *Reservoir Dogs* (1992), *Natural Born Killers*, *Nell*, *Forrest Gump* (1994) and *Waterworld* (1995). Released theatrically in 1998, the movie went unnoticed, but should definitely be on any fan's "must see list," as it is the best showcase of Brown's ability to act completely insane.

Brown also moved onto roles in movies like Roger Corman's *Alien Avengers II* (1997) (a.k.a. *Aliens Among Us*), supplied the voice of Minerva Mink in *Wakko's Wish* (1999) and played a speaker in *Shadow Hours* (2000). She also associate-produced 1998's *Black Sea 213* and *A Place Called Truth*.

In December 1999 she briefly returned to live performance at the Gay and Lesbian Center in West Hollywood. It had been nearly 15 years since her last stand-up routine, but Brown put on a performance to the sold-out shows. "It was great! I loved it," she exclaims about the two-weekend benefit. "The hard part was I didn't have enough time to recover from all the stuff I was doing at the time. I had just completed the pilot for *Strip Mall* and was writing another pilot for FOX. As far as the actual performing, it was fun!"

"There's this weird drama behind putting a show together," she divulges. "I had a band and back-up singers and all of a sudden you've got this group of people who are nuts with each other. The actual performance I loved, but getting the show up and running was quite the epic. Performing is really fun and I do love it. Would I do it again? Probably. I don't have any immediate plans, but yeah, probably."

As her career continues to expand, Brown still feels more comfortable in front of the camera. "It's weird," she says, "because I enjoy writing more than I ever used to. I used to absolutely loathe it. I'd only do it because I needed the material. Now, [it] can be very gratifying. The older I get the more I like it, because it's quiet. Nobody's yelling at me or giving me shit or telling me their opinions. I still think performing is more fun."

With nearly 50 film and television credits to her name, the actress ought to be reveling in fame and fortune. Surprisingly, Brown doesn't necessarily feel famous. "I feel like there's a lot of people who know what I do and appreciate it," she theorizes.

"I don't know if I feel [famous]. I think I started feeling known when I started doing *Just Say Julie*. I began running into people who had more of a general knowledge of what I did. That's when I would go to the grocery store and people would recognize me and know exactly what I'd done.

"Still, the weird part is if you haven't been on TV for a while, people stop recognizing and knowing you. So, are you ever truly 'famous?' I know Julia Roberts has made it because she is totally famous, but at what point does that happen? If you saw one of the Go-Gos walking down the street, would you know who she was? A lot of people probably wouldn't recognize them, yet they were really famous at one time. It's a really strange thing. There's a level where once you're there, you become famous for life. I don't know that I'm there yet."

Would Brown ever want her son to become the fourth generation of her clan to get involved in the business? "*No*," she exclaims, unleashing her contagious laughter. "I wouldn't stop him, but I'm also not going to encourage him. If he got interested in it, I would give him the information I have.

"I think most of my needs in doing this have been met, so I don't have a need, when I look at him, to take this forward. I think people do that [with their children] and put them in commercials and TV. I just want to ask, 'What is wrong with you?!' So if he does it, he does it. I kind of hope he doesn't. I hope he doesn't have to deal with it."

She shifts in her chair, mulling the topic over a bit more. "There are so many insane people in this city. There's so much angst and uncertainty because you never know when you're going to work and I think it makes people insane. He's the happiest little kid and he's so interesting by nature ... I hope he does something where he gets to have fun and use his mind ... not be so intense for him, like show business is. Any time you're working on anything, it's so intense and as time goes on the more I think, 'This is so ridiculous. It's not that serious.' It's hard to turn people off. So, I hope he does something else with his life."

Would the actress consider treading into more unfamiliar territory, away from comedy (though she does obviously have some serious roles on her résumé) and into other genres? "I wouldn't really consider doing an action movie because you have to work too hard," she laughs. "Physical comedy is already exhausting enough. Comedy is sort of my thing. I would like to do more drama, because the older I get the more I would like to do things which are more ambiguous.

"Things which are kind of both comedy *and* drama are very interesting to me. I think there will be more things I do in the future which have more elements of drama to them. Overall I'm more drawn to comedy, because I think if you can do it, there's sort of a gift in there for other people and for yourself where you lighten things up a bit in life and bring out some happiness. It's almost like a Zen thing. You can feel it's a good thing to make people laugh. You've eased something in them and they've appreciated it."

Karen Mistal

Throughout the history of Hollywood, many an actor and actress have made their film debuts in low-budget, campy horror, science fiction and comedy features. Of course they're happy just getting a job, but as years pass and their film résumés flourish, they often hope the "little" film which sent them onto their way to celluloid stardom will vanish. However, it is also a frequent case where said film will surface throughout their career, often dragged out by journalists and night-time talk show hosts as a humbling reminder of pre-fame. In turn, the actor tends to hate the film even more. Ask Demi Moore (*Parasite*), Vanna White (*Graduation Day*), Kevin Bacon (*Friday the 13th*), Brad Pitt (*Cutting Class*), Leonardo DiCaprio (*Critters 3*) or Jennifer Aniston (*Leprechaun*) and they'll often refuse to speak of, or even acknowledge, their early work.

Interestingly, one of today's biggest stars, George Clooney, refuses to speak poorly of his original B-films, which includes *Return of the Killer Tomatoes*. Of course, the sequel to 1978's *Attack of the Killer Tomatoes* is different than the average early-career embarrassment. You see, *Return* strives to be funny ... and it is.

It turned out that several members of the cast went on to additional fame ... and even some notoriety. One of Clooney's co-stars, Karen Mistal (one of the most popular models and MTV video girls of the 1980s), subsequently appeared in such A-list films as *Space Cowboys* (2000) and was a regular on TV shows like *Coach* and *The New Adventures of Beans Baxter*, and guest-starred on *Dragnet*, *The Tracey Ullman Show* and *Men Behaving Badly*, among many others.

The 1980s were filled with a menagerie of B-movies which, regardless of the depth of their plots or the lack of their budgets, were just plain fun. From the hardcore, gore-soaked end of the dead-teenagers horror genre emerged a campy step-sibling ... the bimbo movie. The girls were typically blonde, tanned and big-breasted with incredibly large hair, pinkish-blue eye shadow and big plastic earrings to match their big plastic bracelets. They, *like*, *totally* spoke in a distinct Valley girl manner ... *fur-shure*. In most cases, they were located on some California beach, surrounded by their male counterpart: buff, tanned, blonde and equally vague surf dudes. Their dilemmas were often the result of a romantic misunderstanding and capped off with a lot of sexual innuendo. Basically, they were *Three's Company* in theatrical release form, and given giggle-inducing titles like *Assault of the Killer Bimbos* and *Sorority Babes in the Slimeball Bowl-a-Rama*.

A quick run-down of Karen Mistal's résumé might lead one to assume she was just your average doe-eyed pretty girl. Of course, Mistal did participate in her fair share of cheesecake, often sporting bikinis in fun-loving flicks like *Another Chance*, *Cannibal Women in the Avocado Jungle of Death* (opposite Shannon Tweed, Adrienne Barbeau, and a pre–*Politically Incorrect* Bill Maher), *Killing Midnight* and *Three Secrets*, plus TV's *Baywatch*, *Baywatch Nights* and *Charles in Charge*. Exposing her sexy side has never been a problem for the actress, who began modeling for Eastman-Kodak when she was only 16. Unlike many of her co-horts, Mistal actually has talent, exemplified by a knack for successfully pulling off comedic roles.

"I'm originally from Rochester, New York, and my dad worked for the Eastman-Kodak company," she begins, her eyes still large and innocently beautiful. "So I started modeling for [them]. After graduating high school I came out to San Diego for a photo shoot and ended up falling in love with it and moved out here. I didn't really know how to get started [in the business], so I went the pageant route which I don't know if I would ever [do again]. It was a different time ... it was the 1980s.

Mistal is quick to point out that although she wouldn't repeat those initial steps if given the opportunity, her career did receive a hefty boost as a result. "I was Miss California 1982, and things just started rolling from there. I got a lot of photography work and then commercials. Then it really kicked off when VH-1 started doing music videos. That was my first step into the acting world. My first video was with Michael J. Fox and Julien Lennon for his song 'Stick Around,' then I also did videos for Kansas, Meatloaf and several others."

The model now pursued acting, even though she had originally intended to become a singer. She had trained in musical theater on the East Coast, but upon arriving in the West discovered "it was really tough, and I was traveling and recording my own music to try and get my feet off the ground. So I did a lot of contemporary R&B Top 40 music, more commercial stuff. I traveled a lot and performed in restaurants and weddings, then got booked at some of the bigger clubs. Then I started doing theater again, and I got television commercials like Diet Coke, which were really my first big step into acting.

"Doing stage work [trained] me with the level of acting and entertaining. I love the creativity part of it as much as being on stage and the energy and being able to set different emotions off inside of people. That's what we all try to do. That's our art. We can walk away and have affected somebody's mood for the entire day."

Mistal's doe-eyed appearance and perfect body melded well with her girl-next-door personality and quickly brought her to the attention of Hollywood producers. She spent a season as sexy Cake Lase on the FOX comedy *The New Adventures of Beans Baxter*. The show lasted only one season, but has gone on to cult status as one of the network's earliest guilty pleasures.

While continuing to top agents' lists for music videos, commercials and print work, she landed a bit role in the Bruce Greenwood comedy *Another Chance*. "It's become a cult classic. Actually, I think a lot of my movies have become cult classics," she giggles. "I just remember sitting on the back of a Harley Davidson in a scene with Bruce, and I also did a scene on the beach." Her film debut would become a cult favorite, but it was her second feature, in a lead role, which would ultimately endear her to cult-film fanatics.

"*Return of the Killer Tomatoes* is the one I get asked about the most because it's become such a huge cult classic," she says, smiling. "I think part of its success today is because there were so many great people in it, like George Clooney. When we shot it we ad-libbed a lot of our own lines and just had a good time with it. I don't think any of us knew how big of a cult movie it was going to become. After that I did another cult classic, *Cannibal Women in the Avocado Jungle of Death*, with Bill Maher, Shannon Tweed and Adrienne Barbeau. Bill and I actually still see each other periodically at a lot of functions around town. I even used him to emcee our Heal the Bay [an organization she heads which cleans up the Southern California coastal waters from San Francisco to San Diego –see www.healthebay.com for more info] event least year.

"I've stayed in touch with a lot of these people. Shannon Tweed is married to Gene Simmons [from KISS], and he and my husband do a lot of business in production together. These people keep coming back into [my life]."

Mistal has no ill feelings towards being known as the sexy tomato ... well, perhaps

Karen Mistal formed close friendships with her *Return of the Killer Tomatoes* co-stars Anthony Starke (*left*) and George Clooney (photograph courtesy Karen Mistal).

there should be some explanation. Mistal's character, a beautiful young woman named Tara, loves to clean, cook (especially toast) and serve men, all while dressed in adorable retro–1950s attire. Now, before the women's movement storms in, two things should be made clear. First, her character's submissive 1950s–era housewife attitude was not portrayed as flattering. Second, she was actually a tomato turned into a human … we kid you not! The plot of *Return of the Killer Tomatoes* finds Dr. Gangreen (John Astin of TV's *The Addams Family*), creator of the original mutant veggies, trying to take over the world once again with tomatoes, only now he's transforming them into human replicants. Mistal and a non-homicidal tomato known as F.T. (Fuzzy Tomato) escape to warn the outer world with the help of George Clooney (*The Perfect Storm*) and Anthony Starke (*Repossessed*).

"I never know what's going to happen next with *Return of the Killer Tomatoes* because, aside from George and Anthony—who did some really good stuff—Rick Rockwell, who married Darva Conger on *Who Wants to Marry a Millionaire*, was in the movie … then I found out during the Gary Condit scandal that he was in the movie too! So I had to watch it again and it turns out Condit's a customer in one of the early pizza parlor scenes where George is flipping the dough. How weird is that? You wonder what scandal is going to come out of our cast next! So far I'm in the clear, but you never know," she exclaims in a burst of laughter.

Mistal found all of her castmates to be delightful, and maintains that the four-week shoot in San Diego, California, was a non-stop party atmosphere. She bonded with Starke and Clooney most, referring to the latter as, "Amazing! I still think of him as a very dear friend. He was one of those actors who would still be on the set even when he wasn't in a scene. He was so eager to learn and see the whole process. He could've been off relaxing after shooting a scene for two or three hours, but he wanted to be right there. He loves the business that much. He's just incredible and a really good guy."

She was equally impressed with her director and co-star, John DeBello, who had unleashed the original *Killer Tomatoes* on an unsuspecting national audience in the summer of 1980, with reviewers and audiences alike happily promoting it "The worst movie ever made!" His approach on the sequel was less *Airplane!*-like parody, more satirical on Hollywood, sex and trendiness. "John was a hoot," she guarantees. "This was something he had always wanted to do since he directed *Attack of the Killer Tomatoes*. John has that dry sense of humor which comes at you from out of left field. You never see it coming ... but he's very intuitive and knew exactly what he wanted from the very beginning of the project."

DeBello went on to direct two additional sequels, *Killer Tomatoes Strike Back* (1990) and *Killer Tomatoes Eat France* (1991), but Mistal was never asked to take part. "*Return* did well theatrically, but it only had a limited release. They also branched off into a really popular cartoon series, but, I think for money reasons, they didn't come to any of us to do the voices. However, I do think the character in the cartoon looks an awful lot like me," she says with a snicker.

"It amazes me that regardless of how many other projects I've been in, people always seem to know me most from *Return* and *Avocado*," she laughs. "It's an honor, though. It was such a fun project to do, so I'm really glad people find it totally off-the-wall and appreciate it."

Though *Cannibal Women in the Avocado Jungle of Death* followed up her *Killer Tomatoes* role, Mistal insists her second turn as a ditzy beach bunny was a complete coincidence. "I just happened to get a movie which was very similar in its tone," she shrugs. "One of the producers, Gary Goldstein, went on to do *Pretty Woman* [1990] right after, which just goes to show you my luck in the draw. So, boy, was my time off there!" She shakes her head and laughs.

The actress quickly parlayed her talent for comedy into a gig as a regular cast member of the sitcom *Coach*. As Shari, Mistal was the college roommate to Craig T. Nelson's daughter during the first season. "Craig was so giving," she shines. "After each taping he would present his co-stars a rose or some small keepsake like a bracelet with an inscription on it. If you wanted to do another take or had questions, he'd be right there for you. He was all about the work and doing it right for everyone. He was the sweetest man on earth ... and Shelly Fabares was a darling! I loved her to death."

Unfortunately, Mistal's time on the *Coach* set was only limited to the first season. "Claire [Kelly Fox], Coach's daughter, ended up marrying her boyfriend on the show," she explains. "So the next season they ended up living together in the dorms. She no longer needed a college roommate."

Mistal quickly moved on to roles in other comedies like *The Hogans* (a.k.a. *Valerie, Valerie's Family* and *The Hogan Family*) and *The Tracey Ullman Show*. "I don't think I've ever seen anyone work harder than [Tracey] does. She's such a chameleon. She'd go from one skit to the next with such a smooth flow. She's another one who's a giver. I actually got to work with Paula Abdul during a choreography scene for that show, so it was really, really big for me to do."

Her television and modeling careers were still going strong when Mistal suddenly opted to take her life down an alternate path to become a wife and mother. She remained active in theater, but concentrating on raising her daughter was more important. She considered introducing her daughter into a similar career path, entering her into the world of modeling and commercial work, but ultimately decided that experiencing childhood instead of fame was far more important.

"My [daughter] definitely aspires to be Britney Spears," she laughs. "She's adorable and well beyond her years. She's just recently asked me if she could go on commercial calls. She went on a couple of shoots when she was about four years old, but wouldn't want to pull out her pink ribbon in lieu of whatever outfit she was supposed to put on, and I finally just realized, 'You know what … I've got to let her just be a kid and have a childhood.' If she wants to do it later, after her education, I'm fine with that. However, I do believe in fate, so if she proves to me before then she really has the drive to do it, and things line up, then I won't stand in her way. I would just prefer she get the education first."

Mistal reveals she found her life in turmoil in the mid–90s as her seven-year marriage to a South-African tennis player began to crumble. She found strength and new love in Jamie, a producer of *Baywatch*. Ironically, it was around the same time she had returned to the small screen in two episodes of the jiggle-beach TV series, and an episode of its spooky spin-off *Baywatch Nights*, when their paths crossed. Yet is wasn't until after she'd filmed her episodes when they would finally be introduced.

"When things were really down and I didn't think I would ever meet anybody else and felt my life would never be the same, Jamie came into my life from out of the blue," she smiles softly. "I met him through two writer friends of mine who worked on *Baywatch Nights*. They kept telling me how great he was."

Mistal had also appeared in a TV pilot called *Ocean Avenue*, which was being produced by Pierson-All American, where her now spouse is a television executive. Not realizing each was the person who friends were trying to join them with, the two met at a party where he said, "'Oh my gosh! You're the girl I've been watching from *Ocean Avenue*!' I realized who he was … we hit it off, started dating and were married about eight months later."

With a new source of support and ready to move further ahead with her career, Mistal guest-starred in other TV shows like the sitcom *Men Behaving Badly*, the thriller *Killing Midnight* (1997) and the TV movie *Three Secrets* (1999). Her memories of *Killing Midnight* are surprisingly upbeat, since "I never got paid for it. They sold it … I never got a check."

Mistal laughs and shrugs, "From what I understand, it's available overseas. SAG keeps looking up on it for me. Mickey Rooney was in it, too. We're still struggling to figure out what happened to it. It's a shame. It was a fun movie to do. We shot it all out at sea on a boat during winter. It was freezing, plus I get seasick easily [*laughs*]. However, I got to work with Mickey Rooney, who's another legend. I've been very lucky to be able to [experience] those things."

She was beyond thrilled to work with another set of legendary screen actors via her role as an astronaut in the critical and box office hit *Space Cowboys* (2000), an actioner about a group of retired astronauts trying to help save Earth from a plummeting Russian satellite. "There were two teams of astronauts, the new team and the old one," Mistal explains. "I was on the new team. I shot my scenes for about three weeks. Unfortunately, my one dialogue scene was cut, which was really hard for me, but it's my understanding Clint Eastwood [who directed and starred in the film, alongside James Garner, Tommy Lee Jones, Donald Sutherland and Marcia Gay Harden] shoots a hell of a lot of film. When there's too much, the smaller roles are the first to go. However, I am still in five scenes of the film.

"It was a great time. Clint was very funny and laid-back. He knew what he wanted, would get scenes set up quick, rehearse a couple of times, then shoot it and move right on to the next. James Garner was a total hoot for me. He's also a very generous man. These were the people who didn't have to give you the time of day if they didn't want to. There were no prima donnas."

Though Mistal and her husband have never had an opportunity to work together, she did manage to work with her father-in-law on her follow-up feature, *The Dukes of Hazzard* reunion TV movie. "My father-in-law is the creator and writer of the original [series]," she says, but adds, "I didn't just get [it] handed to me. I had to go in and fight for it. When I went in to the audition at Warner Bros., the casting agents had no idea I was his daughter-in-law until after they hired me. Then I was nervous during the entire shoot, because I'd never worked with my father-in-law before. I was an absolute wreck the whole week before we started shooting. I couldn't eat anything.

"The cast was great, but I didn't get to work with everybody. I was the L.A. mayor and my scene was with Catherine Bach. It wasn't a very long shoot for me, but I really enjoyed it."

Between her ongoing film and television roles, plus caring for her family, Mistal has also tried to remain close to the theater. She recently wrapped the stage production of *Dorian*, based the ageless classic *The Picture of Dorian Gray*. She reports, "I played the role of Gwen here in L.A. It's a musical which is going to be performed in New York off–Broadway. Unfortunately, I won't be going with to New York, because I would have to leave my family behind and I just can't do that. My family is very important to me. However, doing that show is what really got me going again in theater."

Is there a medium she prefers? "Each has special elements all their own," she assesses. "The most fun for me is theater, because every night is different ... you never know what's going to happen. I don't think anything hones your craft more. To go through your emotions during your regular day, then, like it or not, you carry those emotions onto the stage. For me, that is the biggest high. The applause of a live audience ... hearing them laugh ... being able to hear a pin drop if it's a heavy storyline ... it's incredible. When you're up there, you're in another world. It gives me the charge of energy to go out and do other things. I feel like I'm on fire when I'm up there.

"Some people prefer being on a movie set, because they can take their time learning their characters. For me, though, it's just a lot of waiting around. I like things to be moving quickly and more high energy. That's the great thing about doing sitcoms."

Mistal hopes to keep audiences laughing for many more years, and admits she's glad *Return of the Killer Tomatoes, Cannibal Women* and her many sitcoms continue to tickle funnybones. She encourages young performers to follow paths which will help them succeed in both their careers and life. "Do your homework. I don't think

Karen Mistal today (photograph courtesy Karen Mistal).

there is a quick route to getting into this business. Be humble to yourself. Be who you really are. Keep your morals. You don't have to sell out. There are a lot who do, and those are the ones who don't last very long, or get into a lot of trouble. If it's meant to be, it'll work out for you," she insists.

"The public doesn't want to see a fake image of you. They want to see who you really are, so give it to them. Take classes with several different instructors and study your craft. Learn from the people you work with. Don't assume it's all about the money, because if that were the case most of us wouldn't be in it," she laughs.

Are there any projects Karen Mistal hopes to pursue within the next few years? "I've always wanted to do a horror movie," she confesses. "A really good one. I love ghost stories, like *The Others* [2001] and *What Lies Beneath* [2000]. I've never done one. It might be good to have something like that follow you around, like Linda Blair did with *The Exorcist* [1973]. Now *that* was a great movie."

Even if she should never find something the caliber of *The Exorcist* for which she would forever be known, she insists she could do worse than *Return of the Killer Tomatoes*. "As an actress, I wish I'd had something a little more validated, but *Return* is just what happened for me. That's how my life worked out. There are some choices I could have made early on, but I opted for love and wanted to raise a family instead. What's amazing is I've always been able to find work right back into the business. I love acting so much. I don't think I'll ever give it up."

The enduring appeal continues to catch the actress off-guard. After 15 years, and frequent appearances on Comedy Central, the fan base for *Return of the Killer Tomatoes* continues to expand. "One thing which keeps it popular is the title," Mistal believes. "It's so unique. Plus, the plot is so wacky, it's basically about whoever comes up with the craziest, most 'out there' concept and gets it to the finish line first. John DeBello definitely did that. It was one of those things where you just throw it to the wind and are amazed at where it turns up. It ended up being a pretty cool thing in the long run."

Index

Numbers in *italics* represent photographs.